GOLDEN SHRINE, GODDESS QUEEN
EGYPT'S ANOINTING MYSTERIES

ALISON ROBERTS

NorthGate

First published in 2008 by
NorthGate Publishers
3 Court Ord Cottages
Meadow Close
Rottingdean
East Sussex
England BN2 7FT
www.northgatepublishers.co.uk

Front cover illustration:
Pectoral of Sekhmet, Tutankhamun and
Ptah from Tutankhamun's tomb at
Thebes. *Photo courtesy of Kurt Lambelet.*

Half title page illustration:
Pectoral of Nekhbet from
Tutankhamun's tomb. *Cairo Museum.*

Frontispiece illustration:
Hathor and Isis bless the divinized
Queen Nefertari in her temple at
Abu Simbel.

Title page illustration:
Winged solar goddess amulet.
Myers Museum, Eton College, Windsor.

Design: James Lawrence

ISBN 978-0-9524233-24

Printed by KHL Printing Co Pte Ltd,
Singapore

ACKNOWLEDGMENTS

This book could not have been written without the support of others.
My thanks are especially due to the Bet El Trust for a financial gift in
2004 from the estate of the late Patricia Buckle which enabled me to
continue my writing and research. In particular, I would like to thank
Warren Kenton and Joanna Lapage-Browne of the Trust for the
warmth of their encouragement and many kindnesses over the years,
also Pat Rae for her generosity when I most needed it and for her deep
sense of ancient Egypt's artistic beauty, which has inspired me during
our numerous conversations. I am grateful to Gus Gully for the loan of
books from the library of her late father, the Reverend David John
Spurling, and also for sharing with me her healing wisdom. I would
also like to thank Jeremy Naydler for his friendship and support, John
Carey and Jack Herbert for sending me references, and Stephen
Rainbird, who first made me aware of the Holy Saturday homily
attributed to Epiphanius. Stephen Quirke gave generously of his time
to read through the manuscript and I am grateful both for his pictorial
help and Egyptological comments, though any errors are mine alone.

For a long time now I have been most fortunate in having access to the
unique collection of the Warburg Library in London and would like to
thank Jill Kraye and her library staff for their assistance, and also
Christopher Naunton, librarian of the Egypt Exploration Society, for
his helpfulness. My thanks are due to the following for help with the
illustrations: Ann Russmann, curator of the Brooklyn Museum's
Egyptian collection, Klaus Finneiser and Caris-Beatrice Arnst at the
Berlin Museum, Richard Parkinson at the British Museum, Megan
Doyon at Yale University Art Gallery, Shari Kenfield at Princeton
University's Art Museum, Lyn Haward and Robert Partridge.

My special thanks to James Lawrence for the great care with which
he has designed this book and his infinite patience when changes
were needed.

I am indebted to Jay Ramsay for his mercurial advice and to
Elizabeth Hutchins for her sympathetic editing. Thanks also to
Barbara Vesey for proof-reading the book. My son Sam Gladstone
has assisted me considerably with his computing skills. I am also
grateful to Charlotte Kelly for her enthusiasm and encouragement,
and to David Brown and Nicky Bowden for information about
book production.

Finally, this book would never have been without the support
and generosity of my brother John Roberts. I offer him now my
heartfelt thanks.

Alison Roberts

Alison Roberts, *July 2008*

CONTENTS

CHRONOLOGICAL OUTLINE

3000 BCE —

EARLY DYNASTIC PERIOD
c. 3150-2686 BCE

2500 BCE —

OLD KINGDOM (PYRAMID AGE)
c. 2686-2181 BCE

First Intermediate Period
c. 2181-2040 BCE

2000 BCE —

MIDDLE KINGDOM
c. 2040-1782 BCE

Second Intermediate Period
c. 1782-1570 BCE

1500 BCE —

NEW KINGDOM
c. 1570-1070 BCE

1000 BCE —

Third Intermediate Period
c. 1070-664 BCE

500 BCE —

LATE PERIOD
c. 664-332 BCE

GRAECO-ROMAN PERIOD
Ptolemaic Dynasty 332-30 BCE

0 —

Roman Emperors 30 BCE-323 CE

500 CE —

BYZANTINE PERIOD
323-641 CE

1000 CE —

ISLAMIC PERIOD
641 CE-present

1500 CE —

2000 CE —

Chapter 1

QUEEN OF THE SOUTH: A HORUS HOUSE

O Temet, She who is Lady of the Two Lands,
O Uraeus, Lady of Life in the *Per-Wer*,
Hathor, Glorious One of the sky,
At the prow of Re's boat,
Who dwells in Khepri's boat,
May you guide him on the path of eternity,
On the ways of duration.[1]
(Invocation to the Eye goddess in the Horus temple at Edfu)

◀ *fig.1* **The small Golden Shrine from Tutankhamun's tomb in the Valley of the Kings at Thebes. Made of wood overlaid with a layer of gesso and covered with sheet gold, it resembles the archaic *Per-Wer* shrine of Upper Egypt. (Egyptian Museum, Cairo.)**

When, in 1922, Howard Carter excitedly peered through the small opening that he had just made in the wall blocking the entrance to Tutankhamun's tomb, staring into the antechamber's gloom lit solely by his candle, he gasped in amazement at the 'wonderful things' he saw illuminated there. Carter had indeed seen wonderful things, treasures which had lain undiscovered for more than 3,000 years in the Valley of the Kings at Thebes, buried together with a young pharaoh who had briefly ruled Egypt during the 14th century BCE.

One of these glittering 'wonders' was Tutankhamun's small Golden Shrine (fig.1), made of wood and adorned with startlingly informal scenes of the king with his wife, Queen Ankhesenamun, which were worked into thin sheets of gold on a layer of gesso overlaying the wooden interior.[2] This revealed the artistry of craftsmen working immediately after King Akhenaten's controversial reign, in which he had tried to emancipate Egypt from its traditional cults. Moving at rapid speed to fulfil this new vision, which is sometimes interpreted as the beginning of monotheism, Akhenaten and his wife Queen Nefertiti had instigated a period of tremendous social and religious upheaval throughout Egypt. In less than 20 years this remarkable couple had overseen the creation of a completely new capital at el-Amarna in Middle Egypt, dedicated to the supernal solar deity Re, whose ancient sun cult at Heliopolis had provided the inspiration for Akhenaten's new vision. Step by step they abandoned all Egypt's traditional deities, introducing a sun cult entirely focused on the great heavenly orb of the sun, known as the Aten. Beautiful lyrical hymns were composed to give voice to Akhenaten's rapturous devotion to the solar creator who rayed life-giving light and love through the whole of creation.[3]

Akhenaten also completely transformed the old artistic conventions, working out new ways for artists to convey his solar vision, including radically new representations of Egypt's royal couple, which are evident in the superb royal portraiture unearthed by archaeologists from the el-Amarna craft workshops. There also seems to be a new informality in royal art at this time, with Akhenaten and Nefertiti shown together in intimate affectionate scenes or enjoying domestic life with their daughters (fig.3). But this informality is misleading, since every feature of Amarna royal art was carefully designed to portray the royal couple as offspring of the threefold solar creator, showing them as bearers of the sun god's fecund nourishing life for the Egyptian people. Hence, spontaneous though Akhenaten and Nefertiti may seem when they kiss one another in their solar chariot racing through the streets of el-Amarna, their loving gesture openly reveals them to be incarnations of Re and his daughter Hathor-Maat manifesting the all-pervading love that flows through the whole of abundant creation.[4]

To be sure there had been a Heliopolitan royal cult of the sun since Old Kingdom times. And unconventional though Akhenaten may seem, his vision drew extensively on this Heliopolitan mythic world. But what marked his flagrant challenge to Egyptian culture was the ferocity with which he expunged all other traditional temple motifs, especially those connected with the Theban god Amun-Re, completely excluding them from his Amarna royal cult of the sun. Everything to do with dark temple interiors was simply ignored, everything to do with Ptah's craft world at Memphis was abandoned, since Akhenaten had no interest either in cults centred on Ptah's cult images or in priests performing any kind of traditional sacred 'magic' (heka) by word, by rite or by material.[5] For the radiant divine presence was everywhere to behold in the 'love' pervading creation. And no 'separative' act producing opposites, no division which needed to be reunited and healed, could interrupt this flow of radiant solar life.

▶ *fig.2* **Colossal statue of Amenhotep IV/Akhenaten from the destroyed Aten temple complex at Karnak East, Thebes. (Egyptian Museum, Cairo.)**

▶ *fig.3* **Altar relief from el-Amarna showing Akhenaten and Nefertiti with three daughters beneath the life-giving rays of the Aten. Tutankhamun's future queen (here named as Ankhesenpaaten) is seated on Nefertiti's lap, her head tenderly supported by her mother's left hand. (Egyptian Museum, Cairo.)**

CRAFT VISION: AMARNA TRANSITION

Tutankhamun's blood relationship with this controversial Amarna royal family has never been conclusively established, though Ankhesenamun herself was one of the six daughters born to Akhenaten and Queen Nefertiti and lived with them in their new Amarna residence (fig.3). Certainly, Tutankhamun briefly ruled at el-Amarna as Tutankhaten, a name meaning 'Perfect is the Life of the Aten'

or 'Living Image of Aten', before abruptly abandoning Akhenaten's solar city and changing his name to Tutankhamun, 'The Living Image of Amun'.

Even so, although his allegiance once again to the Theban deity Amun-Re is clear, Tutankhamun's name was never to be included with the other illustrious 18th Dynasty pharaohs listed in the Ramessid royal king lists. This was probably denied to him because of his links with Akhenaten's royal court. Far too much water had flowed under the Amarna bridge for the Egyptians ever to have acknowledged Akhenaten's brief but far-reaching revolution. Far too much innovation had severed them from all the revered cities and sacred shrines that had nourished their religious life. And never again were Egypt's rulers to display quite the same exuberant magnificence and certainty that had typified the glorious 18th Dynasty reigns of Hatshepsut, Thutmose III, Amenhotep III and other Theban rulers. The incoming Ramessid kings were concerned far more with restoration, with absorbing the deep trauma of Akhenaten's short-lived revolution and integrating his solar vision into the traditional temple cults.[6]

However, Tutankhamun's Golden Shrine predates this sober Ramessid re-evaluation, belonging to that difficult parting of the ways towards the end of the 18th Dynasty when the royal court, no longer in tune with Akhenaten's ideology, sought to re-establish traditional royal cults. Yet, at the same time, it was a royal court still haunted by remembrance of things past, still tinged with the spirit of Akhenaten's radiant solar vision, which continued to shine over them when they returned to the ancient royal cities of Memphis and Thebes. Indeed, the beautiful Golden Shrine perfectly encapsulates this ambivalent 'restoration' in the time immediately after Akhenaten's extraordinary, if brief, revolution.

Its shape resembles the ancient *Per-Wer* of Upper Egypt, the 'Great House' known from archaic times as the dwelling of the vulture goddess Nekhbet.[7] By the time of the New Kingdom, however, it had become the sanctuary of serpent crown goddesses, notably Hathor-Sekhmet, 'Eye of Re',

and Weret-Hekau, 'Great of Magic', fiery goddesses who held the key to the pharaoh's theophany on the throne of Egypt.[8] Nevertheless, Tutankhamun's shrine is small in size and could hardly have been used in an actual crowning ceremony. More likely, it was intended for a small statuette of the king (see page 12), perhaps originally standing in a palace at Memphis or Thebes, after the return to Egypt's traditional royal residences. Then, after the king's premature death, it would have been buried with him in the Valley of the Kings, together with other objects that had been meaningful in his lifetime.[9]

At first sight the decoration seems to preserve the mood and character of Akhenaten's unconventional reign, with each scene apparently providing an intimate glimpse into the conjugal life of the royal couple. Probably, had Akhenaten not pioneered new art forms at el-Amarna, vividly capturing the affectionate love uniting the solar royal family, these scenes would never have appeared shortly afterwards on the Golden Shrine. For these intimate portrayals of Tutankhamun and Ankhesenamun, of a kind rarely seen in Egyptian royal art, still preserve the radiance of Amarna light and life.

Seemingly oblivious to everything but each other, the royal couple can be observed on the shrine's sides delighting in the sensual pleasures of love and the companionship they share. On the left side of the shrine (as viewed from the front), they hunt together in papyrus marshes which teem with plants, wildlife and the abundance of nature (figs.8, 11), whilst on the right side Ankhesenamun, bedecked in flowing diaphanous robes and solar headdresses, tenderly expresses her affection for the king as she pours a liquid into his cup (fig.13) or adorns him

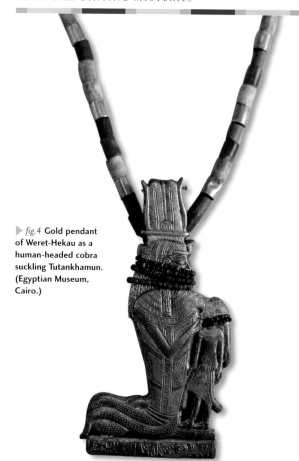

▶ *fig.4* **Gold pendant of Weret-Hekau as a human-headed cobra suckling Tutankhamun. (Egyptian Museum, Cairo.)**

▲ *fig.5* **An unfinished stela from el-Amarna, perhaps depicting Akhenaten and Nefertiti, showing the queen pouring liquid into the king's cup. (State Museum, Berlin.)**

with a scarab-shaped pectoral, bestowing on her beloved an image of the rising sun (fig.28).

All seems to be a haunting remembrance of those intimate portrayals of Nefertiti and Akhenaten (fig.5). But it is deceptive. For on closer inspection this is no Amarna royal couple. Nor is this imagery simply about the couple's private world. These are not just charming, unaffected domestic scenes, as they have sometimes been called. If they were indeed simply 'domestic scenes', why would they be shown on a shrine shaped like the Upper Egyptian *Per-Wer* with 14 figures of Nekhbet swooping across its sloping roof, which is guarded on either side by a winged serpent? And why, as

Ankhesenamun gives her *menit*-necklace to the king (fig.10), would she do so with the following 'undomestic' words:

> Adoration in peace.
> May Weret-Hekau receive you,
> O ruler, beloved of Amun.

Indeed, it is declared nine times on the shrine that the king or queen is 'beloved of the Great-of-Magic', the serpent crown goddess and 'Lady of the Palace' Weret-Hekau. Moreover, deposited within the shrine, along with a gilded wooden pedestal for a statuette of the king, was a bead necklace wrapped in thin strips of linen, its pendant shaped in the form of Weret-Hekau (fig.4). Shown as a human-headed snake goddess, she suckles the king at her breast with her fiery milk, feeding him with the same nourishing liquid that the pharaoh imbibed from mother goddesses at his coronation.[10]

This 'royal' significance is further confirmed in the shrine's inscriptions. Twice Tutankhamun has the epithets 'son of Ptah, whom Sekhmet has born'. He is also 'son of Amun, whom Mut has born' and 'the image of Re'. These three gods, Ptah, Amun and Re, formed the important state triad which emerged in the 19th Dynasty as a response to Akhenaten's threefold creator, linking once again the sun god with the deities of Memphis and Thebes. And their names on the shrine highlight its importance for Tutankhamun as Egypt's reigning king.[11]

HATHOR'S BEADS: SNAKE MAGIC

This is no longer Amarna art, as Ankhesenamun herself makes perfectly clear when she extends her *menit*-necklace and naos sistrum towards

▲ *fig.6* **Detail of Ankhesenamun's necklace from the Golden Shrine. (See fig.10.)**

Tutankhamun (fig.10), for these are cult objects sacred to the sun goddess Hathor (fig.24). Such a powerful ritual gesture, bestowing on the pharaoh all the radiant qualities of Egypt's love goddess, was nowhere to be seen at el-Amarna. But here once again, Egypt's queen encircles Tutankhamun with Hathor's musical sounds and beads, with a solar feminine magic *(heka)* that enhances the king's ritual efficacy and identifies him with the youthful sun god in the horizon, Re-Harakhti.[12]

Undoubtedly, Akhenaten's rites were intensely solar. But these Hathorian cult instruments disappeared from Amarna royal art, at least in their conventional forms.[13] They were far too associated with the female Eye of Re's dangerous magic power in the royal cults Akhenaten had spurned, too linked with material ways of 'capturing' solar attraction in traditional temple ceremonies associated with Ptah's cult images. Yet here they reappear with ever more clarity and insistence. Indeed, Ankhesenamun's *menit*-necklace, with its humanized counterpoise terminating in a crowned female head and divine arms reaching out *Ankh*-signs of life to the king, graphically demonstrates this return to tradition (fig.6). For just as the celestial Aten's heavenly arms had once streamed down from the sky to touch Akhenaten and Nefertiti with light and life (fig.3), pervading the cosmos with radiant love and attraction, so now Ankhesenamun reaches out Hathor's life-giving arms to Tutankhamun, offering the sacred jewels that Akhenaten had blatantly ignored, along with everything else connected with dark temple interiors and cult images.

An immense shift had already occurred during the short span of Tutankhamun's reign. For this 'animate'

menit, which is an early precursor of numerous similar representations (fig.9), is patently a visual riposte to the Amarna solar cult, casting those all-embracing Amarna arms once again within the familiar symbolic gestures of Hathor's traditional love rites. What we have here before our eyes is a Golden Shrine steeped in Hathor's feminine mysteries, a rare glimpse of Egypt's fiery solar queen transforming her consort into the 'anointed king', as perfomed in the highly important New Year rites renewing the pharaoh's rulership and the country's prosperity (see chapter 3). And all the details have been carefully chosen to express this sacred ceremonial life.

Though unacknowledged by his successors in their king lists, Tutankhamun in fact completely reaffirms his respect for tradition in this Golden Shrine. But this is more than simply a straightforward reassertion of the past. For although Tutankhamun's reign saw the return to familiar cults, the 'open-air' spirit of Amarna religious life still streamed through them, creating an unprecedented tension between tradition and Akhenaten's revolutionary ways.

Manifestly, whoever created the Golden Shrine was still immersed in the Amarna world, unable to abandon completely the new artistic vision Akhenaten had so fervently embraced. Here the royal couple's ritual life is still infused with the spirit of Amarna radiance, a fusion so unusual that, for a brief moment in time at the end of the 18th Dynasty, the veil was lifted a little on Egypt's solar mysteries. For every gesture Ankhesenamun makes, though seemingly Amarna in character, is in fact dictated by tradition. Every scene on this golden house has its recognized place in royal ceremony. And never will an Egyptian queen again so openly reveal her temple secrets in a divinization of Egypt's king than here on this lovely shrine. The royal couple, represented in 'domestic' and natural surroundings, may seem casually informal in the gestures they make. But in fact theirs is a ritual magic completely rooted in traditional royal ceremonies. To understand this we need to look more closely at the Golden Shrine's elusive symbolism.

Chapter 2

CHASE OF LOVE: HEART ENCHANTMENTS

> And how are magical operations carried out? By sympathy,
> and thanks to the fact that there is a natural harmony between things
> that are alike and a natural opposition between things that are unlike …
> And the real magic in everything is the Love in it, along with the Strife.
> This is the primary magician and enchanter.[1]
>
> *(Plotinus)*

◀ *fig.7* **Nebamun hunts birds with a snake-shaped throw-stick in the papyrus marshes. He is accompanied by his Hathorian wife holding a garland of flowers and a loop sistrum. Their daughter is seated in the boat and plucks a lotus flower from the fish-laden water. (Wall-painting from the 18th Dynasty tomb of Nebamun at Thebes. British Museum, London.)**

Closer examination of the shrine's royal 'hunting' and 'marriage' imagery soon leads to the conclusion that its purpose is to identify Ankhesenamun with the raging-beneficent 'Eye of Re', Hathor-Sekhmet. Both beautiful and dangerous, this fiery twofold goddess is consort of Ptah, the divine craftsman at Memphis and maker of cult images (fig.27). Indeed, as already noted, Tutankhamun twice has the epithet 'son of Ptah, whom Sekhmet has born' in the Golden Shrine's inscriptions.[2] This 'Eye of Re' is also the sun god's companion, an emanation of Re's glory in the world, manifesting solar energy and power whenever his gaze, his 'Eye', is activated (fig.22). He is wedded to this unpredictable goddess, whose ambivalent female love-fire has the potential to be all-consuming. For the Sun Eye can turn herself either into burning anger or light, becoming now 'red', now 'green', constantly changing her colours as she weaves her web of enchantment through the solar circuit, manifesting the might of her *Ba*-power. There is a continual oscillation between her 'love' and 'strife'. And hence the great alchemy of solar rulership is to transform her rage into radiance, to turn her burning fierce fire into a radiant life-giving force. For hers is

the magical power that compels the sun to rise each day, hers is the 'beautiful face in the boat of millions', inspiring Re 'to illumine the sun disk when he sees her' and sustain the flow of life.

And if Tutankhamun is to rule Egypt effectively, both as Ptah's son and Re's appointed living image on earth, he must remain constantly united with these fiery goddesses—a union typified, above all, by the fiery uraeus rearing up on his royal brow, marking him with the indubitable sign of solar rulership. At stake is leadership exercised by a physically well-endowed youthful ruler, strong and magnetic in personality, able to draw loyal followers close to him and repel those hostile to Egypt.

Everything about the Golden Shrine's imagery is designed to identify the royal couple with this instrumental 'dread' and 'attraction', this 'sympathy' and 'antipathy' that flows through the whole of Egypt—and through the royal marriage. For, on the left side (as viewed from the front), where aggressive themes predominate, Ankhesenamun incarnates as the raging Sekhmet, while on the right side she radiates Hathor's power and sexual attraction. This contrasting royal love and dread, this manifestation of what the Egyptians called *Ba*-power, is

palpably present on the sides of the
Golden Shrine. Furthermore, in complete
accordance with the number seven's
importance in Hathor-Sekhmet's cult,
there are seven different representations
of the royal couple on the shrine's sides.[3]

KINDLING FEAR: ATTRACTING LOVE

This relationship can first be established
if we look at the scenes in the upper
register on the left side, where the couple

are twice shown, once in a papyrus skiff
hunting birds in the marshes and then
standing on land beside the skiff, with
Ankhesenamum supporting her
husband's arm (fig.8). Poised in his
skiff, Tutankhamun holds birds in his
hand, ready to hurl his throw-stick into
the thicket where the quarries hide.
From the Old Kingdom onwards such
bird-hunts regularly appear in private
tomb decoration (fig.7). Though they
seem to be 'realistic' representations of

▲ *fig.8*

**Ankhesenamun sails
with Tutankhamun in
the marshes as he hunts
birds with a throw-
stick. The scene to the
right shows the queen
supporting the king,
who appears securely
'moored' (meni) to her
on land beside the
papyrus skiff. (Upper
scenes on the left side
of the Golden Shrine.
Egyptian Museum,
Cairo.)**

everyday life, conveying the exuberant passions aroused in marshland hunting, several commentators have pointed to a deeper symbolism, associating them with the cosmic destruction of enemies (embodied by the marsh fowl) or even the tomb-owner's regeneration in the afterlife.[4]

Clearly, here in Weret-Hekau's realm, the royal couple's hunting on the Golden Shrine goes far beyond sporting pleasures in the marshes. After all, Tutankhamun's throw-stick is shaped like a 'magic' wand, an instrumental weapon which he needs to wield skilfully if he is to remain the beloved of the magic goddess. Interestingly, votive throw-sticks, frequently adorned with 'eyes' and some in serpent form, were offered at Hathor's cult sites in places like Dendara, Deir el-Bahri, Serabit el-Khadim and Timna by supplicants seeking the goddess's protection and blessings. Occasionally, too, their inscriptions name the Egyptian king as 'beloved of Hathor'.[5]

Indeed, in a striking group of Hathorian offering scenes in the Middle Kingdom private tomb of Senbi at Meir, which are placed above portrayals of the tomb owner spearing fish and hunting birds in the marshes, the bird pools are said to be where the 'Golden One' (Hathor) resides:

> Gold is in the bird pools,
> Gold is in the bird pools
> The places of her *Ka*.
> O be peaceful, O be peaceful,
> Golden One.[6]

'Be peaceful,' request Hathor's musicians, appearing as incarnations of her musical son Ihy, when they bring their bread-offerings to Senbi. Become sustaining *Ka*-life, O 'Golden One', in the watery 'places of her *Ka*', those nourishing 'bird pools', which, according to texts

inscribed around the heavenly sky goddess Nut on a ceiling in the Osireion at Abydos, are located in the outermost limits of the created world, in the marshes of heaven where the *Ba*-birds fly from when they return to Egypt.[7] In other words, what is desired here in Senbi's tomb is to attract the blessings of the propitiated goddess in order to invest Senbi's *Ka* with all her generative life-giving power and transform him into a living *Ba*, reunited with his cult 'image'.

Doubtless, a similar quest to draw nourishment from this fiery goddess underlies Tutankhamun's hurling of a throw-stick and his pose as successful hunter here on the Golden Shrine (fig.8). For, as Wolfhart Westendorf first pointed out, the word *qema* in Egyptian signifies both 'to throw' and 'to create, beget'.[8] And, in fact, the king's 'creative', 'begetting' powers are vividly portrayed in the Hathorian scenes on the other side of the shrine (see below). Furthermore, the king's power to contain the forces in these bird pools, a necessary prerequisite for creative union with the goddess, is graphically conveyed by the wild birds he securely holds, which, on one level, represent the hostile forces of chaos

▶ *fig.9*
Representation of an animate *menit*-counterpoise in Hathor's Graeco-Roman temple at Dendara. The earliest known example of this type of counterpoise occurs on the Golden Shrine (see fig.10).

▲ *fig. 10* Ankhesenamun shakes a naos sistrum and offers her *menit*-necklace to Tutankhamun, empowering him with Hathor's solar attraction. Royal women in Akhenaten's reign were never shown holding a *menit*, though the necklace's new design here clearly displays Amarna influence. Now, for the first time, the counterpoise terminates in an aegis, featuring a female head crowned with a solar horned headdress and human hands holding out *Ankh*-signs of life, echoing the Aten's raying hands bestowing 'life' in Amarna cult scenes. The queen's gesture highlights the return to Hathor's traditional rites after Akhenaten's reign. (Scene on the right side of the Golden Shrine. Egyptian Museum, Cairo.)

fig. 11 **Lower scene on the left side of the Golden Shrine associating the royal couple with Sekhmet's aggressive hunting instincts. Tutankhamun shoots wild fowl, symbolizing the enemies of Egypt, whilst Ankhesenamun sits beside him in a typical posture of Maat and hands him an arrow— Sekhmet's weapon. Beside the king's stool is a lion or lioness. Amidst this chaos, however, the two nestlings sheltering in the papyrus, and the three eggs shown in a nest above them, evoke the duality inherent in the Heliopolitan creative process. Protected by the royal couple's solar strength, this creation provides nourishment, vitality and abundant life. (Egyptian Museum, Cairo.)**

constantly threatening Maat's order. Indeed, the couple's ruling prowess is further confirmed by the hieroglyphs inscribed above the thicket where the quarry hides, to be read 'all life and dominion'. Thus, a whole magical web of solar Eye associations underlies Tutankhamun's wielding of a throw-stick, weaving the royal couple together with the Eye goddess's destructive and creative powers.

Turning now to the right-hand scene in the upper register, where the couple are shown beside the boat, the location suggests that they have 'landed' after their hunting exploits (fig.8). In Egyptian the verb 'to land' is *meni*, and the implication here is that the king is safely 'moored' to his wife. Importantly, too, again by means of visual word-play, this 'mooring' is woven together with the scene of Ankhesenamun extending her *menit*-necklace *(menit)* towards the king in the upper register on the shrine's right side (fig.10). Not only is the hunting king safely moored *(meni)* to his fierce Sekhmetian queen as Egypt's protector, but when she offers him her green-beaded necklace *(menit)*, he is coupled with her in a peaceful love union.

Furthermore, numerous temple scenes show Hathorian coronation goddesses performing a similar gesture with a *menit*-necklace, bestowing on the pharaoh all the 'attraction' he needs to rule Egypt effectively (fig.24). Transforming him into a radiant image of the youthful dawn sun god Re-Harakhti, the 'beloved' as he is sometimes called, these goddesses create his beautiful appearance in the eastern horizon, arousing jubilation and joy in all who behold him.[9] Radiating Hathor's fiery impulses for life, the king 'captivates' hearts, illuminating his enraptured people as the sun of Egypt,

compassionate yet fierce, binding them to him by the love he inspires. For, as the fundamental governing principle underlying solar rulership, this force of love or attraction is the transforming magic through which the king unites the Two Lands.[10]

Here in the Golden Shrine's landscape of light, Tutankhamun's goddess queen encircles him with this Hathorian love, weaving her web of attraction which binds everything together in all-embracing unity. Hence in the shrine's upper register on both sides there is a complex web of 'Eye' associations built around shooting, hunting, mooring and love, subtly reinforcing the couple's solar movement, vitality and life in all its double-sided goddess glory. And it is this deliberate linking of 'sympathy' and 'antipathy' that determines the decoration on the sides of the Golden Shrine. For it is when this ambivalent fiery goddess magic, this *heka*-power to engender both fear and love, freely circulates that these solar rulers truly 'capture hearts' in every way.

DARTING ARROWS: STREAMING LIGHT

The same double-sided meaning runs through the couple's gestures in the lower scenes on each side of the shrine. In the left-hand scene on the left side, the king sits on a folded stool ornamented with lion legs, as Ankhesenamun, who squats on a patterned cushion at her husband's feet, passes him an arrow. With her other hand she points to the quarry, as if urging him to shoot (fig.11). The arrow is well-known as Sekhmet's destructive weapon and its inclusion here surely identifies the queen with the raging Memphite goddess. Moreover, it explicitly shows her to be the active female power, bestowing on Tutankhamun the weapon he needs to

fulfil his shooting instincts and arouse fear in his enemies. Beside the royal stool a lion waits, poised and alert, ready to pounce (or possibly a lioness, given the Sekhmetian ambience)—yet another reminder of the aggressive feline atmosphere surrounding the couple.[11]

The couple's actions are purposeful, controlled and, not least, deadly, suggestive of their rapacious royal natures. Indeed, the Egyptian king's role as archer frequently characterizes his zenithal appearance in the noonday heavens, powerfully manifesting like Re to defend Egypt from intruders. So, for example, Ramesses II is said to be a fearsome archer against enemies, 'like Sekhmet raging in a plague, sending

down his arrows against them'. So, too, the Middle Kingdom ruler Senwosret III is 'one who shoots an arrow like Sekhmet', a skilled marksman able to protect Egypt from that disequilibrium known as *Isfet*—the intrusive strife which is the very opposite of Maat's way, constantly disturbing the balance of creative life.[12]

Significantly, in a similar hunting scene shown on an ornate wooden chest from Tutankhamun's tomb, Ankhesenamun again hands Tutankhamun an arrow. And here the king is named 'beloved of Ptah, lord of Maat', shooting his unerring arrows to uphold the truth goddess's cosmic way of life.[13] Twice on the Golden Shrine

Tutankhamun is again called 'son of Ptah', the ruler 'whom Sekhmet has born', for if Maat is to guide Ptah's creation towards fulfilment, she also needs Sekhmet's shooting prowess to guarantee protection.

But there are also other layers of meaning in Tutankhamun's archery. In Egyptian the root verb *seti* means to 'shoot', 'kindle light', 'set fire to', 'pour water' and, by further word-play, also resembles a word meaning 'impregnate'. It also evokes the 'rays of the sun' *(setut)*. The Egyptians loved to establish multiple meanings through word-play and this is evidently at work in the choice of images here on the sides of the Golden Shrine, since these 'shooting' themes resonate with the lower left-hand scene on the shrine's right side, showing Tutankhamun pouring liquid *(seti)* into the cupped hand of the bare-breasted queen seated at his feet, her hair entwined with the symbolic sidelock of youth (fig.12).[14] In his other hand he holds plants, either mandrakes or persea fruits, which are often difficult to distinguish in Egyptian reliefs, and clearly also a lotus blossom, scenting the air for his beloved queen with its sweet fragrance. Mandrakes, persea fruits and lotus flowers all appear as favourite images in New Kingdom love poetry, though whether mandrakes were included because of their well-known aphrodisiac properties we can but speculate, since little is known about the Egyptian use of mood-modifying substances. But certainly they contribute to the feel of heightened sensuality in the love lyrics.

COSMIC CREATIVITY: HAND OF ATUM

Here on the Golden Shrine Queen Ankhesenamun's receiving gesture further enhances the erotic meaning. For it recalls the 'god's hand', a well-known title of 18th Dynasty queens, referring to the hand through which the cosmic creator, Atum, brought creation into existence on the primordial mound at Heliopolis.[15] Co-existing with his 'hand' in the primal abyss, Atum is the unbegotten origin of all creation, expressed in his name itself, which means both 'Complete One' and 'Not Yet Existent One', the 'Accomplisher' or the 'Accomplished', containing everything within himself. His primordial act, either through spitting or masturbating, releases the divine fluid generating the cosmic Heliopolitan Ennead, beginning with the air god Shu and his female partner Tefenet, an act which was enshrined in the sun city's holiest sanctuary, which housed the sacred *Benben*, the stone of origins. In this eternal cycle of 'Becoming' that has neither beginning nor end, involving a creator god who contains within himself self-renewing, self-regenerating energy, there is a perpetual renewal of creation. And to return to Heliopolis is to return to this centre of unity and creativity, to the mystery of ceaseless renewal and the freshness of the 'first time'.[16]

Ankhesenamun's role as the 'god's hand' here will become clearer once we have followed the king's solar ascension in the New Year ritual, when he enters Heliopolis, renewing the 'old ones' and making them youthful again as 'wearers of the sidelock' (page 43). Suffice to say here, it is this 'hand of the god', before ever heaven or earth had come into being, that stirs Atum's desire to manifest his creative powers. Hence, when Tutankhamun pours forth life-giving liquid into the hand of his braided youthful queen, the gesture completely identifies them with Heliopolitan regeneration.[17] On this Hathorian side of the shrine, every symbolic detail, though

▶ *fig. 12*
Complementary scene to fig.11 on the right side of the shrine showing Tutankhamun pouring liquid into Ankhesenamun's hand. The king holds a lotus blossom and two fruits. The queen, adorned with a uraeus on her brow and an ornate solar headdress, wears a sidelock signifying 'youth' as she sits on a cushion at the king's feet. Though seemingly a glimpse into their private life, the symbolic details encapsulate Heliopolitan cosmic renewal and fruitfulness, with Ankhesenamun appearing here as the 'hand of Atum'. (Egyptian Museum, Cairo.)

seemingly 'intimate' and 'personal', has been chosen to convey royal creativity and life.

In short, everything about this ambivalent Golden Shrine has a double meaning. For even in the aggressive arrow-shooting scene on the shrine's left side (fig.11), the two nestlings sheltering amidst the turmoil in the bird pools and the three eggs shown in the nests above them create a sense of ordered 'life' amidst these raying death-dealing arrows (fig.14). This royal hunting is not about wanton destruction. Rather, to obtain food and nourishment, to generate life, the king must be in touch with propitiated Sekhmetian power that he can then direct against forces bringing cosmic disorder and disease. He must be able to protect both himself and Egypt

▲ *fig. 13*
Ankhesenamun pours liquid into Tutankhamun's cup. The lotus and poppy-pod details shown on the rim represent the decoration inside the cup. (Scene on the right side of the Golden Shrine. Egyptian Museum, Cairo.)

from hostile forces seeking to disrupt the creative flow of life. And this includes the fiery serpent Eye goddess herself, who is quite capable of turning in rage against the king.[18]

In every way, the essential task of this solar-centred royal couple on the Golden Shrine is to align themselves with that very 'first time' of establishing Maat—that primeval wisdom way of 'truth' innate in the original Heliopolitan creation.[19] For without the royal couple's potency and water, without their passionate delight in one another, captured so evocatively in the other scenes on the shrine, the queen's womb would not 'bear fruit' and Egypt would have no food and nourishment, and hence would return to chaos, unable to prosper and flourish. But Egypt's prosperity depends also on the king's

power to unite with his goddess queen 'in peace', ensuring procreative fecund life.

His fiery Egyptian queen is not simply a passive vessel for the king, performing a role which, in the words of one commentator, 'tends to be rather subservient, that of an intimate companion who attends to Tutankhamun's needs'.[20] Nor is she cold and inferior to the male in the order of creation, as the female came to be regarded among later Greek writers, notably the Greek philosopher Aristotle.[21] On the contrary, theirs is a mutual love. These images of Ankhesenamun show her actively providing Tutankhamun with arrows to shoot, rousing his passion as he rouses hers, a Sekhmetian queen who is equal to him in the aggression, the ferocity, the attraction and tenderness of love, a Hathorian solar queen who bestows on him all her fiery goddess power and is utterly united with him in their rulership of Egypt.[22]

SYMBOLIC LANDSCAPES: RESTORATION ART

Not surprisingly, the Golden Shrine's decoration, rich in allusions to the natural world and Hathorian love, finds its echo in New Kingdom private tomb scenes and love poems strewn with imagery drawn from the marshes, hunting, lotus flowers, mandrakes, necklaces and other amulets (fig. 7). Hathor-Sekhmet's rage and radiance pervade the chase of all youthful lovers seeking her golden blessings. Indeed, it is precisely this blurring between 'private' and 'royal' imagery that contributes to the feeling of ambivalence in the Golden Shrine's evocation of royal love. In a sense, it is this ambiguity between these different spheres of private and royal that makes this unusual 'goddess house' so delightful.[23]

Yet, at the same time, there is a certain restraint running through the shrine's emotional intensity. For this is a hidden eroticism, completely veiling the couple's relationship in the secret symbols of love. Here Hathorian love-making is expressed with great subtlety, as it is everywhere in Egyptian royal art, conveyed through the couple's tender looks, the exchange of jewels, the ritual gesture, the underlying word-play and coded imagery, which all contribute to a refined symbolic language of royal love. Indeed, as we shall see, the same subtlety of expression, the same mythic experience of the world, characterizes the enactment of the New Year ritual's 'sacred marriage' ceremonies (see chapter 3).

But what is the unifying theme linking these 'double-sided' scenes with others on the shrine? Undoubtedly their intimate gestures, which are highly uncharacteristic of royal art, are still strongly influenced by the beautiful portraits and affectionate scenes of the Amarna royal family. Nevertheless, such a stylistic comparison with Amarna art, or even comparisons with private tomb reliefs and New Kingdom love poetry, is at the same time extremely misleading. For there is nothing whatsoever in Akhenaten's cult of the sun that could help to explain the overall arrangement of these scenes, including Tutankhamun's anointing on the back of the shrine (fig.26) or Ankhesenamun's identification with the loving-destructive Memphite Sun Eye Hathor-Sekhmet with all its complex mythic allusions.

Nor can the Golden Shrine be explained away solely as an anecdotal revelation of the royal couple's personal life in the palace or the marshes. To be sure, their personal life is crucial. And, as

fig.14 **Detail from fig.11 showing the two nestlings and three eggs in a nest in the papyrus thicket.**

'brother' and 'sister', these royal lovers, like all lovers, live in an enchanted world of loving kinship where the emotional bond between them is as natural as the bond that draws 'a cow to grass, a maidservant to her children, a herdsman to his cattle', linking everything together in a cosmos perpetuating health and life.[24] The difference is that here on the Golden Shrine this loving kinship is utterly royal, belonging in a world where king and queen fulfil their unique roles as Egypt's rulers. By virtue of their service in the royal cult of the sun, they are set apart from their people, as indeed is graphically conveyed when Ankhesenamun shakes her naos sistrum before Tutankhamun (fig.10). For she holds here a cult object sacred to Hathor, one rarely shown in private tombs but played by Hathorian 'daughter' goddesses and priestess queens to propitiate 'angry' deities, confirming their unique status in the temple cults.[25]

Furthermore, the king (or queen) is nine times named as the beloved of Weret-Hekau, 'Great of Magic', the powerful enchantress whose effectiveness depended on ritual activity (fig.4). Indeed, it was through the pharaoh's performance of ritual, through the 'magic' *(heka)* operative in the temple cults, that he derived his extraordinary powers as Egypt's high priest of the sun. And as chief ritualist, he needed to know how to operate with 'the pre-eminent force through which the creator engendered and sustained the ordered cosmos'. It was this 'dynamic energy', this *heka* power, circulating in both the divine and human world that the Egyptian king (or the temple ritualists representing him) sought to channel in the cults, not primarily for personal fulfilment but for the benefit of Egypt. For it was by channelling this power that the cosmic solar king could effect 'the preservation of the creator's universe', a role required of him as Re's representative on earth, the 'living image' of the sun god, authorized to rule by virtue of the cosmic power granted to him at his coronation.[26]

The Egyptians were first and foremost a people of ritual, deeply rooted in the performance of sacred rites. And if we are to see the king's ritual effectiveness in Weret-Hekau's sphere, operating with this magical thread which 'links everything and unites all creatures in a chain of cosmic union', we need to turn now to a divinization ritual of the utmost importance for his rulership of Egypt.[27] This is the New Year ritual, in which the king is anointed with Hathor-Sekhmet's healing oils and completely transformed into the guarantor of cosmic life and fertility, with magical powers to renew the whole of creation and make Egypt live again. For the 'real magic' running through this New Year ritual is, to paraphrase Plotinus, the divine feminine's 'love' and 'strife'. And it is this ritual that, above all, brings alive the beautiful imagery adorning the Golden Shrine, showing it to be not for Tutankhamun's funerary cult and afterlife, but rather a dramatic shrine, deeply immersed in his ritual power as reigning sun king.[28]

RENEWING YEARS: THE ANOINTED KING

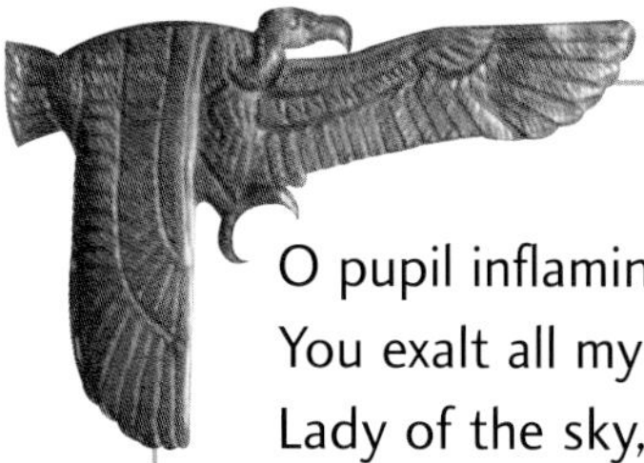

Chapter 3

O pupil inflaming my glorious Eye,
You exalt all my body perfectly.
Lady of the sky, sovereign of the Two Lands…
Lady of fear, the Great One
who causes trembling…
Turn your face towards the deities,
Make the *Rekhyt*-people flourish,
Make the King of Upper and Lower Egypt flourish.
The son of Re, in the life which he lives,
May you preserve him like Re eternally.[1]

*(Atum's invocation to the uraeus from the ritual
for 'propitiating Sekhmet' at Edfu)*

◀ *fig. 15* **Scene on the back of Tutankhamun's throne from his tomb at Thebes showing Ankhesenamun anointing the king. Amarna influence is evident in the couple's intimate pose and the raying arms of the Aten. The Aten's royal names (as known from later Amarna monuments) are also included. (Egyptian Museum, Cairo.)**

Fortunately, this little-known New Year ritual is preserved on a papyrus now in the Brooklyn Museum which forms part of the Wilbour Collection of Late Period Papyri, comprising literary, ritual, healing and technical texts (fig.16). One of the few ancient Egyptian royal rituals to have survived intact, it was rescued from oblivion by the careful work of Jean-Claude Goyon, who entitled it *Confirmation of the King's Power at the Beginning of the New Year* in his publication, though for brevity's sake it will be referred to here as 'the New Year ritual'.[2]

The papyrus is undated. Nor is any specific king mentioned in the text which could help to date it more precisely. Omitted too is the name of the scribe who copied it. But Goyon considered it to be a copy of a much earlier New Kingdom liturgical work perhaps even composed in the Middle Kingdom. For palaeographic reasons, however, he dated

the Brooklyn version to around the end of the fifth century or beginning of the fourth century BCE.[3] Hence, this copy coincided with a period of increasing foreign intervention in Egypt's affairs, notably from Persian kings and subsequently Greek Ptolemaic rulers, who established a new capital at Alexandria at the end of the fourth century. Evidently the Ptolemaic priesthood drew on this New Year ritual knowledge, since, as Goyon observed, certain extracts from the New Year ritual were also inscribed in Ptolemaic temples at Edfu, Philae and elsewhere, sometimes in much greater detail than in the Brooklyn papyrus.[4]

Exactly where the Brooklyn version of the ritual would have been performed in Egypt is unclear. But its anointing, death, rebirth and transformation rites would certainly have required a large temenos with numerous chambers to facilitate the ceremonies. Goyon convincingly suggested it would have been performed in a temple close to Memphis-Heliopolis, though as so little remains of northern royal monuments it is impossible to locate the ritual in any specific building.

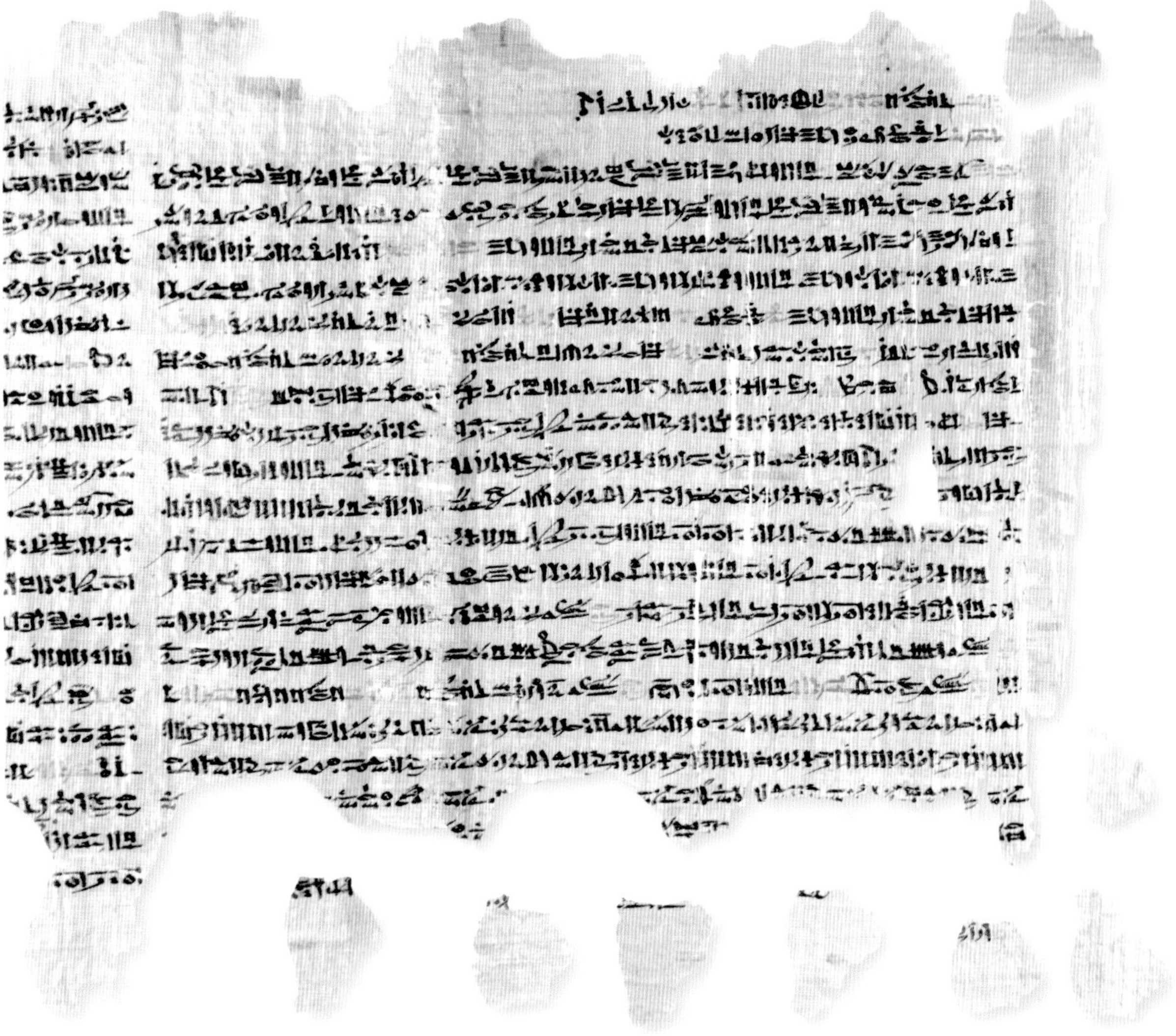

The papyrus itself seems to preserve the form of the ritual for use by a chief ritualist in charge of the elaborate ceremonies—an ownership, however, that has its drawbacks, since it mentions only the directives and incantations he needed

to know for his role in the ceremonies. That the papyrus is incomplete is obvious from the fact that titles of some chants are given without their full content being written down. Nevertheless, despite these limitations, most of the ceremonial detail is preserved, giving us a wonderful insight into the ritual life of Egypt's king at the New Year.

▲ fig. 16 **Opening columns of the New Year ritual papyrus written in a cursive hieratic script typical of the early fourth century BCE. The papyrus records the annual Memphite-Heliopolitan ceremony performed over a 14 day period to renew the king's power, including an anointing rite invoking the solar Eye goddesses. (Brooklyn Museum, New York.)**

29

fig. 17 **Fecundity figure bearing offerings as a gift of the Nile. (19th Dynasty limestone relief in the temple of Ramesses II at Abydos.)**

fig. 18 **View of the Nile inundation near Qena, as seen before the construction of the Aswan Dam prevented the river's natural annual flow. The mud-laden waters covered the agricultural land renewing its fertility, just leaving dry some higher inhabited areas.**

ROAMING LIONESS: DESERT DRYNESS

The ceremonies were long and complex, spanning a period of 14 days at the end of the old year and beginning of the new. In essence it was a commemoration of the coronation, a renewal of the pharaoh's rulership at the death of the old year and rebirth of the new, inaugurated ideally when Sothis/Sirius, the star of Isis, was seen once again on the eastern horizon after a period of disappearance, making its heliacal rising just before sunrise and heralding a new 'counting of the years' in a king's reign, starting on 1 Thoth. The reappearance coincided with the return of the Nile floodwaters associated with Osiris's midsummer rebirth, flowing northwards once again from the south and bringing with them the promise of greenness, renewal and fertility for Egypt's dry, parched land.

But it was always a difficult period of transition, for it was the hottest time of the year, when the sun stood highest in the heavens, having attained its maximum northerly declination. All growth disappeared as the land lay panting in the blistering midsummer heat. It was a time dominated also by noxious deities, particularly Seth, Osiris's fratricidal opponent, instigating confusion in his arid red desert after murdering his brother and seeking constantly to occupy the throne of Egypt. Fiery Sekhmet, too, rampant in her fury, fled through the desert lands far distant from Re at this transitional time. This 'death' of the old year was the prerequisite for the rebirth of life. But the smell of Seth and Sekhmetian blood filled the air. And theirs was the kind of death-dealing separative power that threatened to tear apart Egypt in the unbearable heat. If left unchecked, these harmful energies could bring about real chaos and division. Hence this transitional period was much feared.

A particular danger at this time was the disease brought by the heat and turbulent inundation waters flowing like a river of blood. These returning waters also were unpredictable. Would they be too high or too low? Like a lover bereft of the beloved, the land lay sick as Sekhmet's epidemics raged, her merciless demons plaguing the arid earth, shooting their 'seven arrows' and making uproar. And during this turbulent period of disorder the king, the land and the people all needed to be healed and cleansed from the contaminations of the passing year.

So this goddess of pestilence, who held the power both to burn and bless, needed to be propitiated in order to achieve a safe passage into the New Year. Throughout Egyptian temples, powerful incantations were chanted, both invoking her to reunite with the king and imploring that he be protected from her

dangers. What was desired above all was for this time of division to become a rebirth into unity, a cosmic rebirth restoring the operative pattern that had sustained creation from the very 'first time'. That radiant way of Maat needed to flow into Egypt anew, bringing light, joy and life-giving water once again during the coming year. It was the pharaoh's responsibility as 'son of Re' to ensure this cosmic transition and regeneration in the New Year rites. But to do so his power as Egypt's ruler needed to be renewed and reconfirmed. Reborn in the Heliopolitan place of divine origins, he needed to be reunited with his fiery serpent Eye.

▼ fig.19 **The ibis-headed Thoth pours life-giving water from a vase to purify Hatshepsut. The female pharaoh's figure and name have been hacked out but the god's figure has been left intact. (Detail of an 18th Dynasty relief in the temple of Amun at Karnak.)**

SEKHMET PROPITIATED: EXALTED FLESH

The opening ceremonies in this Memphite-Heliopolitan New Year rite unfold in a similar ritual pattern to the rite of passage confirming the pharaoh's power shown on Theban temple walls.[5] First, the king is purified by priests who enact the ceremonial of the 'House of the

fig.20 **The integration of Seth's turbulent energy in the rulership of Egypt is stated in this hieroglyphic inscription. It reads: 'The years of Seth upon the throne of Horus'. The inscription provides a clear drawing of the Seth animal showing its stiffly raised tail and long curved snout. (Block now in the Open Air Museum in Karnak temple.)**

knots. Holding the centre between these crowns is a figure of Ptah, creator of divine images and archetypal ruler of the Two Lands at Memphis, whose form is drawn on the cloth in ink by a scribe. Next a faience *Was*-sceptre and an *Ankh*-amulet of life are brought to the king as a chant celebrates the restoration of Horus's lunar Eye, the cessation of rivalry between the 'two combatants' (Horus and Seth) and the triumph of the son of Isis on Geb's throne.[6] Then the *Seshed*-diadem for adorning the royal head and a white band are brought, the ritualist affirming the soundness of the king's eyes, his divine vision shining anew in this cosmic setting.

The king is ready to be anointed with the nine sacred oils of the Upper Egyptian 'Great House' (the *Per-Wer* shrine) and the Lower Egyptian 'House of Flame' (the *Per-Neser* shrine), the archaic female dwellings of South and North, where dwell the goddesses investing him with his fiery divine power. And when these oils are first carried before the king, a chant praises Isis's protective death-defying power. For not only was Sekhmet both feared and revered, the Egyptians also feared that the dead, powerful though they were in ensuring growth and sustenance, might also intervene negatively in life on earth during this turbulent time of transition from the old year to the new. Hence, at the start of this anointing, Isis is invoked to ensure that the dead cannot rise up to harm the king or indeed all the deities of Egypt:

> See the protection comes.
> She repels the dead
> So that the dead cannot
> Rise from their confines.

Morning', cleansing the king with water after waking him in his palace at dawn. Following this lustral purification, he is then carried aloft in procession to the 'Shrine of the Great Throne' for the ceremonial robing, where he receives the diadems, insignia and adornments renewing his rulership. And here we indeed step deep into the territory of the fiery serpent goddess, dwelling in her *Per-Wer* shrine.

The ritual begins. First a band of red linen cloth, on which have been drawn 30 White Crowns of Upper Egypt and 30 Red Crowns of Lower Egypt, is wound around the king's throat, and the cords at each end are then securely tied with 60

Rejoice, gods. Rejoice, goddesses…
Go, be victorious
Go, be brave…
The magical protection of Isis
Surrounds the flesh of the pharaoh…7

And the chant concludes by assuring the king that Isis surrounds his body with protection.

Then comes the anointing of the Horus king's flesh with the nine oils. The incantation for the first oil both praises its healing power and invokes the dangerous uraeus serpent rearing up on the solar king's brow, summoning her protection lest she harm him during their reunion:

See the oil comes which exalts the skin,
See the protection comes
Which belongs to the son of Isis,
The unguent which is given
to the pharaoh,
Life, health and prosperity for his body,
When he is crowned as Re,
Sekhmet is on his head,
Wosret [the uraeus] is on his brow,
Shielding him with her terrible fury,
Preserving him with her
mysterious powers,
The Eye of Horus protects
the pharaoh,
Life, prosperity and health…8

Manifestly, this anointing with the protective first oil aims to channel the 'mysterious powers' and 'terrible fury' of the serpent Eye goddess into life-giving health for the king. For the Egyptians ascribed a prophylactic function to oils, incense and aromatic substances, prizing them for their power to propitiate deities, to repel malign influences and to keep

the flesh healthy. Hence the chant concludes by imploring Sekhmet-Bastet to 'save the pharaoh from the impurities, the vexations and all the malevolent furies of this year'. So, too, the protection of Nefertem, the sweet-smelling Memphite child of the lotus flower, is sought. And Horus, 'shoot of Sekhmet', is invoked to encircle the pharaoh's flesh in 'the fullness of life'.

Egypt's ruler needs to be freed from all the contaminations of the passing year, all the malign influences need to be driven off from him and Sekhmet needs to be beseeched to refrain from unleashing her terrible *sekhem*-power. For it is through the pharaoh's healing and anointing that the whole of Egypt can safely enter the New Year, protected by the fiery ambivalent goddess who is both the source of fever in the land and its healing remedy.9

Moreover, everything that the coronation goddesses in the *Per-Wer* shrine do for the king is implicit in this first anointing: they exalt the royal flesh, they protect him with their fury and, though unsung here, they also surround him with Hathorian radiance. Importantly, too, this anointing rite gives a very specific ritual context for the propitiatory litanies invoking Sekhmet

▲ *fig.21* **The solar right Eye protected by the vulture goddess of the South and the cobra goddess of the North. (Pectoral from Tutankhamun's tomb. Egyptian Museum, Cairo.)**

that were inscribed in great detail in Ptolemaic temples. Simply to chant such incantations to the dangerous Eye goddess without any knowledge of their overall place in temple ceremonies would have served little purpose. Crucial to their invocatory effectiveness was the performance of the goddess's rites within a much more extensive ritual process.

▲ *fig.22* **Hathor seated with her partner Re-Harakhti. (Painted relief in Queen Nefertari's tomb at Thebes.)**

Just as Weret-Hekau is named nine times on the Golden Shrine, so the king is anointed nine times with prophylactic holy oils in the New Year ritual. And it is only after he has been united with the dangerous Eye goddess that he is ready to be reconfirmed as the Memphite-Heliopolitan royal priest of the sun. Stretching wide his arms in adoration of the Heliopolitan creator god Atum and Khepri, the solar scarab-beetle of 'Becoming', he is then ready to tread the sacred ground of Heliopolis, 'to approach the earth of the *Benben* temple' in the 'pillar' city, which trembles and is 'on fire' at his coming:

> Earth quakes,
> Geb is on fire.
> The earth of life surrounds you.
> The companions of Atum
> Are protection for your body...
> So that nothing malevolent
> Can destroy you.
> Because the deities protect your body,
> And Heliopolis repels your enemies.[10]

Holding at bay 'Re's enemy'—surely here the malevolent snake Apophis, notorious for his attempts to intrude into the creation of the Egyptian cosmos—the king comes to consecrate the offerings of material creation to a whole host of gods and goddesses, whom he reverences by invoking all their different cult names and shrines in a long litany. It begins with those residing in the shrines on the great throne's west side, headed by the sun god Re-Harakhti, and includes the Ennead of Heliopolis as well as the Theban ruler god Amun-Re. Then the king reveres all those in the sanctuaries on the east side, starting with Ptah, Lord of Memphis. Manifestly, these two great spiritual centres of Memphis and Heliopolis are now firmly held together on either side of the anointed king in a 'union of the Two Lands'.

It need scarcely be said that this kind of ritual would have been completely ignored in Akhenaten's reign. For, in contrast with this 'image'-king, in need of constant renewal like Ptah's temple cult images, Akhenaten was the eternal 'son of Re', not one who had to be repeatedly 'made to live' again through magical initiatory rites. With Nefertiti continually beside him, his perpetual union with the daughter of the sun was openly revealed for all to see. And we need but look at the extensive reassertion

of Ptah's craft wisdom in the aftermath of Akhenaten's reign, as well as the return of the volatile Memphite Eye goddess, constantly weaving her fleshly garments of dread and attraction, to appreciate the trauma that had been caused by separating Memphis from Heliopolis in the Amarna era.[11]

HOLY BREAD: THE SOLAR FACE

But here in the New Year ritual it is through this consecration of offerings to the deities of West and East that the priest-king enters a new sacramental mode of existence. He is the Lord of Rituals, one who is raised into the circuit of the sun through his service in the divine cults, a king now living and moving in harmony with the great heavenly bodies, maintaining the cosmic and social order. And his transfigured

state is celebrated during the next phase of the ritual, called 'The rite of the adoration of Horus which confers the office', which is mentioned also in Graeco-Roman temple inscriptions, especially in Horus's temple at Edfu.

Again the king is anointed. Then, as incense is burned over offerings of bread and beer, a lapis-lazuli star-like adornment is placed at his throat, making manifest his glorious nature as a celestial 'shining one', a radiant *Akh*, whose fiery body is entirely suffused with Sekhmet's *sekhem*-power in the light-filled heaven.[12] A great hymn of praise is chanted, glorifying the pharaoh as the triumphant son of Isis and Osiris who illuminates the horizon of the sky. Who sang this is not stated in the Brooklyn Museum papyrus, but perhaps it was a Hathorian chantress, or even two,

fig.23 **The confirmation of royal power. Here Seti I, holding his name enclosed in a cartouche, reverently kneels beneath the sacred *Ished*-tree of Heliopolis. Behind him stands Thoth inscribing the royal name on one of the leaves. Also present are leonine goddesses. (19th Dynasty relief on the north wall of the hypostyle hall in the Amun temple at Karnak.)**

35

trained in the art of praise-giving and singing like the two Meret-goddesses, the divine Upper and Lower Egyptian personifications of the priestess as singer, whose songs accompanied the rising sun:

Horus appears in the horizon
of the sky,
And the gods rejoice at his sight…
Hail, Horus, Lord of Praises,
To you belongs praise,
To you belong acclamations…
Appear. Be exalted, be exalted,
Be powerful,
Be venerated, be venerated,
O powerful image of every day.[13]

The chant closes with a marked shift of focus as an unnamed deity is hailed with the words: 'May your beneficent face be favourable to the pharaoh.' Then comes the enigmatic statement 'to be uttered for the face of the god in his disk', the divine countenance manifesting the god's glory and splendour, surely here none other than Re's face, the celestial solar father, whose blessing the king now actively seeks as his divinely appointed 'son'. Clearly, here in the ritual, there is another incantation at this point but, alas, the details are not given. Would it have involved a musical priestess shaking her sistrum as she led the king into the divine presence, chanting her sacred utterances for the revelation of the supreme vision, for 'seeing the face of the god'? We can only note that the ritual progression closely parallels Theban temple scenes which show a sistrum-shaking daughter goddess leading the king into the presence of her divine father for the zenithal confirmation of his power (fig.40).[14]

With the beneficent gaze of the sun god now turned to him, this divinized king is indeed in an exalted illuminated state, raised to the very zenith of heaven, where he will eat the sacramental bread. This is accomplished as a priest now draws the design of the emblem of office in resin mixed with saliva on the palm of the king's hand. Then he, the living incarnation of Horus, is given this same emblem in bread, kneaded from dough 'which has not been given to any other human'. As he absorbs this sacramental bread, the very symbol of life, a priest confirms his sacred rulership four times. And this part of the New Year ritual closes with the utterance: 'He is confirmed by the emblem of office when he eats it.' The spirit of the vast cosmos has entered into him, has become alive in him, through this eating of divine bread which invests his *Ka*-body with all its life-giving power.[15]

CREATING BEAUTY: THE IMAGE-MAKER

Chapter 4

Under the apricot tree I woke you.

There your mother conceived you.

There she conceived you, she who bore you.

Place me as a seal upon your heart,

As a seal upon your arm.

For love is as strong as death,

Jealousy as hard as Sheol.

Its darts are darts of fire,

Flaming lightning!

Mighty waters cannot quench love

Nor rivers wash it away.

Should one offer all his possessions for love,

It would be utterly scorned.[1]

(From the Song of Songs 8:6–7, attributed to King Solomon)

◄ *fig.24* **Hathor vitalizes Ramesses II as he touches the sacred jewels of her** *menit-***necklace. (Relief in the hall of Queen Nefertari's 19th Dynasty temple at Abu Simbel.)**

We seem to have left Tutankhamun's Golden Shrine far behind. But with this New Year ritual in our minds, we can now return to its meaning on firmer ground, with a key to interpreting its beautiful 'anointing' imagery and a clearer understanding of its ritual roots.

Turning first to the two reliefs on the back, we see Ankhesenamun 'renewing' Tutankhamun in different ways. In the lower scene she gives two notched palm ribs, the hieroglyphic signs for 'years', from which hang other signs signifying 100,000 Jubilee festivals of renewal (fig.25). They also bear emblematic *Ankh* and *Was* hieroglyphs, so providing a visual parallel to the *Was*-sceptre of dominion and *Ankh*-amulet of life that the king receives immediately before he is anointed during the New Year ritual (see page 32). When he is given these amulets

it is proclaimed that 'Horus has been given his Eye.' His violent conflict with Seth is also mentioned, as is his furious beheading of Isis during the struggle.

Significantly, Tutankhamun, wearing the Lower Egyptian Red Crown, is seated upon a traditional throne, which, according to the inscription behind him, is 'the throne of Horus', a deified throne often associated with Isis as mother goddess. This is the stable foundation on which the king rests as Egypt's ruler. And here Tutankhamun asserts his Horus sovereignty as the queen bestows on him these renewing signs of rulership. [2]

Next we move to the anointing in the scene above (fig.26). Here Tutankhamun sits on a high-backed chair with lion legs which is also decorated with the entwined heraldic plants of Upper and Lower Egypt in open-work between its

legs. This motif symbolizes the 'Union of
the Two Lands', the binding of Horus
and Seth within a united Egypt, together
with all the other paired contrasts
associated with the rivalry between these
two gods. And it means too that the king
is ready for the approach of his
barefooted queen who comes to anoint
him from the garlanded ointment cone
she holds, touching his arm and exalting
his flesh with her fragrant healing oil just
as the king is anointed with the Eye
goddess's fiery oils in the New Year
ritual.[3]

No gesture on this Golden Shrine is
without symbolic meaning. And by
touching the king's arm in this way,
Ankhesenamun becomes completely
identified with Sekhmet, for a beautiful
pectoral from Tutankhamun's tomb
depicts Sekhmet making the same gesture

when she touches Tutankhamun's armlet
on his upper arm, blessing the king
whilst Ptah bestows on him 'life' and
'power' (fig.27). Previously, Akhenaten
himself had worn heavy seals on his
upper arm, each one emblazoned with
the Aten's royal names, stamping his
solar rulership as the divinely appointed
son of Re (fig.2). Indeed, it is during the
pharaoh's New Year anointing with the
fiery nine oils that his name is said to
be in the 'august house' of Heliopolis,
thus authenticating his cosmic rulership
(see page 42). In short, it is by his
anointing with these fragrant oils that his
royal name is 'sealed' in the New Year
ceremony.

Thus, by touching Tutankhamun's
upper arm—specifically in the place
where an amuletic seal was often worn
in the ancient world—Ankhesenamun

▲ *fig.25*
**Tutankhamun
receives two notched
palm ribs from
Ankhesenamun which
bear emblematic
hieroglyphs ensuring
the king 'all life and
power' and '100,000
Jubilee festivals'. The
king wears the Red
Crown of Lower
Egypt and sits upon
the traditional Horus
throne. (Lower scene
on the back of the
Golden Shrine.
Egyptian Museum,
Cairo.)**

▶ *fig.26*
Ankhesenamun anoints Tutankhamun with unguents from a dish containing an ointment cone draped with two lotus blossoms, symbols of regeneration. The king, seated on a throne decorated with a 'Union of the Two Lands' motif, wears the Blue Crown and is guarded above by the vulture of the South. The queen specifically touches the armlet on his upper arm in a similar gesture to Sekhmet's blessing of Tutankhamun shown in fig.27. On statues of Akhenaten from Karnak the Aten's names are engraved into heavy seals on his upper arms (see fig.2). Here these stylistic details are subtly re-echoed in the context of a traditional anointing rite. Just as Sekhmet safeguards the king's Heliopolitan name in the New Year anointing ceremony, so the queen protects Tutankhamun's rulership. (Upper scene on the back of the Golden Shrine. Egyptian Museum, Cairo.)

subtly conveys her protection of Tutankhamun's rulership. The gesture has the added meaning that she herself has come, like a fragrant amulet, to offer her Sekhmetian power to the 'image' king and thus enhance his life, protect him from harm and unite with him in all his actions as Egypt's divinely appointed ruler.[4]

BURNING FURY: LIFE-EMPOWERING EYE

Moving from the back of the shrine to the scenes adorning its sides—that is, following the same direction as the 14 Nekhbet vultures swooping across the roof and the winged uraeus snaking along the roof's sides—we see the twofold implications of this anointing as Ankhesenamun beautifies and adorns her husband, empowering him with all her fiery solar 'dread' and 'attraction'. Here,

as in the New Year ritual, she bestows on him all the magical 'weapons' he needs to rule as a vital solar monarch.

Indeed, all the scenes on the sides of the shrine amplify the anointing themes in the New Year ritual's chants. So, for example, when the king is anointed with the fragrant second oil, Sekhmet is praised as the raging goddess who storms through foreign lands, returning in triumph to Egypt with her trophies 'like the light of the sky', and this return brings protective energy for the Horus king:

You have traversed mountains,
You have dispelled storms…
You assure protection
For Horus, your son, whom you love,
Pharaoh, the son whom you love.[5]

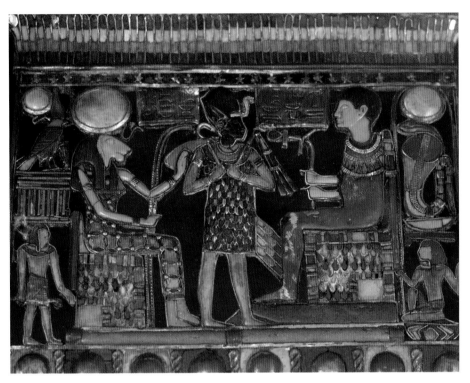

fig.27 Pectoral discovered in a box in Tutankhamun's tomb which probably belonged to the ceremonial regalia worn by the king in life. Inside a kiosk the king, wearing the Blue Crown and a short Jubilee cloak, stands between the enthroned deities of Memphis. On the left Sekhmet holds the sign for 'years' and raises her hand towards the king's armlet on his upper arm, blessing him with an 'eternity of years'. Behind her perches a white-crowned Horus falcon of the South and uraeus. Beneath is the royal *Ka* sustaining the king's life. On the right Ptah bestows Tutankhamun with life and power from the sceptre he holds. Behind him is a rebus for 'millions of years' surmounted by a uraeus. (Egyptian Museum, Cairo.)

Revealing, too, is the chant for the third oil, which praises the serpent goddess Wadjet, hailing her as the might that terrorizes the king's enemies, the 'Eye' that bestows on him 'magical power':

> The might of your terror
> Is upon your enemies,
> O Wadjet,
> She who renews the Two Lands,
> Your magical power
> Is great against all malevolent things,
> Which can harm the pharaoh…
> O, this Eye
> More endowed with power divine,
> More omnipotent than the gods…6

Instantly, such aggressive themes take us to the bird-trapping and arrow-shooting symbolism on the Golden Shrine's left side, showing the royal couple sailing in the bird pools to contact this fiery Sekhmetian *Ba*-power and draw it back to Egypt, channelling it into creative cosmic life and into the nourishing pleasures of solar existence (figs.8,11).

LIVING AND LOVING: SOLAR BECOMING

But this fiery serpent goddess in the New Year ritual is also a 'green' Hathorian power who 'renews the pharaoh in life' and surrounds him 'in the fullness of life', just as the solar queen is shown to be the source of life for Tutankhamun on the Golden Shrine. Thus, when the pharaoh is anointed with the seventh oil, so the chant hails his entry into Heliopolis, the 'pillar city' where the 'great bull' resides (the sacred Mnevis bull), and where, with outstretched arms, the king 'supports the sycamore trees' in adoration of Atum and Khepri. This pillar of the heavenly sky, so the chant proclaims, is 'the image of Khepri, with whom the Ennead are content, whose power is revered', a king whom Atum desires 'should be in his following'.[7]

Likewise, we see Ankhesenamun protectively tying the cords of Tutankhamun's amuletic necklace incorporating a solar scarab (fig.28), protectively encircling him with this Heliopolitan symbol of eternal solar 'becoming'. One of the names of the solar scarab amulet is 'living and loving', an apt name for the vivifying 'knotting' gesture the Hathorian queen makes here on the Golden Shrine.[8] But this heart scarab, supporting a sun disk above, also resonates with Tutankhamun's royal 'name', the 'Lord of Transformations is

Re' (*Nebkheperure*), that 'name of the pharaoh' which, according to the chant for the eighth oil in the New Year ritual, is in the 'august house' of Heliopolis (fig.23). Such a royal name is also celebrated in the opening lines of the beautiful Biblical *Song of Songs* when the female lover chants to her beloved king, 'As for scent, your oils are good. "Oil of Turaq" is your name. That's why maidens love you. Take me with you, let us hasten. The king has brought me to his chambers.' And here we see an Egyptian royal name also 'poured forth' on this lovely Golden Shrine.[9]

Moreover, the Egyptian word for Ankhesenamun's 'tying' gesture is *tjes*, meaning 'to tie' or 'to knot' the cord of an amulet. But it has a whole range of other meanings, including 'knit together' bones, 'form' a body or face and 'reunite' what has been separated. Essentially, then, Ankhesenamun's protective gesture makes manifest her power to 'join' or 'gather together' Tutankhamun's power, making firm his royal person and overcoming any threat of dissolution. Weaving her protection around him, and watched over by a vulture with outspread wings, the divine bird of the great 'mother', she here 'gathers together' Tutankhamun's powers in every way for his renewal of Heliopolitan creation.[10]

Then, as the crescendo of the chants builds, creating a great vortex of power for this solar ascension, so the invocation for the eighth oil praises the pharaoh as 'the one who has unveiled the face of Khepri, who has accomplished the cult of Re-Atum'. This divinized king gives fluids to the Heliopolitan deities, providing them with their offerings. He is now a heavenly king, close to the 'sky goddess Nut and Khepri', whose semen carries the very life essence of the cosmos itself, a king who

▼ *fig.28*
Ankhesenamun knots the cords attached to Tutankhamun's winged scarab pectoral. During the New Year anointing rites the king is praised as 'the image of Khepri' and identified with Re-Atum. (Scene on the right side of the Golden Shrine. Egyptian Museum, Cairo.)

Gives their water to the divine beings
As the messenger of Atum.[11]

Overflowing with fecund fertile life, this 'bull' king makes the Heliopolitan 'old ones' young again, so that they come forth from their caverns rejuvenated as youthful 'wearers of the sidelock' in this heavenly place of divine origins:

They renew themselves when they
see him,
They appear to him like
young children,
And he is powerful when he
sees that...[12]

In this mysterious continuous creation—so graphically portrayed in funerary papyri vignettes of the sun-child encircled by the ouroboros-snake biting its own tail to symbolize 'creator' and 'created' as one—Atum's self-regenerative 'bull' powers are fully at the pharaoh's disposal, streaming forth from him as renewer of creation.

Likewise in fig.12, do we not see the braided Queen Ankhesenamun, wearing her Hathorian lock of hair, squatting at Tutankhamun's feet like a young maiden as he pours his life-giving 'water' into her cupped hand? She who has poured out nourishing liquid into her husband's cup (fig.13) now receives his masculine creative power as the 'god's hand', the divine 'daughter' emanating great attraction and power in these dynamic beginnings of the Heliopolitan cosmos. Together they appear here on the shrine utterly united with Heliopolitan creative life. Kindling fiery renewal for the whole of creation, their rejuvenating love sustains the unending cycle of eternity. Moreover, should Tutankhamun in fact be holding persea fruits here (fig.12), rather than mandrakes, they would be a

highly appropriate natural symbol for his 'water-spell'. Requiring dry midsummer heat to come to maturity, these beautiful and much-loved fruits ripened as the floodwaters returned to Egypt. Hence, they would further enhance the sense of Tutankhamun's fruitful cosmic renewal at this New Year time of the inundation.[13]

Through the divinized pharaoh's creative powers nothing malevolent now harms creation. For, as the chant for the ninth sacred oil proclaims:

He lives from the life that Re lives,
He sees with the vision with which
Re sees,
He hears with the hearing with which
Re hears,
He rules with the ruling power which
Re utilizes,
He fulfils his circuit like Re,
He lands like Atum.[14]

Fully in command of his visionary sight and hearing, the pharaoh is now truly the Heliopolitan anointed one, the illuminated 'pillar' king, destined in every way to keep at bay the sun god's enemy, Apophis, and thus ensure the year's eternal fresh renewal. For he has fulfilled the return to the source required of him in the ritual, a return to the unity and essence of Heliopolitan origins which in itself compels a renewal of life in the ceaseless cycle of regeneration.

RISING JOY:
THE RADIANT CROWN

Just as, immediately after the anointing rites, the pharaoh makes his heavenly ascension in the New Year ritual, so the movement towards the zenith unfolds further on the Golden Shrine in the six scenes depicted on the exterior of the doors. Here the queen manifests as praise-giver, acclaiming her radiant husband in a variety of ways (fig.30). For her beloved, whom she has so richly anointed and adorned, has now become the king worthy of her praise, exactly like the 'Horus, Lord of Praises' in the horizon hymn in the New Year ritual, sung when the pharaoh is again anointed and a star of lapis-lazuli placed at his throat (page 35).

Ankhesenamun has renewed Tutankhamun, has transformed him and vitalized him with all her powers on the back and sides of the shrine. So, too, the Memphite-Heliopolitan deities have been provided with ample nourishment. And now the queen directs the dynamism of her praise towards the exalted king, extolling him on these horizon doors. Above them soars the glorious winged solar disk, Horus of Behdet, connecting the royal couple with both sky and sun. And flanking them on either side are the royal names, inscribed on the door jambs. Those on the left declare the pharaoh's sonship with the Memphite deities Ptah and Sekhmet:

> The perfect god, Son of Ptah,
> Born of Sekhmet, Lady of the Sky.
> King of Upper and Lower Egypt,
> *Nebkheperure*
> (*Translation:* The Lord of Transformations is Re).
> Son of Re, Lord of Appearances,
> Tutankhamun
> (*Translation:* The Living Image of Amun),
> Ruler of Southern Heliopolis,
> Beloved of Weret-Hekau.

Those on the right proclaim his solar filiation as Heliopolitan image of the sun god:

> The perfect god, image of Re,
> Who performs exalted deeds for him,
> The one who gave birth to him.
> King of Upper and Lower Egypt,
> Lord of the Two Lands,
> *Nebkheperure.*
> Son of Re, Lord of Appearances,
> Tutankhamun,
> Ruler of Southern Heliopolis,
> Beloved of Weret-Hekau.

Both proclamations end with the words that the king is the beloved of the 'Great of Magic', a ruler now radiating all the great enchantress's magical rage and radiance. And this love is expressed in the ritual gestures which Ankhesenamun now makes on each door panel (fig.30). In one scene she supports Tutankhamun's arm; in another she brings him flowers, their fragrant scent and colour opening the king's senses to the gifts of health and joy; in another she holds her hands aloft before her face in the typical *dwa*-gesture 'adoration', as the king firmly grasps a lapwing by its wings. This is the ubiquitous *rekhyt*-bird, frequently seen in Egyptian art as a symbol of the king's subjects. As the queen gives praise, so

▶ *fig.29* **The Golden Shrine with doors open to reveal the pedestal and back plinth for a statuette in its interior. (Egyptian Museum, Cairo.)**

fig. 30 **Scenes on the exterior of the shrine's doors showing Ankhesenamun praising Tutankhamun whom she has empowered and 'brought to birth'. (Egyptian Museum, Cairo.)**

the New Year.[15] Yet another scene shows Ankhesenamun shaking a loop sistrum before her enthroned husband, the version of the instrument which was used by temple musicians for praise-giving (in contrast to a naos sistrum, which was used to 'propitiate' a wrathful deity in the temple cults).

The queen's glorification of her husband in these scenes is neither a perfunctory nor servile performance but a summation of everything that has been shown on the back and sides of the shrine. For to give praise and rejoice means to participate in a sacred cosmos filled with 'names'. It belongs to the very act of creation in Memphis-Heliopolis, and any praise-giving, whether it be in honour of a deity, a living ruler or a holy place, releases cosmic potential and life. So, for example, when Ptah, the craft god of Memphis, beholds the beautiful form of Ramesses II, which he has fashioned *(mesi)* in precious metals as Re's divine image on earth, he is overwhelmed by deep joy welling up in his heart. Taking this golden king whom he has 'brought to birth' *(mesi)* in his arms in an embrace of gold, Ptah imbues him with 'jubilation, joy, gladness of heart, delights and rejoicing'.[16]

Tutankhamun, the direct embodiment of the land and his people in the rites, now exerts his sovereignty over his people, incorporating them into this New Year renewal. For the pharaoh's renewal is their renewal, and they completely depend on him for their welfare here at

Likewise here, on these doors of the shrine, we see Ankhesenamun surrounding Tutankhamun with her Hathorian music, perfumes, flowers and jubilation. Like a divine cult image, the king's body has been anointed, adorned and protected by her. And now the king whom she has renewed in the world in every way, whom she has 'birthed' and vitalized, has become the radiant crown of Egypt whom she glorifies through her rejoicing. They are a radiant theophany of male and female, the praiser and the praised, manifesting together as Egypt's rulers beneath the great winged disk which lights up the world. For she who has bestowed on this horizon king everything he needs to exercise rulership is now drawn to him in love and praise through the radiating power of his life-giving 'attraction'.[17]

The doors of the shrine wait to be opened, its contents wait to be revealed (fig.29). Four royal cartouches, each one with a fiery uraeus coiled around it, each one resting on the sign for 'gold', emblazon the inner panels on each side. They proclaim the names of the king: 'The Lord of Transformations is Re' and 'The Living Image of Amun, Ruler of southern Heliopolis'. Beneath, lapwings on hieroglyphic *neb*-signs raise human arms before a five-pointed star, so making an emblematic motif reading 'Adoration of all subjects.' And between these four golden royal names Ankhesenamun brings her adoration yet again before the heavenly king, her name carved in the space between them. This time, however, she approaches the radiant vision of the sun, the Horus of Gold, glittering in the interior of the shrine, a majestic heavenly ruler at the height of his power. The king who has been the object of her praise on the exterior of the doors, who has been

exalted through her acclamations, now actively illuminates her with his shining rays. Standing like a Heliopolitan 'pillar' king, surrounded by the walls and roof of this serpentine 'Great House', a new Horus of Gold shines in the world, entirely fed, nourished and encompassed by his female beloved.

Without the background of the New Year ritual it is very difficult to understand the arrangement of these scenes on the Golden Shrine with their repetition of ritualized gestures which the couple make together. Yet it is only by living their lives according to such ritual patterns that they give their rulership its sacred meaning. As Mircea Eliade observed about the tendency of traditional cultures to live according to ritualized archetypal patterns, 'An object or an act becomes real only insofar as it imitates or repeats an archetype ... everything which lacks an exemplary model ... lacks reality.'[18]

Tutankhamun's Golden Shrine perfectly illustrates this ritualized life of Egypt's king and queen. Though at first sight the scenes may appear personal, individualized and intimate, they are in fact highly stylized and symbolic. Everything Ankhesenamun does for her husband has a cult meaning, which is deeply embedded in the sacramental life they share as Egypt's rulers. And to those deeply versed in royal rituals, these scenes would surely have evoked the New Year ritual's sacred anointing rite confirming the king's power.

They do well to say—and indeed by some divine chance they touch the truth when they say—that lovers are able to return to the light even from Hades. It is true that they do not know where and how this was accomplished; they missed the path, as it were, that Plato through his philosophy was the first of all human beings to discern. There are, however, dim, faint effluvia of the truth scattered about in Egyptian mythology … tiny scraps of evidence.[1]

(From Plutarch's 'Dialogue on Love')

fig.31 **Head of the solar divine cow on a bed from the tomb of Tutankhamun. An inscription on the bed names him as the Osiris king of Upper Egypt and beloved of Isis-Mehet ('the Flood'). (Egyptian Museum, Cairo.)**

We have followed the anointed king's ascension to the zenithal heaven for his confirmation of power as the 'son of Re'. Yet this was not the end of the 14-day New Year ritual preserved in the Brooklyn Museum papyrus but rather preparation for the 'Osirian' phase, in which the heritage of 'the Bull who is shrouded in the august chamber' is transmitted to the anointed Horus king. The 'Bull' surely refers here to the Osirian royal predecessor, or even to Osiris himself, who is depicted in the New Kingdom *Book of Caverns* with his bull-headed entourage in the deepest recesses of the earth, lying in the netherworld darkness as Bull of the West.[2] Indeed, in order to legitimize the pharaoh's rulership at the New Year, it was required that he also renewed his connection with the Osirian realm. Performed in the greatest secrecy, this was a ritual rite of crossing from which the Horus king would return utterly transformed and confirmed in his inheritance, bringing with him the life-giving waters and secrets of eternal renewal.

Possibly Tutankhamun would have had a Lower Egyptian sanctuary shaped like the northern *Per-Neser* shrine and dedicated to the cobra goddess Wadjet to complement his Upper Egyptian *Per-Wer* Golden Shrine. Possibly, too, its symbolic imagery would have related to this Osirian phase in the New Year ritual, for Osirian redemptive rites were closely linked with the Lower Egyptian crown and the north.[3] Moreover, these dual shrines were always paired together, as in Hathor's Graeco-Roman temple at Dendara, where they stood alongside each other on the innermost sanctuary's west side. So, too, the large gilt shrines enclosing Tutankhamun's sarcophagus and coffin in his burial chamber included ones shaped like these northern and southern goddess houses. Nevertheless, no small *Per-Neser* complementing the Golden Shrine was among the objects discovered in Tutankhamun's tomb.

Be that as it may, the confirmation of the Horus king's Osirian lineage was an essential part of the New Year ceremony. It was enacted as the king lay on a bed within a specially prepared chamber in

◀ *fig.32* **Diagram of the House of Life from** *Papyrus Salt 825* **showing an image of Osiris at its centre. (British Museum, London.)**

the 'Place of conferring the Heritage', probably on the last night of the old year. First, however, the New Year ritual text carefully prescribes the preparation of the ritual objects and amulets for use in the ensuing magical operations. Initial rites had also to be performed for the deities of the House of Life, the sacred house attached to temples throughout the country, where statues were created and 'made to live', and where incantations, rituals and medical remedies were all composed and preserved (fig. 32).

Clearly, the New Year ritual has now moved deep into the Osirian world of the Egyptian magical practitioners, those able to enliven lifeless forms and images. For the papyrus states that seven figures—a falcon, a crocodile, an ibis, a baboon, a vulture, a heron and a goat—should be made in clay and then animated by breathing flames into their mouths.[4]

One is reminded here of Michael Psellus, a leading Byzantine Neoplatonist of the 11th century CE, who describes just such a type of magical practice whereby images (of wax and clay) are made to come alive through fire. In his treatise *On Daemons* he wrote: 'Often, too, celestial fire is made to appear through magic; and then statues laugh, and lamps are spontaneously enkindled.'[5] Likewise, these Egyptian statues are now terrifyingly alive, becoming fearsome fire-spitting guardians of the recumbent king as seven offerings are given to them and they are placed in some kind of enclosure of sand to the west and east.

EXCHANGING SEALS: THE TOMB VISIT

Then the rites begin which guide the Horus king through this dangerous redemptive journey. A faience amulet in the shape of a bee, the Lower Egyptian symbol of kingship, is placed at his throat, together with a faience falcon-shaped amulet. A wooden sceptre is placed in his hand. Then the priests are instructed to place four seals beneath his head as the 'heritage of the Bull who is shrouded in the august chamber'. One of these seals is made of wood from the *Ima*-tree, a tree which eludes precise botanical identification, but evidently had Osirian and Hathorian associations (page 69). Indeed, in an archaic royal ritual preserved in the *Ramesseum Dramatic Papyrus*, immediately after Osiris's death has been enacted in the Sethian rite of trampling grain, a Thoth-like ritualist boards the royal boat carrying a branch from the *Ima*-tree and cryptically makes play with its name in his accompanying speech: 'How sweet *(ima)* is that which has come forth from your father.' Probably because it exudes a particular aroma, this *Ima*-branch evokes the life-giving 'sweetness' flowing from Osiris, which the ritual associates with his procreative powers.[6]

According to the New Year ritual papyrus the *Ima*-seal, which is stamped with the name of the earth god Geb (Osiris's father in the Heliopolitan Ennead), must be placed in

> The tomb of the father of a man
> who is alive.[7]

In other words, it must be placed in the Osirian predecessor's tomb by the Horus son as inheritor of the throne in the third generation. Another seal, made of pine and again stamped with Geb's name, is said to belong in the dwelling of the living successor. Two other seals, stamped with effigies of the goddess Maat and the Lower Egyptian goddess Neith, are also placed beneath the king's head.

All is precision. And needs to be. For what is being enacted here is the annual New Year journey to the 'august chamber', during which the reigning Horus king renews a 'contract' with his Osirian predecessor as a powerful legitimization of his rule. To ensure the efficacy of this contract, every detail of the materials used for these seals has been carefully prescribed. For it is Osiris, together with the whole host of royal ancestors and the blessed dead, who ensures the recurrent cycles of nature are restored at the New Year. Hence it is essential for the solar king to renew his relationship with him.[8]

What the pharaoh actually experienced when he lay on the bed in this sleep-like condition is veiled in the utmost secrecy. But the ceremony hints at some form of somnambulistic temple sleep or ritual incubation of the kind that was widely practised in the oracle cults of Graeco-Roman Egypt, often to induce healing dreams. It was also a means of crossing the dangerous threshold of death and contacting netherworld deities. Is it a form of incubation rite here? It looks very much like it.[9]

Certainly, spell 228 of the *Coffin Texts* evokes a redemptive journey to the Osirian tomb. It tells how a person (identified with Horus) goes to the dwelling of Osiris in order to 'enliven his two cobras', to dispel the affliction of the suffering god and to read from the sealed contract that is found there:

> Ah, Great One,
> Enter and tell the collector of writings,
> The door-keeper of Osiris,
> That I have come, being great
> and effective…
> I have come to protect my body,
> and enliven my two cobras,

to sit in the dwelling of Osiris,
and dispel the sickness of the
suffering god,
so that I may appear an Osiris
in strength,
that I may be reborn with him renewed,
and uncover for you Osiris's thigh.
And read to you from this contract
which lies beneath the side of Osiris,
whereby the mouths of the gods
are opened.[10]

Not only must this Horus-like initiate travel to the place where Osiris languishes in order to read from the contract beneath Osiris's side which 'opens the mouths of the gods', but he must also 'enliven' his two cobras. Should he fail to do so, Osiris will continue to suffer and his sickness, arising from Seth's death-dealing blows, remain uncured, thus perpetuating cosmic division and separation. As Rundle Clark observed, the unveiling of Osiris's thigh in the spell must be an oblique reference to the fertility brought by the returning floodwaters. He wrote: 'If the wound in the thigh can be cured, the water and the male fluid will gush forth and life begin again.'[11] For in Osiris's suffering, death and mysterious revival each year lies the secret of the annual renewal of the Nile waters.

RAISING THE CORD: OSIRIS REBORN

Such a quest of 'making the waters flow again', of 'sealing' the pharaoh's relationship with his royal predecessor, lies at the heart of these Osirian New Year rites. For, after the seals have been placed beneath the king's head, the text describes how the chief ritualist then brings two birds close to the king, whose

hand rests upon what seems to have been a loaf or cake called *Bat*. This object had been specifically prepared beforehand from prescribed mineral and vegetable substances and, in accordance with the methods of sympathetic magic, had also been coated with earth taken from the zone of the fields which the inundation waters covered. The king's hand rests therefore on an image which will help him to draw back the life-giving waters to Egypt.

And as the two living birds are brought close to the king, so the chief priest proclaims he has attained the mysterious *Ibhet*-stone:

The mysterious throne of pharaoh, life,
prosperity and health, is the
Ibhet-stone. Pharaoh, life, prosperity
and health, will not surrender
his secret throne of the *Ibhet*-stone.[12]

By means of this redemptive descent the anointed king, who but a while ago has been crowned with all the splendours of the heavenly sun, attains the mysterious stone, the *Ibhet*-stone, identified with his 'secret throne' of rulership.[13] Restraining the hostile forces lurking in this dangerous region, he fulfils this crucial renewal of seals, confirming his link with the vast chain of Osirian royal predecessors. Making manifest the everlasting flow of Osiris's divine influence, the reigning pharaoh reconnects with this deep fount of life, truly becoming the legitimized channel of renewal for Egypt.

Then the priest releases one of the birds (the bird of Horus) with the word 'Go', ordering that a message be taken to Horus declaring that the king is in the process of consolidating his position, stretching his cord and driving in his

▶ *fig.33* **The release of the waters harmonized with the return of sun and stars at dawn. In the upper register the goddess Maat sails with Khepri in the solar boat towed by six spitting cobras towards the eastern horizon. Energizing the return to life each cobra appears with human arms holding the boat's prow rope. In the register beneath, the owner of the papyrus Bakenmut kneels in worship before a chthonic snake, 'the lord of very secret faces', wearing the White Crown of Upper Egypt. The serpent is named as 'the great god, the flow of the primordial waters', the tremendous burled power controlling the waters in the deep abyss. Before him Horus the Elder leans on his staff. On the far left Bakenmut praises the glorious rebirth of life. Standing within the solar globe are the ram-headed Atum and Khepri, the polar gods of West and East in the solar circuit. From the globe a vivifying shower of light falls upon two fish-like mummiform figures and a human head emerging within the horizon. The descent of the sun into the depths of earth leads to the annual renewal of the waters and return of the celestial stars. (Scenes on the papyrus of Bakenmut. Egyptian Museum, Cairo.)**

mooring-post. The other bird is ordered not to allow any enemy of Horus 'who is at the head of the Ennead' to chase him from his throne.

With this flight of Horus's messenger bird, so everything in the ritual is now directed towards returning the pharaoh from this dark tomb. And to this end, as the spell from the *Coffin Texts* already quoted says, Horus must 'enliven his two cobras'—must rouse the serpent whose fire will guide him safely to the land of the living. Or, as another netherworld-traveller declares in a *Coffin Text* spell 'I have come here so that I may turn my snake, that I may raise the uraeus and that I may cure the great god [Osiris] of that which he has greatly suffered.'[14]

Here in the New Year ritual seven marsh plants are first brought to the pharaoh, together with seven sheets of papyrus, the number of efficacy in Egyptian ritual practice. The king then inhales the scent of these marsh plants before cutting their umbels. Why he does so is not stated. But the seven sheets of papyrus suggest some kind of execration rite, probably directed against the cosmic enemy Apophis, since sheets of papyrus were commonly used in Egyptian magical rites, inscribed with the enemy's name or image in fresh red ink.[15]

That the ceremony had some kind of protective function can be conjectured from the brief enigmatic instructions concerning the next rite, involving the

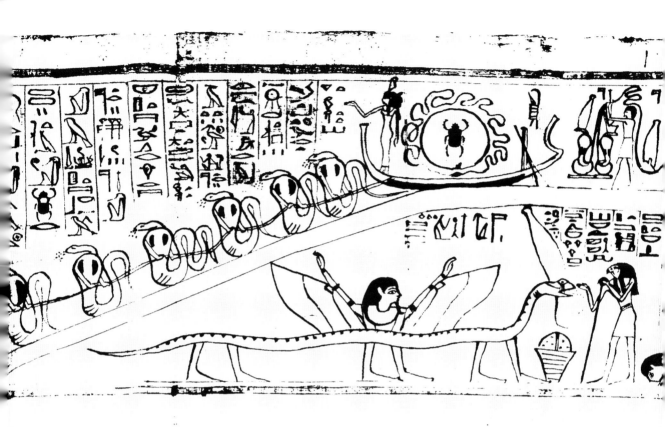

raising of the bow warp towards the sky and a gesture towards the stake *(menit)* of the boat. There is also an allusive reference to Sekhmet. But, alas, none of the important ceremonial details is included in the papyrus.

Nevertheless, the meaning becomes apparent if we look to spell 276 of the *Coffin Texts* for 'taking shape as Hathor' in the Osirian realm. Here the shining 'equipped' traveller powerfully manifests with the 'Lady of the Horizon' on his brow and the 'Lady of Offerings' within him, having 'taken her bow warp' and the 'great oar within the shrine'. This shape-shifting goddess who sails in the sun boat makes this Osirian initiate a powerful 'protector' of the Eye of Horus,

worthy of respect among the assembled deities.[16] And in this New Year rite of passage what can this ritual 'raising of the cord' mean other than that the powerful serpent uraeus, the fiery goddess, now rears up to the sky (fig.33), coiling her neck like the rope of a boat and spitting fire at those seeking to harm the ascending king whom she is now bringing back from the Osirian depths? For in the *Pyramid Texts* the resurrected king frequently invokes the feminine stability of the 'great mooring-post' *(menit weret)* when he seeks to be ferried across the difficult terrain to the eastern horizon. She it is who guards this up-and-down flow of powerful life forces along the heaven and deep earth axis when her serpentine power ascends. Sometimes the serpent goddess is called the 'braided one'. And the Egyptians loved to play with words associating hair braids, the cords at the prow and stern of a boat and the snake coils of the uraeus.[17]

Here in the ritual, however, all is veiled in cryptic allusions to a ceremony intended to bring the pharaoh into the boat of Re so that he can participate in the sun god's perpetual rejuvenation and resurrection. There then follows a brief statement which speaks volumes:

Horus shines, Horus shines. The Tired Heart appears as chief of the altars.[18]

When this powerful Horus king shines, so the 'Tired Heart' (an epithet of Osiris) manifests as 'chief of the altars', according to the rites in the 'Festival Ritual'—again, however, without the details being preserved in the New Year ritual papyrus. The meaning, though, is clear enough. As the Horus ruler returns from finding the stone, so Osiris is mysteriously beheld, 'healed' and reborn. For it is through the Horus king's entry into the hidden vault that Osiris's eternal nature becomes manifest, truly revealed as nourishing life on Egypt's holy altars, the rejuvenating New Year pure water 'that returns at its time', bringing renewed food and prosperity to the whole of Egypt. But it is a revelation completely dependent on Horus's power to unite 'peaceably' with the fiery serpent Eye goddess whose cords both bind the king's enemy to the path of destruction and provide his umbilical link to life when she rises up to the sky. She is the fire in the stone, the heart of earth, who holds the secret of return to life from this shrouded 'bull' chamber.[19]

CELESTIAL WATER: LIQUID SKY

Such an initiatory experience charges the returning king with immense power: the power to heal and to bring back the waters of life that make Egypt live again. But, like a shaman, he also returns as one who has been in contact with dangerous netherworld spirits. Moreover, he is now completely inflamed with the magical raging female heat that he has roused for his return. Such contact means that before he can function safely within the order of Egypt, he must be ritually protected and Sekhmet propitiated. Evidently he has remained in the sacred enclosure where this Osirian 'sleep' is enacted over several days, for it is specifically on the fifth day of the New Year that these prophylactic rites take place, together with a robing of the king.

A priest first brings a stem of papyrus, that heraldic plant of Lower Egypt and symbol of the fiery cobra goddess Wadjet, evoking her green flourishing life and peaceful state. For it is this Eye goddess who needs now to surround the pharaoh with all her health-bestowing goodness, green growth *(Wadj)* and protection as her serpent energy rises once again fully to the crown (fig.34).[20] Brought too is the boat of Seth, that erstwhile opponent of Osiris and Horus whose strength the king has gained and whose boat here shows his 'redness' to be now safely integrated into the order of the Two Lands. For if the annual inundation of the Nile is to flow creatively, it needs the fiery 'contentment' of male and female 'red' deities in every sense.[21]

The king takes the papyrus's umbel in his hand, grasping its green freshness, whilst the chief ritualist takes the lower end of the long papyrus stem in order to perform the ritual for protecting the pharaoh four times. Whether incantations were chanted at this point is not stated in the ritual papyrus. But it is not hard to imagine that this rite invoked the protection of the fiery serpent Eye goddess.

Next the king is ritually robed and adorned. Amulets are placed on the front of his clothing, specifically fastened with six threads made of red linen, of the kind in which it is said the king is also clothed. A sceptre symbolizing his dominion over foreign lands is placed in his hand and white sandals on his feet.[22] Then, once again, the Sekhmetian rite of raising the rope is performed. Amulets of the West are brought to him—a turquoise *Wedjat*-Eye no less, and a *Heh*-jewel of faience, an amulet symbolizing millions of years. These are now placed in the solar king's right hand with the words:

> When Re shines in his shrine
> He says to his Serpent Guide...
> 'Truly, the heaven of this Heliopolis
> has become the well of every god...'[23]

The text is elliptic, but its meaning is clear. For this is the reappearance of the solar 'Red King', possessing the power to span both earth and sky and move between the worlds completely reunited with his female 'Serpent Guide' (fig.35). Communing with his female snake, Re proclaims also that his 'magical power is victorious', marvelling at how the highest heaven of Heliopolis has become the 'well of every god', at how the highest has come down to the lowest in this flooding forth of heavenly water upon a celestial earth. United with his mystic guide, he commands the vertical axis of the world, the pillar of Heliopolis which 'simultaneously gives access to the lowest depths of the cosmos and to the greatest heights of heaven'.[24]

fig.34 **Statue of Sekhmet holding a papyrus stem symbolizing her 'green' propitiated state. (Temple of Ptah, Karnak.)**

▲ *fig.35* **In the centre of this earring from Tutankhamun's tomb is a carnelian figure of the 'Red King' holding a sceptre. He comes forth flanked by two uraeus snakes. Above them soars a winged Horus falcon. (Egyptian Museum, Cairo.)**

▲ ▶ *fig.36* **Vignette of a swallow perched on the primordial mound from chapter 86 of the *Book of the Dead*. The accompanying text associates the reborn initiate with the daughter of Re. (21st Dynasty papyrus of Ankhesenmut. Egyptian Museum, Cairo.)**

Now this red-robed adorned king is ready to leave the place of conferring the heritage to consecrate a whole host of offerings to all 'the gods of the caverns, to the guides of the netherworld, to the companions of Horus, to the Kings of the South and to the Kings of the North'. In short, his first ritual act after finishing this ritual crossing into the Osirian chamber is to feed those who dwell in the cavernous realms, including all the former kings of Egypt. The offering list naming the recipients is long and includes many different manifestations of Osiris in all the netherworld's 12 regions. And having done so, the pharaoh then stops at the shrine of the House of Life, offering to the 'god who is in his disk'.

Whereas in the ritual's first phase he offered to the deities of East and West (see page 34), in this regeneration phase it is the deities of North and South to whom he offers. Hence there is a fourfold dynamic between the cardinal points or four quarters in the ritual, held together by the Heliopolitan king and his 'Serpent Guide' at the point of confluence where the streaming forces of heaven and deep earth meet.

SPEECH OF THE BIRDS: SHINING REUNION

Finally, the climax of the ceremonies takes place as nine living birds, 'birds of Re', are brought before the divinized king, paralleling the nine sacred oils with which he was anointed at the beginning of the rites. Amulets, too, are brought: a falcon of gold, a vulture and a turquoise cat. Each bird is then anointed, though only the first bird, 'the living falcon' of the year, is specifically anointed with olibanum, as 'is done for the god'. Each bird then approaches the king with its head reverentially turned back, its gaze averted from a ruler now actively

radiating the full force of the regenerative powers he has acquired in the rites.

It is in bird form that the heavenly beings alight in their earthly temples, returning as *Ba*-birds in order to unite with their cult images. And it is as *Ba*-birds that they soar forth god-like to heaven, set free from the body, eternally reborn into life and light. Here, at the close of the New Year ritual, Egypt's Horus king manifests all the regenerative unifying might of his heavenly solar *Ba*-power, which he now actively controls and directs.

As each anointed bird is brought, including a vulture associated with Nut's protection as 'mother of the two brothers' and a kite honouring Isis as mother of Horus, so its wings are ceremonially placed around the pharaoh, protectively encircling him whilst the manifold powers he has gained in the ritual are acclaimed. Significantly, the sixth bird's chant hails the *Ibhet*-stone, the mysterious throne that is reached in the Osirian tomb.

And then comes the seventh bird. It is a swallow—that lovely darting Hathorian bird shown standing on the sun boat's prow as herald of the dawn. And, as this bird is anointed with sacred oil, she is hailed as:

The swallow unveiling her face when
she speaks to Re,
She has found Re rising up to meet her,
The cup-bearer who has given fresh
water and bread.[25]

Finding her beloved Re, whom she has so
lovingly sought, she unveils her face to
speak with him, the nourishing 'cup-
bearer' bringing 'fresh water and bread',
opening a new horizon for the dawn
birds. And like the 'green bird' praised in
the chant for the first hour of the day in
the New Kingdom 'Ritual of Hours', she
shows the way to the golden dawn:

O light of the sky, O light of earth,
You who dawn peaceably…
You who shines on the breast of Ptah,
If you give me my flight,
Then I shall find exit with the children
of my mother.

Manifesting like a winged protectress
adorning Ptah's shining breast, this divine
swallow, light-bringer for sky and earth,
soars forth 'peaceably', becoming the
flight-giver for the 'children of my
mother'. She is also 'the one with the
golden tresses' sailing in Nun, bringing

▶ *fig.37* **Inlaid counterpoise which
was attached by straps to the
pectoral of Sekhmet, Tutankhamun
and Ptah shown in fig.27. The king,
seated within an ornate kiosk with a
papyrus-shaped column on either
side, is offered a sign of life by the
winged goddess Maat. She is the
symbol of balance, truth and order
in the solar circuit and Ptah is often
called 'lord of Maat'. Tiny gold fish
hang from some of the gold and
glass bead tassels beneath.
(Egyptian Museum, Cairo.)**

forth new life when the egg breaks and releases the primordial placental waters:

> The one who shines
> The one with the golden tresses,
> Who sails in Nun,
> She who gives orders for your delight,
> Your egg is broken beside you
> And I am the newborn.

What clearer proof do we need than these glorious 'swallow chants' of the reborn king's return with Hathor, his propitiated 'Serpent Guide', soaring forth at the New Year with his beloved 'golden-tressed' companion, spanning the worlds of heaven and earth?

Finally, (though the text breaks off abruptly at this point), as the ninth bird is brought, all these 'birds of Re' are hailed as bringers of life, health and protection.

Then the king receives the sacred collar of gold. The name of this collar is *shashayt*, an epithet of Hathor (in her manifestation as Maat) during the Late Period.[26] And so, in the climactic moment of the ritual, the sun goddess herself adorns the shining Red King, her necklace protecting his heart, completely united with him in this marriage chamber. He has won the treasure hard to attain, the glittering jewels of gold brought by the nine birds of light. Crossing all boundaries between the living and the dead, the royal regenerator of time ensures creation 'becomes young' again, eternally reborn. The pharaoh in need of renewal at the beginning of the rites has become Re's living divine image, an image created by Ptah, the lord of Maat, manifesting all his heavenly power in the eternal cosmic order (fig.37). There is fire in the stone, transformational fire which, when worked with creatively, becomes the source of eternal renewal. Truly, by living through those age-old Egyptian New Year rites of 'making statues live', transforming them into divine presences infused with regenerative *Ba*-power, the divinized king has found union with his goddess queen, Re's heavenly golden 'daughter of the sun'.

Welcome in peace, Lady of the Two Lands,
Sovereign of men and women,
Lady of the universe in the sky and on earth.
When you shine, earth is strewn with raying light,
The deities accompany you in the sky,
Fearing your pestilence.
The deities carry you on earth,
Bowing before your *Bas*,
The deities of the *Dwat* tremble,
Because of the terror of your might.[1]

(From the ritual for propitiating Sekhmet at Edfu)

◀ *fig.38* **Fourth Dynasty diorite statue of King Khafre from the valley temple of his pyramid complex at Giza. Perched on the throne behind is a beautiful figure of the Horus falcon protectively enclosing the king's head with his wings. (Egyptian Museum, Cairo.)**

François Cumont once described the loss of the 'liturgic books of paganism' as the most disastrous in 'the general wreck of ancient literature'. For what we can glean is only, he says, 'a dim reflection of the religious ceremonies'.[2] He was, of course, referring primarily to the mystery religions that sprang up throughout the Roman Empire, but his words hold true for ancient Egypt, since much about Egyptian ritual life is unknown, only a fraction of the temple rituals that must once have been performed having been preserved on papyri. Even when we see ceremonies depicted on temple walls, it is very difficult, without a corresponding ritual papyrus, to reconstruct how they might have been enacted.

But not everything has gone in ancient Egypt. For, although no papyrus has so far been discovered describing the actual coronation ceremony, in this unique original New Year ritual document the veil of secrecy is lifted surrounding the

pharaoh as Egypt's 'anointed one'. He it is who reunites high heaven and deep earth at the turning-point of time, delivering Egypt from all the ills of the passing year. Binding together everything that has been 'separated' when the death-dealing powers have raged, Egypt's divine sun king creates the world anew.

His is the royal flesh sanctified by the fiery nine oils at the beginning of the ritual, sealing his unique name on the holy *Ished*-tree in Heliopolis and his sonship with Re. Protected like a divine cult image, the king acquires Re's attributes during this anointing, reuniting with the fiery serpent Eye goddess who coils around the sun god's head as the venomous cobra, both his fierce protectress and the destroyer of enemies. Indeed, it is this anointing with the nine holy oils, uniting him with the fiery divine feminine, that 'stamps' his rulership with its solar character, sealing his sonship with Re and setting him apart from the Egyptian people.

It also presages his ritual entry into the Osirian tomb. For on him falls the responsibility of journeying to the fountainhead of life, to the place where his buried predecessor lies, the 'Bull shrouded in the august chamber', in order to renew the seals of rulership. And through this renewal, the waters mysteriously flow again, bringing fertilizing power to Egypt's thirsty earth.

So, too, during this 'tomb' phase the pharaoh reaches the sacred *Ibhet*-stone. His secret throne becomes the living stone that is attained anew each year during these perilous Osirian rites. Though it is unclear precisely what kind of stone the *Ibhet*-stone might have been, diorite has been suggested. So, too, have amethyst and the green smaragdite.[3] Interestingly, in a late magical incantation it is an 'emerald' *(smaragd)* that is specifically connected with Osiris's Heliopolitan tomb (see page 79). But clearly, whichever stone it was, 'finding the stone' confirmed the Horus king's rulership at the New Year, as it did for the 18th Dynasty ruler Thutmose IV, whose confirmation of power, according to an inscription on a naos now in the Cairo Museum, also required him to discover a stone. The text tells how Thutmose found a 'stone in the manner of a divine falcon when he was a youth', an endeavour resulting in Amun commanding him 'to perform the kingship of the Two Lands'. Evidently, a quest for stone lay at the heart of the Horus king's rulership.[4]

But this New Year ritual is not just about the living Horus king and his quest for the stone. For when the fiery female serpent returns the pharaoh from the tomb, a king now blessed with the power to hold together high heaven and deep earth, so the 'Tired Heart' (Osiris) mysteriously appears, the hidden divine source of life, food and fertility, now resurrected and alive as 'chief of the altars'. This revelation of Osiris's resurrected powers is at the heart of these New Year unification mysteries. Indeed, it is through the Red King's power to move between heaven and deep earth, to travel along the Heliopolitan vertical axis of the world with its up-and-down flow of forces, that the 'hidden' Osiris can truly reveal his life-giving powers. Though once dormant, this 'Bull shrouded in the august chamber' now actively nourishes cosmic life, releasing the desired floodwaters.[5] Every dimension of the cosmos has harmoniously come together, deeply and truly alive in this regenerative New Year life process.

HEALING DIVISIONS: SEKHMET'S REMEDY

Yet this revelation of Osiris's reborn vitality depends completely on Hathor-Sekhmet's magical raging heat. For to regenerate Egypt the anointed king must awaken the Eye goddess's fiery power, not only to raise himself to the Heliopolitan sky at the beginning of the ritual but also when he soars forth from the darkness of the Osirian tomb. Her love and desire must fill his heart if he is to make manifest his celestial nature. She it is who moves him between the 'opposites' of heaven and deep earth. Both when the king ascends to the zenith and when he returns from the darkness of the tomb, her power moves him between the worlds. Indeed, it is only through channelling her energy effectively, releasing her 'greenness' and flow of 'sympathy' in the world, that the 'pillar' king can heal divisions, creating anew the stable axis between heaven and deep earth.

Dangerous though this rousing of serpent energy may be, it is essential if

there is to be a great interchange and flow of power between above and below in this most secret sanctuary where the 'hidden things manifest'. As the sun god Re marvels to his female Serpent Guide (see page 55):

> Truly the heaven of this Heliopolis has become the well of every god.

Every New Year this Heliopolitan axis linking heaven and earth needed to be ritually re-established in order to be protected from destabilizing forces that might separate 'above' from 'below'. In the course of living everything is used up, depleted of energy, so every 'image' needs

◀ *fig 39* **The Heliopolitan union of heavenly sun and deep water embodied by Amun-Re in two reliefs in the great hypostyle hall at Karnak. In a scene on the west wall (south side) Amun-Re is seated on a throne as ruler of the waters, indicated by the ripples beneath the throne. Behind him stands Mut, the mother goddess of Thebes. To the right members of the Ennead, accompanied by the king (not shown here), raise their arms in praise. By contrast, a large scene on the west wall (north side) shows Isis as solar goddess shaking her sistrum whilst leading Seti I into Amun's presence for the zenithal confirmation of his solar power (fig.40). Behind Amun stands Mut and to the right is their son, the moon god Khons. These 19th Dynasty reliefs exemplify the reintegration of the Theban deities into Heliopolitan ritual traditions after their cults were suppressed in Akhenaten's reign.**

◀ *fig. 40*

to be reanimated in the passage of time and 'recharged' with its divine potential. Even, according to the New Kingdom *Myth of the Destruction of Humanity*, Re himself grows old and his *Ba* withdraws from his body, returning his divine image to its elemental form and bringing separation from his beloved Eye.[6]

Fleeing through the land at the close of the year, Sekhmet leaves 'poison' everywhere during this 'death' time. But paradoxically this fleeing goddess is both the source of the raging epidemics plaguing the feverish 'red' earth and their healing. For, like the inert Osirian god Sokar, the 'golden remedy [*pekheret*] in the temples' who, lifeless though he may seem, in fact contains the source of regeneration, so this fiery Eye goddess is in every sense the healing New Year cure—the kind of 'charm', called *pharmakon* by the Greeks, which could be either healing or poisonous depending on how it was used.[7]

As indeed the late antique alchemist Olympiodorus well knew in his treatise *On Soldering Gold*, when he referred to the liquid of 'the Egyptian with the tresses of gold' (Hathor-Aphrodite) as 'bitter and styptic' (see page 81). This volatile Eye goddess could bring both burning pain and healing, both love and death, being the medicine that could heal the pain that she herself had inflicted. Not surprisingly, then, we find 'priests of Sekhmet' as highly skilled medical practitioners dealing especially with fevers, blood disorders and diseases of the heart and knowing how to channel the Eye goddess's anger into life-giving medicine, both in the cults and in their healing medical practices.[8]

These priests knew that love was strong medicine, that to love something meant wanting it to live and that love had the power to transform. For Hathor's

fiery impulse for life lived on and on, through all the pangs of separation and death. But to find this 'medicine of life', the Eye goddess's power had to be actively sought. For it was when this fleeing goddess returned 'in peace', becoming again the solar king's true beloved, his 'charm' and 'great of magic', that the real healing began, replenishing him with vitality and drawing everything endangered with separation into their love union. Indeed, we find the same healing wisdom flowing through New Kingdom love poems, with their soothing medicinal mixtures prescribed for lovers, softening their flesh and healing their wounds, their 'lyrical' ingredients being no different from those prescribed for remedies in Egyptian medical texts.[9] For medicine, magic and religion were all of a piece in ancient Egypt.

▲ *fig.41* **View eastwards towards the second pylon and great hypostyle hall in the temple of Amun at Karnak.**

63

Hence the importance of the incantations when the pharaoh's flesh is first anointed with fragrant oils, bringing an inrush of the Eye goddess's fiery energy. He needs to draw her to him in order to revitalize himself and draw sustenance from her life-giving power. But these chants are also directed towards restraining her burning anger, lest it should turn hostile and 'poison' him, thus preventing the flow of her exuberant unifying love.

Just as Sekhmet's priests, and also Graeco-Egyptian alchemists, operated creatively with the forces of 'sympathy' and 'antipathy' flowing through the whole of nature, so here in the New Year ritual we see this healing magic operating on behalf of Egypt's king.[10] And, in turn, he himself becomes a kind of 'medicine man', whose healing regeneration of time cures the sick and raises the dead, drawing forth the Osirian elixir of life from the tomb. Mingling together all the cosmic separated elements through his healing 'charms', birthing all the 'opposites' destined for combination into flowing light-filled unity, he is in every way the uraeus-encircled god incarnate on earth, the divinely appointed son of Re, reborn into unity with his loving–destructive solar Eye.

THE YEAR'S MIDDAY: A SHADOWLESS SUN

Curiously, this Memphite-Heliopolitan New Year union between heavenly sun and deep water brings to mind a cosmic natural phenomenon in Egypt much remarked on in Hellenistic and Roman times. The first-century historian Pliny the Elder, quoting the mathematician Timaeus, described in his *Natural History* how the Nile inundation was drawn forth and overflowed through the power exerted on it by heat. This occurred,

Pliny said, when the Dog star (Sothis/Sirius, the Isis star) reappeared at the time when the sun entered the sign of the Lion (the astrological sign of Leo). It was then, Pliny said, that the sun stood in a vertical line directly over the Nile source, 'at which season in that region shadows entirely disappear'.[11]

The same knowledge is preserved in Heliodorus's third-century novel *Aethiopica*, in an episode when the local people of Syene show Hydaspes, the king of Ethiopia, a deep well that measures the Nile's flow, marking the ebb and flow of the waters. They also tell him how their sundials give no shadow at midday, since the midsummer sun is directly overhead and shines upon the water at the bottom of the well. Heliodorus says that it is for this reason that the people of Syene call the Nile the source of all fruitfulness, the saviour of Upper and Lower Egypt, bringing down new soil every year.[12]

▶ *fig.42* **Water streams from two vases held by the inundation god Hapy seated within a rocky cavern completely enclosed by a great serpent. (Detail of a relief on Hadrian's gateway at Philae.)**

How long such a well had been there at Syene we do not know, though ancient Nilometers are found throughout Egypt for measuring the ebb and flow of the Nile waters, on which all life depended. Nevertheless, both the Classical authors must have had in mind a famous well in ancient Syene (Aswan) into which, at midday on the summer solstice, the sun's rays descended perpendicularly, illuminating the depths of the well and casting no shadow, thus proving that Syene was located under the tropic.

Curiously, it was in connection with this Aswan phenomenon that Eratosthenes (c.275–194 BCE), keeper of the great library at Alexandria in the reign of Ptolemy III Euergetes, discovered his famous method for calculating the circumference of the earth with only the slightest margin of error. He knew that, at the summer solstice, the sun at Syene cast no shadow from a perpendicular gnomon, in contrast to the gnomon in Alexandria, which, at exactly the same time, cast a shadow with a measurable angle. According to Cleomedes, gnomons were used for the calculations. But Eratosthenes may well have had access to the kind of information which Pliny and Heliodorus refer to, for solstitial observations clearly interested Ptolemaic expeditions to this southern region of the tropic.[13]

Perhaps underlying his 'scientific' calculations was a much older Memphite-Heliopolitan wisdom that had been preserved in this solstitial well at Syene. For in the New Year ritual we find a similar zenithal solar illumination of deep well water bringing forth the desired inundation. To be sure, ancient Egyptian ritualists, immersed as they were in a mythic sacred world, experienced this midsummer relationship between sun and water quite differently from later Greeks, leaving it to people like Eratosthenes to develop a 'scientific' understanding of these cosmic rhythms and mysteries. The ancient Egyptians had a very different conception of the dynamic processes of the cosmos, an 'all-pervading belief in the magical nature of things', as Erik Iversen called it, that was utterly unlike Western 'scientific' or 'philosophical' explanations of phenomena.[14]

Clearly, the Egyptians perceived the relationship between sun and water particularly acutely when the midsummer sun was at its highest exaltation in the noonday heavens and at its northernmost point in its annual circuit. To them, however, its deep meaning could be experienced each new year when the divine Horus sun king illuminated the zenithal heavens without shadow and ritually brought this solar light deep down into his Osirian predecessor's dark inaccessible cavern, the life-giving 'august chamber' where lay the eternal source of renewing water. It is this divine connection between the heavenly sun and the 'well of every god' that illuminates the New Year ritual. Quite possibly, then, the famous well at Syene, located closest to the source of the Nile floodwaters, was constructed to embody this Heliopolitan solstitial wisdom and channel its sacred influence throughout the region—a mythic well so renowned that it subsequently inspired Eratosthenes to make his famous empirical observations.

PALACE PRIESTESS: QUEENSHIP RITES

Interestingly, Heliodorus also reports there was a similar well at Memphis. And it is surely to the Memphite-Heliopolitan region, rather than to Aswan far away in the southernmost part of Upper Egypt, that we should locate the Brooklyn papyrus's complex New Year ritual. For, although it is impossible to locate the ceremonies specifically within any known Egyptian temple, in all likelihood they would have been performed in one of the huge sacred precincts in the north at Memphis or Heliopolis which have long since disappeared. Certainly, the ritual would have required a vast sacred temenos incorporating a robing and 'anointing' chamber. It would also have needed a spacious court with shrines on the east and west sides for the Memphite and Heliopolitan deities and a throne dais, perhaps a pavilion standing on a platform and approached by steps. It would also have required a special 'tomb' chamber with a bed for the Osirian 'sealing' rites close to a court with shrines on the north and south for the ancestral kings and deities. In short, a temple on a lavish scale would have been needed for these elaborate ceremonies.[15]

There is also another conundrum here. For, despite the fact that Re communes with his 'female guide' about the wondrous union of high heaven and deep earth, we have rarely referred to the participation of any priestesses or royal women in the actual ceremonies. How so? After all, it is the serpent Eye goddess who empowers the Horus king throughout. And, as Lana Troy observed, the power to move between the opposites is repeatedly connected to the 'ritual role of the royal women' whose generative power as daughter-wife-mother sustained the pharaoh's rule.[16] But who, it may be asked, embodies this Hathorian divine feminine in the ritual?

Here, unfortunately, we have to face the limitations imposed by the nature of the New Year ritual papyrus itself, which seems to have been written as a

ceremonial guide for the chief priest in charge of the ceremonies (see page 29). Important details, at least from a modern-day standpoint, are omitted, for example who actually anointed the king and sang the chants during the anointing. The ritual papyrus simply states that each oil is brought and then the relevant incantation follows. Whether this involved the queen (or high priestess), we cannot determine with certainty. But surely this anointing rite would have required a feminine presence for its efficacity, especially as it is Ankhesenamun who is shown anointing the king on Tutankhamun's Golden Shrine (fig.26) and in the beautiful scene decorating the back of his throne (fig.15).

We have already referred to the zenithal chant for 'seeing the face' of the god (see page 36). Again, who chanted this is not stated. But it is not hard to imagine the queen as priestess shaking her naos sistrum at this point in the ritual, creating a great vortex of sound to transport the king into his solar father's divine presence. Nor do we know who glorified the horizon sun king immediately before this zenithal revelation. Again, it could well have been female chantresses, singing like the dual Heliopolitan Meret-goddesses chanting their songs for the rising sun (see page 36).

There are other reasons for reaching such a conclusion. In the 22nd Dynasty Sed Festival scenes of Osorkon II, originally carved on a granite gateway in the temple at Bubastis, the queen, royal princesses and a high priestess are all prominent during various ceremonies, which include rites for the appearance of the king in the *Per-Wer* and also his ritual descent into the tomb. Often performed as a ritual of regeneration after a ruler had completed 30 years on the throne, but not exclusively so, these festival scenes give a tantalizing glimpse into the Sed Festival, portraying numerous processions from shrine to shrine without ever really revealing the nature of the rites performed there. Nevertheless, the queen is never far from the king's side, walking in procession with him, accompanying him when he makes offerings to various deities, shaking her sistrum as he burns incense and watching, accompanied by princesses, when the nobles come to adore their ruler. Women called 'singers' also appear when the king's power is confirmed.[17]

Similarly, scenes in Kheruef's tomb at Thebes show Queen Teye standing behind the enthroned goddess Hathor and Amenhotep III during acrobatic night dances for Hathor performed at the close of Amenhotep III's first Sed Festival. According to an accompanying inscription, Teye is 'in the following of the king, like Maat in the following of Re'. She is, in other words, the solar 'guiding' principle in the rites. Elsewhere in the tomb she is portrayed ceremonially sailing with Amenhotep III in the solar night boat, the king being attired in his Sed Festival robe. She also accompanies him, together with Hathorian sistrum-shaking princesses, when the Osirian *Djed*-pillar is raised, surrounding the rite with Hathorian musical energy and vitality.[18]

Were all these royal women simply passive bystanders during these rites of renewal, without any prescribed ritual function? It scarcely seems plausible, especially as we know from other sources that the high priestess at Thebes, the 'God's Wife of Amun', actively participated in musical rites of propitiation in temples, as well as rites for the dedication of offerings and execration rites aimed at destroying

fig.43 Painted limestone statue of Meritamun, who was both daughter and great royal wife of Ramesses II. She holds a *menit*-necklace and is crowned with a coronet of solar cobras. On her brow are the paired cobras of Upper and Lower Egypt. The statue lacks the queen's name, but an identical statue bearing Meritamun's name, though ten times the size, was discovered at Akhmim. (Egyptian Museum, Cairo.)

Egypt's enemies. Surely, in order to be efficacious, this New Year ritual would have required the queen's participation. Or, if not the queen, then the temple high priestess would have embodied the Eye goddess's power throughout the ceremonies.

NEW YEAR CEREMONIES: A NINEFOLD PROCESS

Ceremonially, the New Year ritual incorporates nine distinct phases as befits a Memphite-Heliopolitan ritual linked with Atum and his Ennead:

1 The king's purificatory lustration, perhaps in the royal palace.
2 The lunar foundation of Egypt: the bestowal of insignia in the 'Shrine of the Great Throne', symbolizing the triumph of Horus over Seth and restoration of the Moon Eye.
3 The solar anointing with nine fiery oils in the 'Shrine of the Great Throne' and the cosmic king's actualization of Heliopolitan creative life.
4 The king's cult service of the Heliopolitan and Memphite deities of West and East. The glorification of the celestial horizon king as son of Isis and Osiris.
5 The zenithal confirmation of the king's power as 'son of Re' and the eating of the sacred bread confirming his solar rulership.
6 The entry into the Osirian tomb, the quest for the water-bearing *Ibhet*-stone and the renewal of seals legitimizing the rulership of Horus on Geb's ancestral throne.
7 The rites for the return from the tomb, raising the rope for Sekhmet and the manifestation of Osiris's resurrected life-giving power.
8 The rites for the 'greening' of Sekhmet, the clothing of the Red King and his cult offerings for the ancestral rulers of South and North and the deities in the *Dwat*.
9 The glorification rites incorporating the 'litany of the birds' when the nine birds are brought before the divinized solar king, celebrating his command of all the cosmic healing powers acquired in the ritual. The gift of the golden necklace uniting him with the truth goddess and divine 'daughter of the sun'.

This ninefold ritual process falls into three distinct phases marked by three 'unions' of the king and Eye goddess. First, the king is brought into union with her as the 'anointed one' in order to ascend to the zenith, fully invested with solar life and light after being renewed like a terrestrial cult image. Secondly, after his entry into the Osirian tomb, the shining Red King returns utterly transformed, completely encompassed by his Serpent Guide and ritually clothed in a red garment with white sandals on his feet and a sceptre in his hand. Thirdly, in the 'litany of the birds' at the close of the ritual, Hathor-Maat's golden necklace is bestowed on the pharaoh. He is then the divinized 'King of Gold', the 'tenth' Heliopolitan power amidst the nine birds, appearing with the solar truth goddess in this New Year cosmic regeneration of time, his heart utterly in balance with Re's heavenly 'daughter' as their glorious union finds its consummation.

And, as the nine anointed birds are brought in turn before the Horus king, each one with its head reverently 'turned back' in deference to his power, so the chants recapitulate the nine phases, thus ritually re-enacting the rites, which are here experienced in their completed form. What was potentially present at the beginning now manifests its eternal cosmic nature, reaching completion in all its shining gold. The king, renewed but a little while ago by the goddess, now actively shines forth with the divine daughter of the sun, his healing regenerative power flooding into the world and filling it with vital creative energy.

Hovering over Egypt with outspread wings, the royal falcon's golden gaze radiates deep into the celestial earth, drawing everything within it upwards to

the heaven above—an Egypt resurrected in a living body, transparent to the light, its radiance made manifest, rising to new life in a flowing golden liquid dawn. The highest has indeed come down to the lowest, and the lowest has reached up to the highest in a great interchange of heavenly and deep earth energy, bringing renewal to the whole of cosmic life. For this return from the tomb renews the seasons. It replenishes the flowing inundation river and the cyclical movement of sun, moon and stars in their celestial heavenly circuit. Everything threatened with 'separation' is reunited and healed in this annual rebirth of time.

So the archetypal pattern of the New Year ritual is formed by three royal 'marriages' and nine phases, with the anointed Horus king himself representing the Heliopolitan 'tenth' power. Through his ritual 'ascent', 'descent' and 'return', he becomes the vanquisher of death and eternal renewer of the years as at the very 'first time' of creation, radiating true healing efficacy for the whole of a regenerated Egypt.

KINGSHIP AND DIVINITY: THE PILLAR AXIS

The whole feeling of this New Year ritual is very different from the New Kingdom ancestor ritual which I described in *My Heart My Mother*.[19] For instead of a ritual composed around food offerings, the heart and the lighting of candles, we find here highly complex magical rites

performed on the king's person, a divinization ritual akin to temple rites performed for a cult statue and involving purification, anointing, ritual clothing, amulets and talismanic objects. So, too, there are highly charged ceremonies, including the king entering a trance-like state upon his bed to renew the Osirian seals of rulership, guided by the priests surrounding him. Even birds are included in the ritual. Everything is carefully prescribed throughout, including the specific materials to be used for amulets and seals (see page 49).

To the Egyptians everything in creation had its own special set of complex correspondences and affinities within nature. Hence ritualists needed to know which things belonged together, which were 'sympathetic' to particular deities and which might 'repel' hostile forces. To give one example from the New Year ritual, the Brooklyn papyrus carefully prescribes the ritual objects to be used during the Horus king's descent to the tomb. Thus, the *Bat*-object which the king holds during these secret tomb rites (see page 51) is to be compounded with *Ima*-wood and other prescribed ingredients, as well as coated with mud from the zone of the inundated fields.[20] Accordingly, two of the four seals used in this descent to the tomb are to be made from wood of the *Ima*-tree (see page 50).

This was no ordinary tree. For, whilst its botanical identification is uncertain, it clearly resonates with Osiris's life-giving

▲ *fig.44* **Vignette from the** *Book of the Dead* **showing members of the Heliopolitan Ennead seated behind Re-Harakhti and Atum as witnesses to the weighing of the heart. Seth and Osiris are omitted and on the left are Horus, Hathor, Hu and Sia. (Papyrus of Ani. British Museum, London.)**

power (see page 50), as well as Hathor's radiant charms and 'uniting' power, the name of the tree itself evoking her 'charm' *(ima)*. Evidently, it is this 'charm' that radiates when the raging Eye goddess peacefully returns to Re in the *Myth of the Destruction of Humanity*, since the myth explains how her

▼ *fig.45* **Colossal 19th Dynasty granite statue of Ramesses II from the Ramesseum at Thebes. (British Museum, London.)**

homecoming creates the beautiful women in the town of Imu, a place punningly connected by name with 'charm'.[21] Wherever there is a 'love union' Hathor's 'charm' flows. Hence inscriptions in Seti I's temple at Abydos tell how 'charm' and 'attraction' fire Horus's heart with desire to serve Osiris, uniting the reigning king with his Osirian predecessor.[22]

Trees, stones, minerals, plants and metals—all could powerfully capture a deity's activity, imparting this in the temple cults whenever Ptah's Memphite craft skills transformed them into magical ritual objects. Clearly, if the mud-laden *Bat* and seals were to be efficacious in the New Year ritual, creating a 'water-pouring' bond between the Horus king and his predecessor, they needed not only to be inscribed with the correct name but also to contain active Hathorian ingredients, carrying her fragrance and unifying 'charm'.[23]

Indeed, different kinds of efficacious 'sealing' rites, both to 'protect' and 'authenticate' the pharaoh's rule, are crucial throughout the New Year ritual. When the king is anointed with the nine fragrant oils, Sekhmet's amuletic protection surrounds his body, guarding his royal 'name', his spiritual essence, which is sealed on the Heliopolitan *Ished*-tree. Likewise, when he ingests the sacred bread of 'office' at the zenith, Re's solar rulership becomes a nourishing 'sealed' force within his *Ka*-body (see page 36). So, too, when the Horus king renews the seals of rulership in tomb darkness, he 'seals' his Osirian royal lineage. At stake is the confirmation of the king's authority in every way, the 'marking' of him anew as the divinized royal priest of the sun, the bodily heir of Re-Atum and his 'living image' on earth, responsible for realizing the sun god's divine presence throughout the cosmos.[24]

This brings us to that oft-repeated statement about the Egyptian king, namely that he was never considered to be a human being, that he was simply and solely divine. This is surely an over-simplification, since it is important to realize that, by New Kingdom times, his origins were both 'human' and 'divine'. He was a mortal king who travelled the same 'way to the Osirian ancestors' that all his people could travel, as represented in the New Kingdom *Book of Night*. But he was also the divinized incarnate 'son of Re', an initiate king.[25]

This twofold character of the Egyptian pharaoh—both human and divine—was particularly emphasized from the Middle Kingdom onwards when the 'human' element crept into religious experience and Osirian religion extended far more widely into the populace at large. No longer was it simply enough for the pharaoh to rule by divine decree. He had to be seen to exercise justice and mercy towards his subjects, who were bound to him by ties of loyalty and affection. And, as the *Book of Night* so graphically shows, all humans, including the pharaoh, could follow that path of the heart that led to the ancestral Osirian realm.

Hence we find very different ritual ways of working in ancient Egypt's complex temple life. But what we see here in the New Year ritual is a very specific solar divinization designed not only to reconfirm the solar basis of the pharaoh's power, but also to regenerate everything in the cosmos endangered with 'separation' from the divine source in order to bless the land with plenitude. 'I am in heaven, in earth, in water, in air. I am in animals and in plants; in the womb, before the womb, after the womb, everywhere,' marvels Tat in Treatise 13 of the *Corpus Hermeticum*,

when Hermes Trismegistus initiates him into the mysteries of regeneration. It is the arrival of 'truth' that brings this radiant vision to Hermes's divinized initiate, who now no longer experiences the world in 'three bodily dimensions', for he has been spiritually reborn into the cosmic unity of 'life and light' engendered through the power of 'the ten'.[26]

Such too is the unification mystery experienced when nine winged

▲ *fig.46* **Atum inscribes Ramesses II's name on the Heliopolitan sacred tree. (19th Dynasty relief in the Ramesseum at Thebes.)**

companions surround Egypt's 'anointed king' at the close of the New Year ritual, the Heliopolitan 'tenth' power reborn into unity when the 'truth goddess' arrives (fig.37). In Roman times, when the Egyptian temple mysteries had become more accessible to people outside the temples, Hermes Trismegistus, the Hellenized incarnation of the ancient Egyptian wisdom god Thoth, seems to have taught a similar unification wisdom to his initiates. But here in the New Year ritual it is still the Egyptian pharaoh, his white-sandalled feet touching the ground and his crown in heaven, knowing 'what is in its heights and depths', who enacts these regeneration rites on behalf of his people.[27]

It was a task he shared with no other human, save the goddess queen participating with him in the mysteries of solar rulership. Indeed, it is specifically stated in the New Year ritual papyrus that the sacramental bread the king eats when his divine 'office' is confirmed is bread made from dough never tasted by any other mortal (see page 36). Appointed to rule by Re, the pharaoh thus has his light-filled *Ka*-body

nourished with solar creative energy, enabling him quite literally to 'perform the works of Re' on earth for the welfare of his people.

As such, he is a sacred king, a functionary, not a personality, symbolized above all by the uraeus serpent rearing up on his brow. For it is when he takes to himself the fiery power of the loving-destructive Eye goddess that he transcends all limitations of personality to become Re's divinized son. Mediating between above and below, the cosmic 'pillar' king rouses his serpent to influence the whole course of nature at the turning-point of time. He is the uniter of realms. Drawing forth the waters of life from the tomb, he serves as unique representative of the land and his people, bringing them rebirth and healing at the New Year. And it is the first part of this ancient regeneration ritual that is woven into the veil of symbols adorning Tutankhamun's beautiful Golden Shrine, both pointing to and yet hiding these ancient Memphite-Heliopolitan 'royal marriage' mysteries of love and union between Egypt's anointed king and goddess queen.

Chapter 7

OPEN DOORS:
BECOMING ROYAL

I am Isis, ruler of every land. I was taught
by Hermes and with Hermes I devised letters...
I divided earth from heaven. I showed the ways
of the stars. I brought together woman and man...
I revealed mysteries to the people ... made right to
be stronger than gold or silver ... I am queen of rivers,
winds and seas ... am in the rays of the sun ...
I overcome fate ... Hail, O Egypt that nourished me.[1]

(From a Greek aretalogy of Isis discovered at Cyme)

◀ *fig. 47* **Cleopatra VII, the last queen of Egypt, appears as the solarized Isis in Philae temple.**

How long the Egyptians continued to celebrate the New Year ritual once the country came under Greek rule is unclear. But given that the Brooklyn Museum papyrus preserves a version of the ritual in use during the Late Period, it was certainly being enacted in Egyptian temples shortly before the Ptolemaic dynasty was established in Alexandria, after Alexander the Great took control of Egypt in the late fourth century BCE.

Egypt's social and religious life had always found its focus in the king, depending on him to create unity. But the Egyptian priesthood's distaste for the incoming Greeks is also well known. To be sure, Ptolemaic rulers in Alexandria wore native forms of dress in ceremonial life. Some were even crowned according to Egyptian customs, which gave the Ptolemies considerable cultural prestige with other rulers, including the Seleucid dynasty in Antioch. They also courted the native priesthood's support to bolster their claims to the Egyptian throne, as is evident in the magnificent Upper Egyptian temples built between Philae

and Dendara in the Ptolemaic era, which proclaimed the hegemony of the far-distant Greek rulers in Alexandria (fig.48).

The support of the Egyptian priesthood was crucial to the Ptolemies. But in a Hellenized Egypt in which an administrative elite functioned increasingly independently of the temples, it contributed to a slow erosion of traditional ways, as well as priestly apathy towards Ptolemaic kingship, especially in Upper Egypt where widespread unrest surfaced from time to time among a rebellious population.[2]

Yet Egypt would still have needed its sacred rites of renewal. And rather than allowing Maat's way of life to be completely eroded, the native priesthood was fuelled by a deep desire to maintain what the Egyptian king had once upheld.[3] Hence we find extracts from the New Year ritual being inscribed in Ptolemaic temples, and at times being given in more detail than in the Brooklyn papyrus, particularly in the Horus temple at Edfu (fig.52). There they were integrated into the annual Heliopolitan

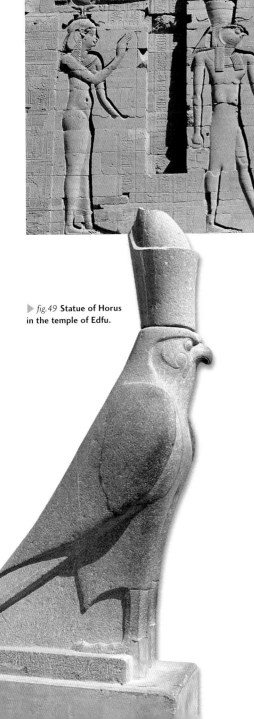

fig.48 Relief on the second pylon of the Isis temple at Philae showing Ptolemy XII offering to Horus and Hathor. He was the father of Egypt's last queen, the famous Cleopatra VII.

fig.49 Statue of Horus in the temple of Edfu.

enthronement rites renewing the 'Living Falcon' as Re-Harakhti's terrestrial image. Certainly, it is the reigning Greek king who is shown performing the cult rituals on Edfu's temple walls. But there is a subtle shift of focus. For this royal New Year ceremony has been modified so that it relates to the temple cult image, which is invested with all the 'royal' attributes of a Heliopolitan Horus king (fig.49).[4]

These Ptolemaic temple practices were by no means in decay. But we need only consider an inscription on the exterior of Hathor's early Roman-period temple in the Philae temple complex to appreciate the underlying changes (fig.50). For here it is explicitly said that this temple, which is called the 'Enclosure of Calling', is a 'royal' building, being formed on the potter's wheel as a 'perfect house', a solar royal house exercising 'the kingship of Re'. And when 'its beautiful mistress [Hathor] beholds it, so she rejoices'. Clearly, here at Philae this lovely gem of a temple, with its rites honouring the return of the 'goddess in the distance' and her role in the temple's Birth House, now represents Re's solar rulership. Moreover, exactly as Khnum had once formed the king on his potter's wheel in the New Kingdom royal birth cycle together with Hathor (fig.73), now he forms this Philae temple on his wheel. Manifestly, as at Edfu, what is emphasized here is solar rulership as a 'priestly' rather than a 'royal' art.[5]

▲ *fig.50* **View through the temple of Hathor at Philae. Here rites were performed to celebrate the return of the pacified Eye goddess to Re after her wanderings in the Nubian desert.**

To be sure, the Egyptian priesthood had always been able to conduct rites on behalf of the pharaoh and represent him in the cults, even instituting their own Theban theocracy at the end of the New Kingdom. But what we see here in Graeco-Roman times is a much bigger shift, undertaken by a priesthood living in an increasingly Hellenized Egypt, subject to a resident foreign ruler and with a Greek-speaking population in its upper echelons. The consequences were far-reaching.

Once Egypt became a province of the Roman Empire at the end of the first century CE, with Rome's emperors ruling the country from afar, assisted by local administrations in Egypt loyal to Rome, the problems intensified. Moreover, once these rulers began to use Egypt's temple income for their own purposes, the economic basis on which Egyptian temples had always existed, including the status of the priesthood, was significantly undermined. It was a severe blow to the Egyptians, a 'lost structure of life', as Roger Bagnall called it.[6] Temple closures became inevitable, especially from the fourth century onwards, after Constantine had become the first Roman emperor to embrace Christianity, though the Isis temple at Philae held out until the sixth century before finally being closed between 535 and 537 on the orders of Justinian (fig.51). By this time the transformation of pagan into Christian culture had been mainly achieved.

Was this sacred New Year ritual destined for oblivion amid the tensions which engulfed Egypt in these early centuries of the Christian era? So it would seem if we accept such a drastic over-simplification of the transition to Christianity. But such a view ignores the profound influence Egyptian religion continued to exert on the new forms of spirituality evolving under the Roman emperors. It is little understood just how far, and for how long, these age-old royal anointing mysteries continued in most remarkable, if often unnoticed, ways—though it is far beyond Egypt's sacred temple precincts that we can best detect their abiding influence.

TEMPLES IN TRANSITION: SEEKERS OF WISDOM

It has long been argued that Egyptian temple rites became 'democratized', particularly in Roman times, when what had once been royal cults, closely

guarded by priests, were increasingly made available to individuals outside the temples. Here is not the place to discuss this important 'democratization' process in detail, especially as it is extremely difficult to disentangle all the social changes that led to this gradual annexation of traditional royal rites. But eventually, when Egypt was ruled from afar by Roman emperors, there was an unprecedented diffusion of ancient Egyptian cult knowledge, which made it available to people seeking personal salvation through mystical knowledge or *gnosis*.[7]

The spread of the Isis mysteries throughout the Roman Empire, the rise of healing and oracle cults in Graeco-Roman Egypt and the emergence of Hermeticism all contributed to this diffusion of Egyptian wisdom. And whether through actual ritual enactments or interiorizing the ancient rites in the temple of the soul to create a 'temple within', individuals now had the potential to become 'royal' through initiatory teachings, experiencing both their own 'enthronement' and the

discovery of the divine spark of life whilst alive on earth.[8]

Nowhere perhaps is this development more vividly conveyed than in Apuleius's famous second-century account of an initiation into the mysteries of Isis at the close of the *Golden Ass*. Here the solarized Lucius, having first experienced secret rites that have taken him to 'the very gates of death', gloriously appears in the heart of Isis's sanctuary at Corinth. Crowned with palm leaves and adorned like the sun, he stands on a wooden dais before a statue of the goddess, holding a flame before the crowd of people who have come to acclaim him 'like when a divine statue is unveiled', clothed like the sun.[9] This may be a literary rendering of an Isiac initiation, but it betrays Apuleius's familiarity with the widespread mysteries of the Egyptian goddess. What had once been a confirmation of the Horus king's unique power was now openly being transferred to initiated individuals, transforming them into cosmic illuminated 'royal' persons able to realize their own authentic spiritual nature as divinized living statues.

fig. 51 View of Philae temple looking towards the Kiosk of Trajan. The temple was built in the Ptolemaic and Roman periods and is now relocated on the island of Agilkia. It was eventually closed in the sixth century CE by the Roman emperor Justinian and subsequently occupied by Christians, who carved Coptic crosses and inscriptions on the walls.

fig. 52 View of the beautifully preserved Horus temple at Edfu where extracts from the New Year ritual were inscribed on the walls. It was closely linked with Hathor's temple at Dendara and the goddess made a great festive voyage each year to Edfu to celebrate her union with Horus.

fig.53 **Scene at the top of a stela belonging to the Phoenician Chaiapis, chief of police at Memphis, who is depicted as a foreigner with close-cropped curly hair and beard, and wearing a long fringed robe. Yet he is seated like an Egyptian before a table of offerings. To the right is the goddess Nut in her sacred sycamore tree and behind him is the goddess of the West. This unusual stela, found in the Memphite necropolis at Saqqara, illustrates the integration of Phoenicians from the Syrian coast into Egyptian cultural life during the third century BCE. (State Museum, Berlin.)**

More difficult to detect is the role of the native Egyptian priesthood in this gradual 'democratization' and shift away from traditional ritual settings. But confronted with a cult life increasingly undermined by changing social conditions, some must surely have participated in this transmission beyond the temples. After all, it was the priests who had always guarded these temple secrets in their 'Houses of Life'.[10]

So, too, culturally integrated foreigners, living at places like Edfu and Memphis, could have played a significant role. There were well-established Phoenician and Jewish quarters in Memphis populated by people still retaining links with their original homeland. Indeed, there is sporadic evidence that foreigners, including Phoenicians (fig.53), with their long history of cultural links with Egypt, were able to serve in the cults during the Ptolemaic era.[11] Interestingly, in the early

second century CE a much underestimated Phoenician in the Levant, Philo of Byblos, emphasized the relationship between Egyptian and Phoenician traditions. He also displayed knowledge of the Hermopolitan cosmogony and Thoth's identification with the Greek Hermes, which is indicative of the wider diffusion of Egyptian cult knowledge into the Levant, Syria and Palestine.[12]

In short, the evolution of this 'democratization' of Egyptian royal rites and spread of temple wisdom was diverse and complex, within a Hellenized world spawning numerous groups and sects, some profoundly influenced by ancient Egypt, some undoubtedly hostile to it. It also mingled together different traditions, sometimes creating strange hybrid forms typifying the fluidity that existed in Hellenistic-Roman times. But what it did, above all, was to make traditional Egyptian cult knowledge available outside the temples in ways which would have been unimaginable in New Kingdom times.

ALCHEMY'S STONE: EMERALD LORE

And if themes in the New Year ritual have a familiar ring to those versed in Graeco-Egyptian, Islamic and European alchemy, it is hardly surprising, since alchemists have always revered Egypt as a major influence on their tradition. Indeed, to discover 'the stone' lies at the heart of alchemy, or the 'royal art', as it is sometimes called. Over and over again, alchemists refer to the precious stone, the treasure hard to attain, which is the goal of all their work. Thus, the renowned early fourth-century alchemist Zosimus of Panopolis (Akhmim), quoting from an earlier alchemist called Ostanes, says:

Go to the waters of the Nile and there you will find a stone that has a spirit. Take this, divide it, place your hand in its interior and draw forth its heart. For its soul is in its heart.[13]

How are we to understand this strange command to find a stone in the Nile waters and draw forth its heart? Surely, in the light of the Egyptian king's discovery of the *Ibhet*-stone in the New Year ritual and his return with the Memphite 'heart' goddess Hathor-Sekhmet, it is legitimate to ask which ancient Egyptian secrets Zosimus still preserved behind his enigmatic words in the early fourth century.

Or again, yet another alchemist says:

Visit the interior of the earth, and by purification you will find the secret stone.[14]

Clearly, to this much later European alchemist, visiting the interior of the earth reveals 'the secret stone'.

Indeed, the pharaoh's New Year ascent to the zenithal sky followed by his descent into the tomb perfectly exemplifies the later *Emerald Tablet's* famous alchemical maxim: 'Ascend from earth to heaven and descend again from heaven to earth, and unite together the power of things superior and inferior.' It is by means of this ascending and descending journey that the alchemical work of unification comes to completion. Or, as the *Emerald Tablet* succinctly concludes: 'Perfect is what I have said of the work of the sun.'[15]

This is not simply a quest to replicate heaven on earth, as if in a mirroring of separate realms. Rather the aim is to experience a complete unification of 'above' and 'below' in which every material form, whether it be human, animal, plant or stone, is woven together within a unitary world unfolding its living truth. Or, if we transpose this unifying work into the ancient Egyptian New Year ritual, we see it expressed when Osiris's resurrected life flows forth, bringing nourishment upon Egypt's temple altars, and Re proclaims to his female Serpent Guide how the 'heaven of this Heliopolis' has become the deep 'well of every god' (see page 55).

Curiously, in a Graeco-Egyptian magical incantation preserved in a first-century papyrus from Oxyrhynchus, mention is made of the 'true emerald' at Heliopolis in the context of Osiris's tomb. Issuing threats about what might happen if his wish to attract a girl remains unfulfilled, the magician says he will go into the 'house of *Benben* and to Heliopolis' where he will 'twist the bones of the sacred phoenix' and every day:

I will pour true oil on the true emerald
(smaragd) where your tomb
is, and I will open …where Osiris lies,
the greatest, in the inaccessible.[16]

Hostile in intent though this incantation
may be, and aimed solely at gratifying
the magician's own personal desires, this
love magic draws on very specific
Heliopolitan cult knowledge to
accomplish its aim, not least an 'emerald'
associated with Osiris's 'inaccessible'
tomb.

Perhaps then it is not so strange, after
all, that a key alchemical text should be
called the *Emerald Tablet*. For in both
alchemy and ancient Egypt there is a
quest to reveal the interior tomb secrets
and make the 'hidden things' appear.[17]
Yet some commentators have been far
too ready to ridicule the claim that
alchemy is a genuine transmission from
the Egyptian temples and in doing so
have missed vital clues concerning the
spread of Egypt's ritual knowledge into
the Hellenistic and Roman world. For
have we not here in the New Year ritual
alone a quest for the stone and
manifestation of the Red King as in
alchemy—a king, moreover, who has
previously lain in a trance-like state with
his hand resting on an object coated with
Egypt's black earth, that 'black earth'
revered by alchemists in their quest for
regenerative living water? Crucially, too,
the king seeks a mystical marriage with
his divine queen, uniting with a female
love-fire, a 'green' fire of desire, that
brings new life. All these were themes
beloved of later alchemists.

BETWIXT AND BETWEEN: LOVE'S MEDIATION

They were also mysteries known to
Plutarch, steeped as he was in the ancient

Egyptian Isis and Osiris cults. In his
'Dialogue on Love' he refers to a return
with the Egyptian love goddess from
Hades, saying that anyone who cares to
track down 'the tiny scraps of evidence'
in Egyptian mythology will find the truth
that Plato knew, concerning how 'lovers
are able to return to the light even from
Hades'.[18] He also explains how the
Egyptians reverence not only a heavenly
and earthly love but also believe that the
sun is a 'third' love as Eros associated
with the Greek love goddess Aphrodite.
Or, if we give them their Egyptian names
(which Plutarch omits), Re-Horus and
Hathor. Plutarch goes on to explain how
this Egyptian 'love' comes like a 'mystic
guide' to lead a Hades-dweller
heavenward:

It is Love who graciously appears to lift
us out of the depths
and escort us upward, like a mystic
guide beside us
at our initiation.[19]

Much later, the alchemist Olympiodorus
also alludes to this Egyptian 'mystic
guide' in his treatise *On Soldering Gold*,
written in Greek during the fifth or sixth
century CE. Amidst his wide-ranging
commentary on the work of earlier
alchemists, he juxtaposes two ancient
oracles of Apollo, the first one
graphically describing Osiris's tomb,
where the god lies heavily bandaged in
the sphere of 'lead' with only his face
uncovered:

But what is the tomb of Osiris? Lying
there is a corpse swathed in bandages,
with only the face visible. And
interpreting Osiris, the oracle says:
Osiris is the closely confined tomb,

concealing all the limbs of Osiris,
whose face only is visible to mortals
…Thus he fetters and binds the
All of lead.[20]

By contrast, the second oracle's theme is
a love-union between the 'male of the
chrysocolla' and the 'woman of vapour',
whom Olympiodorus explicitly identifies
with the 'Egyptian with the tresses of
gold' (Hathor). She is, too, the 'Cyprian',
in other words Aphrodite residing in her
copper-bearing island of Cyprus (fig.54).
Indeed, copper is the metal that
alchemists frequently identified with the
love goddess. It is her fluidity of life and
movement, her 'divine water', both
'bitter and styptic', Olympiodorus says,
that flows as a solder in this alchemical
gold-making, binding the separate
elements together and transforming the
'male of the chrysocolla':

Place him with the woman of vapour
until he has been transformed.
This is the divine water, bitter and
styptic, the one which is called
the liquid of Cyprus and the liquid of
the Egyptian with the tresses of gold.
With this smear the leaves of the
luminous goddess,
Those of the Cyprian, the Red
One…[21]

To be sure, Olympiodorus here
deliberately veils his meaning in
alchemy's highly coded language,
mingling together a craft process for
soldering gold obtained from the 'land of
the Ethiopians' with a love union
between male and female. But this is not
the work of 'some muddle-headed
charlatan', as he has been called, since it

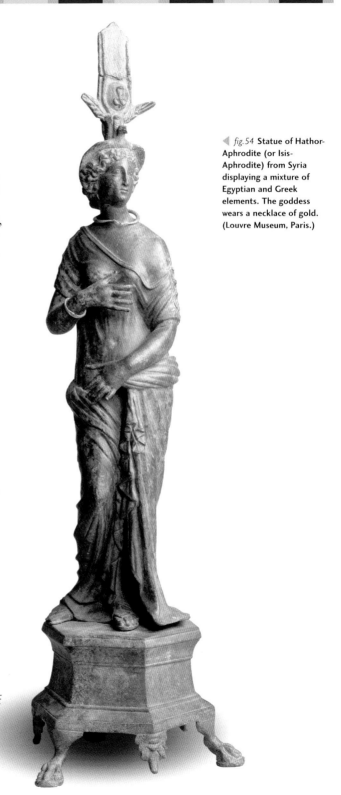

◀ *fig.54* **Statue of Hathor-
Aphrodite (or Isis-
Aphrodite) from Syria
displaying a mixture of
Egyptian and Greek
elements. The goddess
wears a necklace of gold.
(Louvre Museum, Paris.)**

is a very conscious juxtaposition of two older oracles.[22] Moreover, in the light of Plutarch's dialogue about the Egyptian Aphrodite and lovers returning to the light from Hades, it is no coincidence that he mentions the love goddess and a 'marriage' immediately after describing Osiris's tomb.

True alchemist that he was, Olympiodorus allegorically projected this union onto an ancient technique of uniting separate pieces of gold in which 'chrysocolla' (a ground copper carbonate in the form of powdered malachite) was used as the solder, including by craftworkers in ancient Egypt. Called *wadj* by the ancient Egyptians, a word also meaning 'green', 'fresh', chrysocolla was obtained from copper-mining desert regions presided over by Hathor.[23] Manifestly, like Plutarch, Olympiodorus knew her 'green' attraction to be the great alchemy in this Osirian gold-making. But he was also firmly rooted in alchemical craft language, hence this skilful weaving between the art of soldering gold using chrysocolla and allusions to a sacred 'marriage'.

Just as the Horus king first entered the Osirian tomb to obtain the stone, before rising forth with the propitiated 'green' Eye goddess Hathor-Sekhmet, the 'one with the golden tresses' as she is called in the New Year ritual (see page 58), so this 'green' love union between the 'male of the chrysocolla' and the copper goddess is utterly founded on Osiris's tomb. Olympiodorus may have interpreted this strange craft-based imagery allegorically, but even at this late date, in these 'tiny scraps of evidence' we can discern the same 'marriage mystery' of love and death that Plutarch transmits, with its deep roots in the Memphite-Heliopolitan mysteries.

Indeed, Plutarch himself talks about flowing 'divine water' in his 'Dialogue on Love' when he states that just as the sun gives nourishment, light and the power of growth to the body, so this gleaming ray of love which can be experienced by contemplating beautiful human forms nurtures souls. Furthermore, whenever souls keep this light, warmth and radiance, excluding its raging element, 'as if it were literally fire', then they will find a 'marvellous and fruitful circulation of sap, as in a plant that sprouts and grows, a circulation that opens the way to acquiescence and affection'.[24] Blending together the language of botany with his language of the Egyptian 'third' love, Plutarch beautifully encapsulates divine 'attraction' and 'sympathy' as the source of harmony and beauty in the world. And whether through its workings in the soul or the process of tending and nurturing plants, it is this nourishing 'green' power, circulating 'where the immortal is blended with the mortal', that makes transient life eternal.[25]

Nevertheless, it has to be said that Plutarch's 'mystic guide' is essentially 'lunar' and 'passive'. For Aphrodite is 'ineffective by herself', he says, and 'without illumination' until lit by Eros as the 'active' masculine sun.[26] It is a passivity that starkly contrasts with Hathor's dynamic solar power in the Egyptian cult, and with Olympiodorus's elusive 'woman of vapour' who flows through alchemy, the 'Red One', both 'bitter and styptic', both death-dealing and healing, a 'woman who flees' as she is sometimes known. This fluid light goddess is easily stirred, difficult to stabilize, yet hers is the unifying power, hers is the 'sympathy' that unites everything together like pieces of gold.

In the Hellenistic world inhabited by Plutarch, Egypt's solar goddesses had been extensively subsumed into the

fig.55 **Aegis surmounted by the solar crowned head of Hathor or Isis flanked by a Horus falcon on each side. The rows of plant and fruit decoration convey the circulating fruitful life bestowed by the encircling goddess. (Petrie Museum, University College London.)**

widespread Isis cults, their fiery power being increasingly brought into line with Greek perceptions of the female as 'cold' and 'passive' and Isis as a lunar goddess. Perhaps, too, the Greek dislike of Egypt's animal deities, typified by Plutarch, played into this obscuring trend. After all, he must have known Hathor's manifestation as cow and Sekhmet's as lioness. Certainly, the balance between the solar and lunar aspects of Hathor and Isis that was so central to their roles in Hathor's Graeco-Roman temple at Dendara tipped very decisively towards Isis in the Hellenistic world.[27] Yet curiously, hidden though Hathor's name may have become, this Hellenized sistrum-shaking Isis, crowned with her uraeus and solar-horned headdress, in fact embodied many of Hathor's fiery magnetic qualities. 'I am Isis,' she majestically declared in the Greek aretalogy discovered at Cyme quoted at the beginning of this chapter. But this Hellenized universal goddess of many names, with all her shape-shifting manifestations, still remained united to Hathor in her deepest essence, as did alchemy's female guide, her fire creatively fuelling the alchemical work, the flame within the flame at the heart of the green stone.

Probably, Plutarch had Isis in mind when composing his 'Dialogue on Love', though he also remained faithful enough to the Egyptian solar tradition. For we have seen this same propitiated 'mystic guide' in the New Year ritual, this fiery 'green' goddess mediating between heaven and the Osirian depths, ever desirous of bringing forth flourishing new life. Circulating freely like vital sap in trees, in plants and all living forms, hers is the 'affection' at the heart of creation, the radiant elixir of life, the green 'emerald' bringing forth flowing living water from the tomb. Surely, despite all the philosophical Greek style, despite all the veiling of Hathor-Sekhmet's real name, a genuine Egyptian core shimmers through Plutarch's mediating 'third' love.

OUT OF EGYPT:
A CHRISTIAN MYSTERY

Chapter 8

> As for scent your oils are good.
> 'Oil of Turaq' is your name;
> That's why maidens love you.
> Take me with you, let us hasten,
> The king has brought me to his chambers.
>
> *(From the Song of Songs 1:2–4, attributed to King Solomon)*

fig.56 **A third-century portrayal of Christ's midday meeting with the Samaritan woman beside the well when she recognizes him as the Messiah or 'anointed one'. She holds a vase and Christ is painted in a scarlet chlamys which is unique in early fresco painting. During the Egyptian New Year ceremony the anointed king also wore a red robe when he appeared as ruler of the vertical world axis, uniting the Heliopolitan heavenly sun with the 'well of every god'. (Fresco in the catacomb of Praetextatus, Rome.)**

In the light of this diffusion of Egypt's temple secrets, we need to look again at Queen Ankhesenamun's anointing gesture on the Golden Shrine (fig.26). For hers is a gesture that strangely recalls much later representations of Mary Magdalene in Christian art. Her vessel, or *alabastron*, filled with precious ointments for anointing Christ, became her ubiquitous symbol from the Middle Ages onwards.

Curiously, a feminine rite of pouring balm to anoint Jesus is recorded in all four canonical books of the New Testament, its purpose being variously conveyed by the gospel writers. The account in the Gospel of Luke (7:36–9) tells how an unnamed woman, a sinner, comes to Jesus whilst he is eating a meal in a Pharisee's house, bringing oil of myrrh in a flask to anoint his feet, wiping them with her tears and filling the room with her fragrance. Though an ill-regarded social outcast, this woman can still lovingly recognize Jesus's true nature. And he in turn displays great compassion towards her, blessing her with forgiveness. Indeed, it is she who enables him to live out his prophetic purpose as 'anointed one', which he earlier proclaimed in Nazareth, when he quoted

from the words of Isaiah: 'The spirit of the Lord is upon me because he has anointed me ... to bring good news to the poor ... release for prisoners ... sight for the blind ... and to proclaim the year of the Lord's favour.' This role is made manifest when this female outcast anoints Jesus (Luke 4:16–20).

By contrast, in the Gospels of Mark (14:3–9) and Matthew (26:6–13), an unnamed woman pours her fragrant oil over Jesus's head whilst he is eating a meal at the house of Simon 'the leper' in Bethany. By anointing Jesus's head in this way the woman confirms his royal and priestly nature. Indeed, through this anointing he becomes Christ, a name deriving from the Greek *christos*, meaning 'anointed one'. And this transformation occurs two days before the Jewish Passover festival and last meal which Jesus will share with his disciples before his crucifixion. Certainly he accepts the woman's anointing as a preparation for his 'day of burial', implicitly linking it with death and the tomb. He also says her act will be forever told 'in memory of her' whenever the gospel is proclaimed (Mark 14:9).

This 'royal' anointing, specifically in a leper's house, must have caused shock waves among the Jewish authorities with their zeal for the law. Lepers were outcasts, their access to the temple being heavily restricted because of the fear of impurity. Moreover, according to the Hebrew Bible, leprosy could be a sign that someone had encroached on Mosaic tradition and the prerogatives of the high priesthood. Thus, when Miriam, together with her brother, the high priest Aaron, questioned the sole right of Moses to receive direct revelation from God, she was afflicted with leprosy for seven days (Numbers 12:1–16). The same fate befell King Uzziah (2 Chronicles 26:18) when he tried to burn incense in the temple against the wishes of the high priest.[1] Hence the woman's anointing of Jesus in a leper's house not only powerfully confirms his 'royal' priestly nature as 'anointed one' but also represents an implicit challenge to established Judaic traditions.

In the Gospel of John (12:1–8), however, it is Mary of Bethany, the sister of Martha and Lazarus, who lovingly anoints Jesus's feet with her ointment, wiping them with her hair and filling the room with fragrance. Here she performs this loving rite whilst Jesus is eating a meal at a banquet in Bethany, shortly after he has raised Lazarus from the dead, and does so six days before the Passover meal. Hers is an anointing that Jesus again says has been done for the 'day of my burial'. And when he rides into Jerusalem on an ass or colt the next day, not only does Mary anticipate the people's acclamation of him as their king and 'anointed one', she also reveals her knowledge of his imminent death and resurrection.

Significantly, it is Mary Magdalene, sometimes identified with Mary of Bethany in Christian tradition, who becomes the first witness to the risen Christ, finding him near the empty tomb in the Easter garden where life rises anew.[2] Hence, in John's gospel, Christ's royal entry into Jerusalem and his death and resurrection are encompassed by two Marys, one who anoints him and one who is the first to witness his coming forth from the tomb. Of all the gospels, John's presents this anointing in the context of a distinctive royal progress, displaying a ritual pattern remarkably similar to Egypt's New Year ritual: initiation by 'anointing', then the 'acclamation' of Jesus as king in the temple city, his last 'meal' with his disciples, followed by his passion, redemptive 'death' and 'resurrection', witnessed by Mary Magdalene, which enables his divinity to shine through.

SOLOMON'S SEAL: PHARAOH'S DAUGHTER

Where did this anointing episode come from, each time performed by a woman and, in three of the canonical gospels, implicitly linked to the tomb and healing, either by taking place in a leper's house or when Jesus had brought Lazarus back to life? For although the prophetic expectation of the Messiah or 'anointed one' had long been alive among the Jewish people, anointing by a female cannot be explained in terms of Judaism. Nor can this symbolic anointing of Jesus's body for burial, which though a Jewish custom, is here specifically performed as though it were an embalming ritual for the living Jesus, with all its echoes of Egyptian rites.

Undoubtedly, anointing was an age-old rite of kingship which was widely practised in the Near East for many centuries before Christianity, so there would have been a general familiarity with its royal significance. But despite the importance attached to the anointing of

▶ *fig.57* **This is the earliest surviving image of Mary Magdalene and shows her with two other female figures (the third is scarcely recognizable now) moving towards a large sarcophagus. The women, dressed like brides, hold burning torches as they bring light to the tomb where Christ is buried. They also carry spice bowls identifying them as ointment bearers. (Detail of a wall-painting from the third-century house church at Dura-Europos, now in Yale University Art Gallery.)**

kings and priests in the Hebrew Bible, there is little evidence, other than veiled hints in the wisdom tradition associated with King Solomon, to suggest that this was ever a female-guided rite.

Nevertheless, in the opening lines of the *Song of Songs*, attributed to Solomon, we find the 'bride' praising her royal lover's 'name', poured out like 'oil of Turaq', and expressing her desire to join the anointed fragrant king in his marriage chamber (see page 86). Throughout this intensely beautiful song, with all its erotic imagery highly reminiscent of ancient Egyptian love poetry, anointing with fragrant oils is a powerful symbol pervading the lovers' quest for union, as is the 'amuletic' revelation of the beloved, whose love 'is as strong as death' when she is placed like a seal upon her lover's heart (see page 38).

When this song was composed is uncertain, but it became woven very early into the Christian mystical tradition.[3] In his commentary on it, Hippolytus (*c.*170–*c.*235), a bishop of Rome, identified the women seeking Christ in the garden with Solomon's bride or Shulamite seeking her bridegroom, a link which continues to be celebrated even today during the feast day of Mary Magdalene on 22 July, when the verse beginning 'Place me as a seal upon your heart' is sung to celebrate her love for Christ.[4] Nevertheless, it was a seal that, for centuries, an ancient Egyptian goddess queen had placed upon the heart of her beloved king at the New Year. And, veiled though it may be, this Solomonic tradition displays a whole network of symbolism evocative of Egypt.

Indeed, Solomon's kingship is itself royally confirmed by a woman during the legendary visit of the Queen of Sheba, who travels from the south to his court to test his wisdom with riddles and marvel at his court's magnificence. Bearing her gifts of spices, gold and precious stones, she communes with Israel's famous wise king, speaking to him from her heart to ascertain his wisdom (1 Kings 10:1–13). Curiously, this episode follows closely after Solomon has established 'Pharaoh's daughter' in her house near to his temple, which he had built in Jerusalem with the help of Phoenician craft expertise (1 Kings 9:24). This royal building activity, which established Solomon's glorious reputation as temple-builder, bears the stamp of Phoenician and Egyptian craft wisdom, 'bound in its conception and its completion to a foreign wife and her own house'.[5] Likewise, it is a foreign woman, the Queen of Sheba, who glorifies Solomon's divine kingship with her gifts, acclaiming him as Israel's divinely appointed ruler whom God loves, wise in judgement and justice for his people.

Such was the intensity of this meeting between Solomon and Sheba that it created an enduring fascination with the 'queen of the south' that evolved under Christian, Jewish, Islamic and Ethiopian influences to become a powerful current of love wisdom. Indeed, Jesus himself invokes the 'queen of the south', saying she will rise up in judgement against his accusers who decry his healing work (Luke 11:31).

To be sure, it is never stated that the Queen of Sheba anoints Solomon, yet everything that this southern queen brings with her is a fragrant gift that transforms a ruler into an 'anointed one'. The parallels with Maat's blessing of Egypt's 'anointed king' need scarcely be elaborated (see page 58). Nor the similarities with the meeting between Hathor and Re where she unveils her face to commune with him in the 'litany of the birds' at the close of the New Year ritual (see page 57). The gifts of this golden goddess were extremely important

to the Egyptian kings, whom she showered with her exotic fragrances from the southern regions as 'Lady of Punt', yet the meeting between Solomon and his own 'queen of the south', with all its aura of 'Pharaoh's daughter' and solar confirmation of kingship, has always been seen simply as a Biblical episode.

As has the anointing of Christ. Yet it is in an Egyptian royal ritual that was still preserved in Upper Egyptian temples not long before the New Testament gospels were written that we find the most direct parallels to this anointing. It is also in Egypt that we find the female linked with the power to overcome death and rise from the tomb. Is this a coincidence? Or is to ignore these similarities simply to suppress the possibility of early Christianity's links with ancient Egypt?

JEWISH WISDOM: ISIS REGINA

Nor would such an Egyptian influence be at all implausible, since there was a good deal of interaction between Egyptians, Greeks and Jews in Hellenistic and Roman times. Indeed, a large number of Jewish refugees had fled to Egypt after the Babylonian occupation of Judah in the early sixth century BCE, settling in places like Memphis, Edfu and Elephantine, where they came under the influence of native Egyptians but also strongly retained their own Jewish traditions. Subsequently, Alexandria attracted a large Hellenized Jewish community, which was well integrated into the cultural life of the Greek capital.

The *Wisdom of Solomon*, which was written in Greek and was probably composed for a Hellenized Jewish community in Egypt around the turn of the millennium, typifies this cultural interaction. Here Wisdom (Sophia) is presented as the lover and beloved, known only to the king. She is a world-soul leading individuals to God, with whom the maturing king seeks a mystical marriage. It has been suggested the author was familiar with Greek hymns to Isis, and John Kloppenborg tellingly observed how a mythic pattern of Egyptian kingship underlay this Jewish wisdom book, writing:

> The mythic power which informed Egyptian royal ideology is captured and transformed for Judaism.[6]

But there are signs of Egypt's royal 'mythic power' in Judaism long before the first century. 'Egyptianizing' elements of the two-winged sun disk and four-winged scarab seem to have been adapted as a royal emblem of the kingdom of Judah during the time of King Hezekiah in the late eighth century BCE, a period of intense contact with Egypt.[7] Commentators have also observed the similarities between Psalm 104 in the Hebrew Psalter and Akhenaten's longer hymn to the Aten, and the likely influence of Egyptian solar goddesses on 'Woman Wisdom' in the Hebrew Bible's Book of Proverbs.[8]

For just as the Memphite Sun Eye, Hathor-Sekhmet, is the instrument of Re's divine energy and royal power in the solar circuit, so, too, Wisdom both guarantees the rulership of kings and makes manifest God's creative activity in the world (Proverbs 8). Ever delighting him and ever at play, she appears alongside the divine craftsman from the very first time of creation. Whilst stopping short of advocating a direct historical connection with Egypt, Othmar Keel nevertheless observed the many similarities with Maat in the Egyptian solar cult, the playful 'daughter of Re' whose

harmonious guidance sustained a solar creation shaped by Ptah's craft skills.[9]

This Biblical Wisdom figure is particularly at home in the wisdom tradition attributed to Solomon, the archetypal wise king for the Jewish people, if one who ultimately failed to follow the law. Remarkably, Solomon's very first act as ruler was to marry 'Pharaoh's daughter', for whom he provided a palace close to the temple he built in Jerusalem. Notwithstanding the antipathy to Egypt in many parts of the Hebrew Bible, this Egyptian lady, according to *The Oxford Bible Commentary*, 'plays a surprisingly large role in the story of Solomon'—as indeed had another 'Pharaoh's daughter' in the life of Moses, when she discovered him abandoned as a baby amongst the reeds of the Nile and compassionately reared him as her son in the Egyptian palace (Exodus 2:5–10).[10] According to Stephen, the first Christian martyr in Jerusalem, Moses was 'trained in all the wisdom of the Egyptians', becoming a powerful speaker and man of action. Evidently, to this first-century Christian anyway, an upbringing in the Egyptian palace was an auspicious training in wisdom (Acts of the Apostles 7:20–22).

THE SAMARITAN WOMAN: JACOB'S WELL

Of course, all this royal anointing and wisdom symbolism could be explained away as a similar response to a shared Near Eastern tradition of kingship, not necessarily evidence for any special relationship between Egypt and early Christianity. But it is not so simple. A carefully crafted episode in the Gospel of John's fourth chapter (John 4:1–42) suggests a much deeper connection with Egypt. So far it has never been conclusively established where John's gospel was composed, though it has always been considered as somehow different from the three synoptic gospels. Early evidence for its existence comes from papyri discovered in Egypt, though an old tradition associates it with Ephesus. Antioch and Alexandria have also been suggested as its place of origin.[11] Regardless of where it may have been first written, however, it is certainly a healing gospel, particularly noted for its sacramental outlook and celebration of abundant life in all its material fullness—in water, in bread, in wine and the life-bearing vine.

The episode in question follows immediately after the mention of Jesus's ritual activity (baptism) and his appearance as 'bridegroom' in the third chapter. Then the theme shifts to his journey in Samaria, where the Samaritans had become a firmly established, if enigmatic, group by the first century, believing themselves to be the authentic representatives of Mosaic religion, with their own temple on Mount Gerizim. Whilst his disciples go to buy food Jesus stops in a place called Sychar, resting beside a spring called 'Jacob's well', a name that intimately connects it with the revered ancestor of the people of Israel. Here he encounters a Samaritan woman who has come to draw water (figs.56,60). The time is stated quite specifically: it is 'about the sixth hour', which is perhaps an unusual time to travel, as it is at the sun's moment of culmination, the hour of 'standstill' as the ancient Egyptians called it, when a sense of suspension and cessation of movement prevails in the noonday heat.

Jesus asks the woman to give him water. Taken aback that a Jew should ask a Samaritan for a drink, she enters into an ambiguous double-layered conversation with him in which Jesus tells her he can give her 'living water' drawn from an 'eternal spring always welling up for eternal life'. Applying his words primarily to her earthly needs and thinking that her long treks to the well may soon be over, she asks Jesus to give her this abundant water. But he tells her first to go home and bring her husband to him. When she truthfully replies she does not have one, to her amazement he then discloses his knowledge of her previous five husbands and her present companion, with whom she now lives, though not in marriage. Furthermore, he tells her that a new form of worship is coming where the Father will be worshipped 'in spirit and truth' which will be neither on the holy mountain of the Samaritans nor in Jerusalem. He then reveals to her that he is the longed-for Messiah, the 'anointed one'. At that moment the disciples return and the woman, amazed at these revelations, hurries away to bring her townspeople to Jesus.

So, when the heavenly sun is highest in the sky, shining upon Jesus and this Samaritan woman beside an ancestral deep well, there is the extraordinary revelation of Jesus as the 'anointed one', offering believers, whether Jew or Samaritan, a share in the flowing water of eternal life. It is the moment when Jesus, whom the gospel will shortly proclaim as the healing 'saviour of the world', also promises a new form of worship. And we find exactly the same combination of 'zenithal sun' and ancestral 'deep well' in the Egyptian New Year ritual when the fiery goddess transforms the king into Re's heavenly 'anointed one'. In both, there is the vision of the exalted divinely appointed son at the vertical axis of the world, the cosmic king bringing abundant new life and eternal water to his regenerated people.

▶ *fig.58* **Drawing of the Samaritan woman beside the well from a third-century house church at Dura-Europos, a Roman outpost on the middle Euphrates river.**

specific reference to the 'sixth hour' recalls Jesus's earlier appearance in Samaria at exactly the same time, thus weaving together his two appearances as anointed king.[12] But now, wearing his purple robe of royalty he is perceived through completely different eyes. Where once he was acclaimed by the Samaritans, there is now rejection and suffering. Moreover, his death is imminent, as is his burial in the tomb, from where, after three days, he will rise again, appearing to Mary Magdalene in all his resurrected glory, making manifest his life-giving redemptive powers. That earlier 'sixth-hour' appearance of Jesus as 'anointed one' in Samaria, with its promise of eternal living water, is now unfolding its deeper truth, being expressed within a royal ritual pattern remarkably similar to the unfoldment of the Egyptian New Year ritual (see chapter 9).

Importantly, too, the encounter with the Samaritan woman hints at a 'marriage' mystery, a spiritual 'rebirth' in her deepest soul through her relationship with Jesus as 'bridegroom'. For it is after Jesus has opened the eye of her heart to his unique presence in the world that it begins to dawn on her that he may indeed be the bearer of divine glory. Already she has had five husbands and she is now with a sixth partner, an allusion to her marital status that some commentators see as a riposte to the 'adulterous' ways of worship in Samaria.[13] But seven is also a highly significant number in John's gospel, with its seven signs or miracles revealing Jesus's power at work in the world. Moreover, previously, in the third chapter, Jesus has been called 'bridegroom'. The underlying implication is that this truthful woman is now being invited into a very different relationship with Jesus as the 'seventh'—a 'marriage'

There are still more Biblical parallels with the Egyptian New Year ritual. In the second half of John's gospel Jesus appears again as the 'anointed one' in an episode which is closely attuned to his previous appearance beside Jacob's well. Here it is preceded, however, by Mary of Bethany explicitly anointing him before his acclaimed entry into Jerusalem as king, entering upon the royal road which will ultimately lead to his death (see page 87). In Jerusalem Jesus shares his last meal with his disciples. Then comes his trial. And it is precisely at 'around the sixth hour' that he is presented to the hostile Jewish people as their king, clothed in a purple robe and wearing a crown of thorns, shortly before he is handed over to be crucified (John 19:14).

Every detail in this carefully composed gospel illuminates the deeper meaning woven into the narrative and this very mystery that will bring rebirth into eternal life. For seven is also the number symbolizing spiritual 'rebirth' and 'completion' in Hellenistic mystery religions and Hermeticism, and this theme of 'being born again' recurs throughout John's gospel.[14]

MYTHIC EGYPT: EVER-NEW WORD

Seven is also a sacred number in ancient Egypt, especially in Ptah's creation at Memphis. According to inscriptions in the Graeco-Roman Horus temple at Edfu, seven creative words or 'utterances' call the world into being, a sevenfold sounding in the primordial depths which is already attested in the *Coffin Texts*.[15] Indeed, the famous prologue of John's gospel which celebrates creation through the 'Word' (Logos) and the glorious appearance of the 'Father's only son, full of grace and truth', manifesting divine creative power as the 'Word made flesh', brings to mind the lengthy praise of Ptah's creation in the *Memphite Theology*. Inscribed on the 'Shabaka Stone' now in the British Museum, this account of Ptah's creative activity, which is inserted between episodes dealing with the transference of power to Horus as Osiris's heir and his redemptive rescue of Osiris, tells how the Memphite divine craftsman calls creation into being specifically through his 'heart' and 'tongue'. Working in complete harmony with Maat's way of wisdom, Ptah fashions the earth's varied substances to establish all Egypt's rituals and sacred cults, including the Heliopolitan divine images in their places of worship.[16] So, too, it is the cosmic Horus king, enthroned upon the ancestral seat of his grandfather, Geb, who ensures Re's 'light' and 'life' flow through Ptah's wisdom-filled creation.

As James Allen observed, 'The opening words of John's Gospel, devoid of their Christian implications, could easily have been appreciated by the Egyptian author(s) of the "Memphite Theology" as a summary of their own view of creation.'[17] To Henri Frankfort this Memphite mode of creation was the 'true Egyptian equivalent' of the gospel's creative Word.[18] Yet ironically, most New Testament commentators overlook the prologue's 'Egyptianness', planting it firmly within the Jewish Wisdom tradition or the Platonic philosophical discourse of the Greek-speaking world.[19] To be sure, in his remarkable fusion of Jewish faith with Greek thought, the highly regarded Jewish philosopher Philo of Alexandria also elevated the eternal Logos and Wisdom as the divine Word identified with the first-born Son of God.

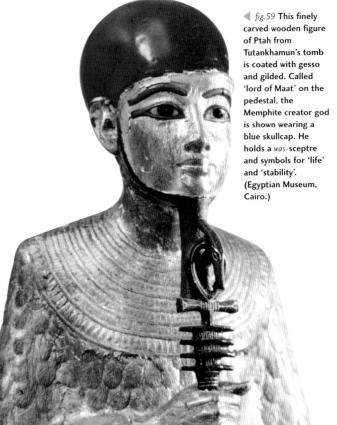

fig.59 This finely carved wooden figure of Ptah from Tutankhamun's tomb is coated with gesso and gilded. Called 'lord of Maat' on the pedestal, the Memphite creator god is shown wearing a blue skullcap. He holds a *was*-sceptre and symbols for 'life' and 'stability'. (Egyptian Museum, Cairo.)

But however much Philo may have drawn on royal traditions current in the Wisdom schools of Alexandria, his allegorical approach to the spiritual mysteries encoded in Hebrew Scriptures is certainly not oriented towards the performance of ritual. Philo taught about symbolic meaning and the soul's search for God, the divinity within which can be experienced deep in the human soul, but his allegorical approach is not, first and foremost, about temple-building, craft activity and ritual. By contrast, in John's sacramental gospel Jesus very specifically promises a new form of worship—and does so within a context highly suggestive of Egypt's New Year 'anointed king'.

According to J. M. Hull, Egyptian perceptions of an initiate king possessing healing power and ruling by cosmic authority were extremely important in shaping early Christianity. He compared the emanation of Christ's divine power in the world to that of an ancient Egyptian king whom Amun-Re authorized to rule as his divine representative on earth (fig.40). He wrote, 'Christ is like the divine king; he will suffer no permanent depletion of his energy because he is directly sustained by the divine Father of all.' Referring primarily to the Theban theology of Amun-Re, Hull was clearly in no doubt as to the influence of Egyptian divine kingship in early Christian life.[20] Had he looked at this episode beside the well in John's gospel, he would have found further confirmation of his view, for the gospel's highly creative author seems to have skilfully recast Egyptian New Year royal wisdom so that it is uniquely centred on Jesus as the 'anointed one', the divine son and revealer of God's presence in the world.

Undoubtedly, the rich mythological content of the New Year ritual is entirely absent. Nor are there any signs of Egypt's traditional deities in their magically animated world. Indeed, the ancient temple wisdom has been thoroughly 'de-mythologized', as happened more generally in Hellenistic times, making it all too easy to miss the 'Egyptianness' in this encounter beside the well.[21] Yet Jesus's majestic appearance, illuminated by a zenithal sun shining deep into ancestral life-giving water, is so evocative of the Heliopolitan New Year cosmic king, the ritual atmosphere so specific, that surely this is more than simply a coincidence?

Moreover, here Jesus inaugurates a new religious era for humanity. How might early Christians have understood his promise of a new form of worship? And what might this revelation beside the well have meant in early Christian sacramental life? There is little surviving evidence regarding Christian worship in the first and early second centuries. Nevertheless, we need to turn now to a Christian gospel not included in the New Testament, the *Gospel of Philip*, which was discovered at Nag Hammadi in Upper Egypt. Unorthodox it may have become in later times, but this unusual gospel sets out a 'New Year' form of worship that displays once again a remarkably similar pattern to Egypt's age-old anointing ritual, albeit now dramatically transformed in meaning.

Chapter 9

SACRAMENTAL LIFE: PHILIP'S GOSPEL

> For what is now called the Christian religion existed even among the ancients and was not lacking from the beginning of the human race until 'Christ came in the flesh'. From that time, true religion, which already existed, began to be called Christian.[1]
>
> (St Augustine)

◄ *fig.60* **Another early painting of the meeting between Christ and the Samaritan woman when he promises a new form of worship (see also fig.56). Here, as she stoops to draw water from the well, Christ is shown seated on a stone holding an outstretched scroll from which he is reading. (Early third-century fresco in the catacomb of Calixtus, Rome.)**

The *Gospel of Philip* came to light around 1945 when a hugely important group of ancient religious texts unexpectedly surfaced in Upper Egypt, discovered by two local farmers, the brothers Muhammad and Khalifah Ali al-Samman, who stumbled across them whilst searching for fertilizer close to the rocky cliffs at Nag Hammadi. Not long after the discovery of Tutankhamun's Golden Shrine in the Valley of the Kings at Thebes, another chance find, this time a collection of more than 50 diverse writings, uncovered lost secrets from Egypt's desert sands.

These intriguing texts, copied on papyrus sheets and known collectively today as the Nag Hammadi Library, were written in Coptic, the old Egyptian language in its final stage, as used by Christian descendants of the ancient Egyptians, whose script primarily incorporated the Greek alphabet but also six characters deriving from demotic to express sounds particular to Egyptian. Some treatises in the cache were clearly pagan, some Christian, some gnostic, and there were even extracts from a Hermetic treatise and Platonic writings, all stashed away in an earthenware jar and hidden in a cave not far from Hathor's holy cult site at Dendara.[2]

Who originally owned them we can only speculate. But suddenly, thanks to these Egyptian farmers, a whole collection of early manuscripts, probably buried sometime around 400 CE and including gospels not incorporated into the canon of the New Testament, showed early Christianity to be far more diverse than anyone had ever suspected. Indeed, it seems that during the first centuries of Christianity there were very different ways of following Christ, with the Christian spiritual life being much more of a personal matter than it subsequently became, being pursued in small groups which sprang up everywhere, with quite varied ritual practices and beliefs.

The considerable excitement aroused by the Nag Hammadi discovery was increased still further by gospel references to Mary Magdalene as Christ's beloved companion, her role in some texts being far more dramatic than in the canonical gospels, sometimes to the intense jealousy of the other disciples. According to the *Gospel of Philip*, the Saviour loved Mary Magdalene 'more than all the disciples' and 'used to kiss her often'.[3] And it is this uncanonical gospel that particularly concerns us here.

FIERY OIL: NAMING POWER

Though preserved in an Upper Egyptian dialect of Coptic, the gospel's author shows familiarity with both Greek and Syriac, which has led to the scholarly

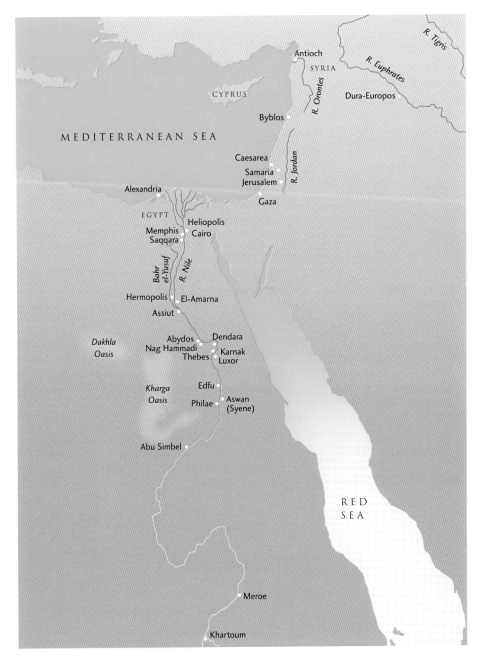

consensus that it was probably composed in Syria, perhaps in the Hellenized cosmopolitan city of Antioch, a leading cultural centre rivalling Alexandria in its magnificence. Founded by Seleukos I after Alexander the Great's conquests, Antioch was where the name 'Christian' was first applied to believers (Acts of the Apostles 11:25–6). It was also particularly renowned for its development of Christian liturgical expression and sacramental life. And it was to Antioch, as well as to Byblos and Cyprus, that followers of Christ had migrated in the late first century after hostility had broken out towards them in Jerusalem and Judaea (Acts of the Apostles 11:19–21). However, precisely when the *Gospel of Philip* was originally composed is uncertain; dates ranging from the second century to the latter half of the third century have been proposed.[4]

This is in many ways a 'New Year' gospel, very much attuned to nature's seasonal rhythms, the passing of winter and coming of summer, which, in contrast to the Egyptian river Nile-based culture, was celebrated in the Syrian region in March. Thus, the gospel says that when the wind of the world blows, 'it brings the winter. When the holy spirit breathes, the summer comes.' Or again, 'What comes out of the winter is the summer.'[5] It is with this coming of summer and rebirth of the world that Christ's triumph over death is harmonized in the *Gospel of Philip*.

For this critical turning-point of the year, the passing of the old year and arrival of the new, the time of death and resurrection for all living things, was when neophytes were often initiated into the Christian community, through rites inaugurating their 'summer' regeneration and flourishing new life. Unlike the four canonical gospels, however, which preserve details of Jesus's public life, death and resurrection, the primary emphasis of Philip's gospel is on ritual as a cult and social reality, the efficacy of which depended on relationship with heavenly life. Repeatedly, the gospel spirals around core ritual experiences, which the author interprets, probably in order to help Christians deepen their understanding of the Christian 'mystery'

and the nature of the 'divine kinship' and spiritual life into which they had been initiated. In short, he states what it means to be 'regenerated' in these initiatory rites. For without this knowledge, the power of the rites remained hidden and inactive.

And it is to the theme of 'anointing' that the author repeatedly returns, calling it 'a spiritual love of wine and fragrance', which is identified with fire. 'The fire is the anointing, the light is the fire', he says. But this is not a fire 'without form'; rather it is the kind of fire 'whose form is white, which is bright and beautiful', a dynamic fire 'creating beauty' in a cosmos where 'love builds up', bringing a 'knowledge of truth' that makes hearts free.[6]

So, too, just as 'Christ was so named because of the anointing' which he received in 'the bridal chamber', it is specifically through anointing that initiates 'are called Christians' and incorporated into a chain of initiation in which 'the Father anointed the son, and the son anointed the apostles, and the apostles anointed us'. Unlike other names, moreover, which are ineffective and powerless, when the new name 'Christian' is uttered, everything 'quakes'.[7]

It is this fiery anointing, not baptism, that seals Christians in a spiritual lineage handed down from Christ through the apostles and then to everyone, granting spiritual blessings to its members. At this Christian turning-point of time all can become 'anointed ones'. All can receive Christ's life-giving love, the healing energy 'creating beauty' which floods into everything porous enough to receive it, rendering the 'image' completely transparent due to the light invested in it. Yet we see the same 'naming' power at the pharaoh's fiery anointing when his cosmic royal name is inscribed on the sacred *Ished*-tree and the whole of

Heliopolis 'quakes' at his coming.

This 'gift of the name' brings union with the holy spirit, understood in this gospel as a feminine power whose 'children are many'. This feminine emphasis continues in the naming of the triple Marys as Christ's companions:

There were three who always walked
with the Lord: Mary his
mother and her sister and Magdalene,
the one who was called
his companion. For Mary is his sister
and his mother and his companion.[8]

Here is a generational triad, at once both personal and mythic, reminiscent of the three Marys who stood by the cross at Jesus's crucifixion in John's gospel (John 19:25). But it is also suggestive of familial kinship in ancient goddess cults and Wisdom's relationship with her royal spouse in the *Wisdom of Solomon* (see page 89). Moreover, it is a mythic pattern that Isis proclaims in a Greek aretalogy found at Cyme on the coast of Asia Minor (modern-day Turkey). In keeping with the Hellenized world in which this litany belonged, she proclaims her father to be, not Geb, but the Greek Kronos, though her husband-brother and her son are certainly Egyptian. Thus she declares: 'I am eldest daughter of Kronos. I am wife and sister of King Osiris. I am she who finds fruits for the people. I am mother of King Horus.'[9] Ever transforming, ever changing, this cosmic mother-sister and wife is an omnipotent world-creating goddess, the life-giving source of regeneration for her royal partner, with whom she shares the deepest kinship. Likewise, the *Gospel of Philip* is anchored in a similar 'kinship' mystery mediated by three Marys as the Lord's mother-sister-consort.[10]

DURA-EUROPOS: THE THREE MARYS

Whoever painted the hauntingly beautiful wall painting discovered in a Christian house church at Dura-Europos, a Roman garrison town on the west bank of the Euphrates in present-day Syria, also honoured three Marys (figs.57,62). Evidently third-century Dura Christians had adapted a mud-brick house for their meetings and religious practices, using a room in its northwest corner for their sacramental rites. Here, on the room's north wall, three women are shown, clothed like brides in their flowing white veils and white robes (the third is scarcely visible), moving towards a huge white sarcophagus surmounted by a star at each end, a blazing torch clearly visible in the hand of the first two women, illuminating the red-purple background of the tomb's darkness. Each woman also carries a spice bowl, identifying them as fiery ointment bearers come to light up the tomb as first witnesses of Christ's resurrection.[11]

At the room's west end was the baptismal font, located within a painted columned niche, its vault strewn with stars and its back wall adorned with a representation of Christ as the good shepherd, which has John's gospel as its source (fig.62). Shown also are small figures of Adam and Eve. Looking immediately to the left after they had entered through a doorway in the south wall, these early Christians would have seen, too, a sketchily drawn figure of the Samaritan woman at the well, holding a rope as she stooped to draw forth the water of 'eternal life' (fig.58). Again it is an image specific to John's gospel.

Interestingly, between the two doors on the south wall there was also a niche, which Carl Kraeling suggested would have contained the sacramental oil. If so,

▶ *fig.62* **The reconstructed 'baptistery' in the Christian house church at Dura-Europos showing the scene on the north wall of the three Marys approaching the sarcophagus. At the room's west end is a shrine enclosing a baptismal font surrounded by a brightly painted arch adorned with floral and fruit motifs. Represented on the back wall is Christ as the Good Shepherd and a much smaller scene of Adam and Eve. (Reconstruction in Yale University Art Gallery.)**

this niche, with its paradisiacal garden painted above and a scene of David fighting the Biblical giant Goliath below, is precious evidence for the anointing rite that must once have been performed for early Christians in this far-flung Syrian region, a 'naming' rite that initiated them into the wider Christian community, transforming them into 'anointed ones' with prodigious power to protect themselves from Goliath-like hostile forces.[12] Carefully written in Greek beside the niche were the words 'Christ Jesus is yours, remember Proclus', perhaps inscribed by a donor who had supported this house church and had himself experienced this sacred anointing rite.[13]

Placed directly across on the north wall was the beautiful, though now sadly damaged, painting of the three Marys, which would have graphically conveyed to initiates the regenerative healing

meaning of this fiery anointing in the marriage chamber. (fig.62) Here before their eyes these Christian initiates would have seen those words in the *Gospel of Philip* unveiled:

> Whoever has been anointed
> possesses everything …the
> resurrection, the light,
> the cross, the holy spirit. This is
> what the Father gave to them
> in the bridal chamber and they
> received it.[14]

Very little is known regarding the spread of Christianity to Dura-Europos, a town strongly influenced by Greek language and culture, where archaeologists also found evidence of a Jewish synagogue and Hellenistic mystery cults. But here, in this discreet house church, Jesus's promise of a new worship to the

Samaritan woman had evidently become a very tangible ritual reality by the mid-third century, as it must have done in numerous other small house churches established throughout the Syrian region.

ABOVE AND BELOW: A FIVEFOLD SEALING

It is this ritual life, strengthening and revitalizing Christian initiates, that deeply concerns the *Gospel of Philip*'s author. For, in a somewhat startling statement, the gospel tersely sets out a form of Christian worship incorporating five sacraments. Startling because its form shows a remarkable similarity with the ancient Egyptian New Year anointing rite:

> The Lord has done everything in a mystery: A baptism and an anointing and a eucharist and a redemption and a bridal chamber.[15]

Immediately after setting out this sacramental 'mystery', the gospel describes the unification of heaven and earth, the 'making the inner as the outer', which is here clearly linked to Christian ritual practice:

> The Lord said, 'I came to make the things below like the things above and the things outside like the things inside. I have come to unite them in that place'.[16]

However these five sacraments, namely 'baptism', 'anointing', 'eucharist', 'redemption' and 'marriage', may have been actually celebrated in early Christianity, this is a 'mystery' which forms a unity, even perhaps five different phases of a 'complex initiation ritual' sealing an initiate's identification with Christ.[17]

The ritual thread linking these five sacraments together has proved elusive, but, as yet, no one has looked to ancient Egypt for an explanation. Yet despite the Christian context, this fivefold sacramental 'mystery'—occurring in a New Year gospel attuned to the awakening of life from death in cosmic nature, with 'the coming forth from winter' into summer and concerned with the Christian initiate's regeneration—looks remarkably similar to the pattern of the Egyptian New Year ritual, albeit divested of specific Egyptian mythic or cult allusions. Had not the pharaoh also

▲ *fig.63* **Drawing of the three Marys approaching the sarcophagus.**

first been completely purified with water, then anointed with fiery oil? And had he not then been given the consecrated bread to eat at the zenith before the redemptive entry into the Osirian tomb where he discovered the stone? And did not this ritual also culminate in a 'marriage chamber' rite when the Horus king gloriously united with his golden-tressed divine consort Hathor-Maat, whose necklace completely encircled him in light, righteousness, love and truth?

In both the *Gospel of Philip* and the ancient Egyptian New Year ritual, there is the unification between above and below, between the key elements of fire and water, creating beauty in the world. But where once the Egyptian king sought a healing union between the opposites, now the quest is for the Christian initiate to open a light-filled heart to Christ and experience his unifying power through the influx of fiery healing love. It would be too easy simply to explain away the similarities as signs of a general religious

atmosphere in the early Christian era drawing on widespread Near Eastern myths of a dying and resurrecting god. But this Christian anointing 'mystery'—in a gospel steeped also in alchemy, in Mary Magdalene's key role in Christ's life, in 'rebirth through the image', in the holiness of a world made flesh and purification through water and fire—follows a very distinctive Egyptian ritual pattern, unlike anything to be found in traditional Jewish sources.

Initially, of course, to anyone unfamiliar with Egypt's anointing rites, these five sacraments could easily appear to be simply a Christian ritual development expressed in a fivefold canon typical of the Jewish tradition of arranging sacred writings, for example in the first five books of the Hebrew Bible known as the Pentateuch or 'five books of Moses' that formed the basis of the Torah.[18] Certainly, this fivefoldness in the *Gospel of Philip* would have resonated with the Judaism from which

fig.64 **Isiac procession preserved on a mosaic fragment from Antioch perhaps dating to the third century CE. To the right is a female figure holding a sistrum near an open door. Another female figure, probably an Isiac priestess, wears a white robe with a vertical sash adorned with a lunar crescent, a typical Isiac garment. Behind them two other female figures are discernible in the procession. (Hatay Archaeological Museum, Antakya.)**

the various Christian communities were emerging. Moreover, it also recalls the five seals associated with baptism and the power over death mentioned in the so-called 'Pronoia hymn' in the *Apocryphon of John*, which was bound in the same codex as the *Gospel of Philip*. Interestingly, too, bearing in mind alchemy's significance in Philip's gospel (see chapter 10), Graeco-Egyptian alchemical treatises record how the alchemists Cleopatra and Zosimus of Panopolis taught a 'five-step' process of 'gold-making', which Régine Charron compared with the *Apocryphon*'s hymn and five seals.[19] Hence, this fivefold sacramental arrangement is not unusual. But, at the same time, its sequence of rites also displays a remarkable similarity with the mythic pattern of Egypt's royal New Year ceremony.

ANTIOCH'S MOSAICS: HERMES AND ISIS

Here we need to look more closely at Egyptian influence in Syria. For the likely origins of Philip's gospel in the Syrian region locate it in an area that had enjoyed a lively cultural interchange with Egypt for centuries, Syrian deities having entered the Egyptian cults as far back as the New Kingdom. In the Ptolemaic era there was a hugely important network of trade routes between Syria, Arabia and Upper Egypt, linking them by the shipping of spices from the East, as well as aromatic incense, fragrant resins, ivory and other luxury goods from southern regions, which came via the Red Sea and desert trade routes. Hellenistic Syria's wealth derived partly from trading with these goods, especially at Antioch, which was strategically located in the fertile plain of the Orontes river north of Phoenicia's rocky coast, at the junction of trade routes to Egypt,

Palestine, Damascus, the Aegean and the East.

But this was not just a trading connection. For with trade came the Egyptian cults, and by early Roman times the Isis and Sarapis cults had evidently spread throughout the Levantine coastal regions, reaching further northwards to Antioch. Indeed, according to Libanius, the cult of Isis had been introduced to Antioch in the reign of the Syrian king Seleukos II (246–226 BCE), who had asked for a healing statue of the goddess to be sent there from Memphis after she had appeared to him in a dream. Evidently Seleukos wanted an Isis statue not from Greek Alexandria but from the age-old royal capital of Memphis, which evidently still retained its religious prestige in Hellenistic times.[20] Ptolemaic Memphis might have been overshadowed by Alexandria's political and economic importance, but its priesthood still preserved Egypt's 'royal' traditions as they had always done. Indeed, the introduction to the Greek Isis aretalogy discovered at Cyme states it was copied from a stela in Memphis which stood by the temple of Hephaistos (the Greek Ptah). And it was this kind of aretalogy, praising the 'goddess of many names', that helped to spread Egyptian 'royal' wisdom throughout the Mediterranean world and bring increasing numbers of worshippers into the Isis cults.

Whether Isis was, in fact, established in Antioch as early as Seleukos II's reign is unclear, since it is extremely difficult to piece together the origins of her cult in Syria and Phoenicia, where the evidence is very dispersed and sporadic. But certainly this universal goddess, whom the Greek aretalogies praised for providing all the sacred cities, the shrines, the cult images and rituals, all

▶ *fig.65* **The 'mors voluntaria' mosaic probably dating to the third century CE. This unique mosaic originally formed part of the floor of a room in the so-called 'House of the Mysteries' at Antioch. The identity of the female figure on the left, wearing a wreath in her hair and holding a torch over her left shoulder, has been much debated. She is almost certainly Isis (or an Isiac priestess), not Demeter. To the right is Hermes holding his familiar caduceus in his left hand. The man in the centre is naked except for his elaborate headdress and a red cloth over his shoulder (the red colour is still preserved on the actual mosaic). This cloth is an important clue to the scene's 'Egyptianness' since a red cloth was traditionally associated with coming forth to new life in Osirian regeneration rites. Here Hermes beckons to the initiate with his sceptre, and the open door behind him suggests that the man has already undergone the 'death' experience and is now moving towards glorious rebirth in the Isis mysteries. (Princeton University Art Museum, Princeton.)**

the languages, the laws, the love and justice-making in the world, appears on coins in the mid-second century reign of Antiochus IV. Interestingly, too, a late second-century priest at Athens, responsible for interpreting the incubatory dreams which were sent by Isis and Sarapis, came from Antioch.[21]

A Roman-period mosaic which was discovered at Daphne, not far from Antioch (fig.64), leaves no doubt as to the presence of Isis in the region. Here an Isiac procession moves towards an open door, headed by a woman holding Hathor's sacred sistrum. Following her is a white-robed regal figure, wearing a sash adorned with a lunar crescent and stars, a typical Isiac garment in this period.[22] Perhaps she is Isis, but possibly an Isis priestess, followed by two figures impossible to identify because of damage to the mosaic. The scene is Egyptian, that we can be sure. Sadly, however, its ritual context is lost. For nothing remains that can positively be

identified as an Isiac temple in the largely destroyed ancient site of Antioch, other than possibly in the port city of Seleucia, where, in a Doric temple with a crypt, a damaged bronze statuette of the goddess was found. But numerous fragments of lamps decorated with figures of Isis and Sarapis provide evidence enough for their cults in greater Antioch.[23]

Even more thought-provoking, however, is a floor mosaic from Antioch itself (fig.65). Here a male initiate is flanked on the left by a female figure who holds a torch over her left shoulder and wears a wreath in her hair. To the right is Hermes, standing before an open door, which is perhaps the entrance to the tomb or perhaps the entrance to the upper air. Like Thoth in ancient Egypt (fig.66), he carries his fiery staff with its twin coiling snakes emblematic of healing, its upper half still visible above the damaged part of the mosaic, clearly identifying him as the Greek god.

MYSTIC GUIDE:
THE LAMP OF LOVE

In his study of the mosaics from Antioch soon after they were excavated, Doro Levi had no hesitation in identifying the scene as an initiation into the Isis mysteries, calling it the 'voluntary death' and 'crowning moment' of the mystic journey involving a 'ritual death and the following resurrection to divine glory'.[24] Indeed, Levi named the site where the mosaic was discovered as the 'House of the Mysteries of Isis', strengthening his interpretation by associating the ships portrayed in another damaged floor mosaic from the same house with the *Navigium Isidis*, a great sailing festival held in honour of Isis in March. This was when the boat of Isis sailed forth, inaugurating the summer and start of the sailing season along the Mediterranean coast wherever there were Isis cults.

Others have interpreted the mosaic differently, identifying the torch-bearing female as Demeter rather than Isis.[25] But the absence of any links between Demeter and Hermes is an awkward stumbling-block, especially as Isis and Hermes are linked together in the Greek aretalogies praising Isis. 'I am Isis, the ruler of every land,' declares the goddess in the Cyme aretalogy (see page 74). And she goes on to say how she received the teaching from Hermes 'and devised letters' with him, as well as 'revealed mysteries to the people'. Greek in expression, but probably Egyptian in origin, this important litany clearly links her with Hermes.

Diodorus of Sicily, writing in the first century BCE, could not have stated the matter more clearly. In the first book of his *General History* he wrote how it was Isis and Hermes who together instituted 'religious ceremonies' and 'secret rites' for Osiris, in order 'to exalt the power of the god.'[26] Certainly, the early second-century writer Philo of Byblos understood Hermes to be an incarnation of the Egyptian god Thoth.[27] If a Levantine author knew this, someone seemingly also very familiar with Thoth's Hermopolitan cosmogony, why should we doubt the 'Egyptianness' of this 'Hermes' mosaic further north at Antioch?

Moreover, according to Doro Levi's detailed description, the initiate wears a red cloth over his left shoulder. (fig.65) If so, then it would further strengthen the rite's Egyptian roots.[28] For this Antiochene initiate is adorned with a cloth whose colour had for centuries symbolized the New Year coming forth of a Horus king from the Osirian realm (see page 55). He may be about to enter the death chamber. But more likely, crystallized in this floor mosaic, as Levi first saw, is that profound transitional moment when an Osirian initiate, not yet fully robed, nor yet fully reborn, is coming forth from the tomb with all its New Year promise of regenerated life.[29]

Where once an Egyptian priest, steeped in all Thoth's incantations and cult wisdom, guided the king through these rites, now it is Hermes. Though whether we identify the female torch-bearer here in fig.65 as goddess or priestess, matters little. For here before our eyes surely is an incarnation of the Egyptian love goddess, the 'mystic guide', as Plutarch called her (page 80), the same light-bearer whose fiery power gloriously brought forth a regenerated king from the tomb.

Here at Antioch these age-old Egyptian rites seem to have become a deeply Hermetic mystery, indicative of the burgeoning Hermeticism that took root in Syria, including at Edessa and Harran. Though it was also a development which was to see outbursts of considerable negativity towards Egypt among groups hostile towards its cult traditions.

To see this rampant hostility towards Egypt in full flood we need but mention the well-known *Hymn of the Pearl*, or *Hymn of the Soul* as it is sometimes called, known in both a Syriac and Greek version, which was inserted into the third-century apocryphal *Acts of Thomas*. Described as a 'charming oriental tale' in *The Oxford Bible Commentary*, the hymn's anti-Egyptian sentiments have been tacitly accepted by scholars when discussing its charm.[30] Yet its theme of a youthful eastern prince's quest for the 'stone' (a pearl), which lies in the snake-encircled waters of Egypt (fig.42), suggests its origins were far more complex. Indeed, it seems to have been composed by someone displaying more than a passing acquaintance with the Horus king's search for the *Ibhet-stone* in the New Year ritual.

The prince is sent to find the pearl in Egypt by his royal parents in the East, so that he can inherit the kingdom and his name be proclaimed in the 'book of the valiant ones' (or 'book of life' in the Greek version of the hymn). When he arrives at his Egyptian destination he first sees a beautiful youth, an 'anointed one' and 'a son of my race', residing amidst Egypt's 'unclean ones', close to where the pearl's snake guardian dwells. But even this youth cannot protect the prince from the trickery of the Egyptians and the deep sleep he falls into because of the heavy food they give him. Significantly, it is the power of a sealed letter that ultimately wakes him, a letter sent by his royal parents in the East to remind him of his royal nature, calling on him to 'rouse himself from sleep'. Manifesting in the form of a great eagle, the king of birds, this letter alights near the prince, waking him. And, having read the letter

and charmed the pearl, he then travels eastwards with his treasure, guided by his letter's 'voice' and 'love'. Interestingly, it is a female who appears as a guide in the Greek version, giving the prince an oracle before taking him towards the light of the East. There he is drawn towards his richly bejewelled robe, which he had left behind at the start of his journey, a royal robe painted with an image of the king—a robe, too, which is alive and endowed with 'movements of knowledge', making manifest the unity of the 'two in one' as the prince reunites with his 'image'. Finally, confirmed in his power and reintegrated into his royalty, the victorious heir's reunion with his father completes his redemptive journey.

Despite its utmost contempt for ancient Egyptian 'impurities', this hymn, which is thought to have been composed somewhere in the region of Edessa (present-day Urfa in eastern Turkey), has all the ring of an author very familiar with Egypt's anointing tradition. And, moreover, someone who was very keen to take this ancient treasure 'out of Egypt'. For we have seen a similar 'quest for a stone' in the New Year ritual. We have seen, too, how priests brought a great bird close to the sleeping Horus heir to proclaim his royal power. And how he was adorned in a resplendent red robe after his return from the tomb, a return that brought the revelation of a unification mystery. All this precious ancient wisdom seems to have been reformed in the *Hymn of the Pearl*. Indeed, it seems to have been intentionally subverted and made into a rival eastern 'royal confirmation of power', stressing the dangers of falling asleep entrapped in Egypt's material realm. Certainly, it is a redemptive journey more in tune with a dualistic world view that is known to have flourished among people living in the Mesopotamian region, including ascetic Christian communities inclined towards 'Thomas' teachings. But what it also demonstrates is the potency of the Egyptian 'anointing' tradition among people in the Syrian region during the third century.[31]

A RITUAL HERITAGE: EARLY CHRISTIANITY

We can now return to the *Gospel of Philip* with new eyes. For the two mosaics from Antioch encapsulate the spread of the Isis cults into the wider Syrian region during the Roman era, and the attraction they held for Hellenized people still steeped in ancient cult traditions. It is not difficult to imagine that Egypt's ritual wisdom might have been dramatically transformed into a Christian 'mystery', thus fulfilling the sacramental needs of early Christians, some of whom may well have been initiates in these ancient mysteries.

Even if, as some have suggested, the gospel is not the work of a single author, but a collection of short excerpts gathered together over time from unknown works, its sacramentalism follows the same distinctive pattern as the Egyptian New Year ritual.[32] Indeed, the very fact that it includes an archetypal feminine pattern of mother-sister-consort (see page 99) which is distinctly reminiscent of the Hellenistic Isis cults should alert us to its Egyptian mythic roots. As should its interest in creating living images and finding heavenly rebirth through the 'image'. For it is participation in heavenly life, as the ancient Egyptians well knew, that makes both the 'image'-body and the rites efficacious and alive.

Undoubtedly, the *Gospel of Philip* was composed by someone able to use a

Greek discursive mode of thought and conceptualize a ritual experience in a way that was quite unlike ancient Egyptian mythic expression. Someone, too, who was able to make judicious use of the ancient tradition, stripping away its characteristic mythic and 'magical' dimensions. Consequently, the gospel's 'Egyptianness' is extremely well hidden and difficult to detect, as doubtless the author intended it to be. But there are simply too many Egyptian undercurrents for us to ignore what Jean Doresse called its 'rare mystical speculations'.[33] For the same pattern of sacramental rites had been practised for centuries in the Egyptian temples, in a New Year cosmic drama centred on an anointed king as the son of Re, a divine sun king completely encompassed by the Memphite loving-destructive goddess with whom he soared heavenwards from the tomb in the regeneration of life.

It would have been essential to develop new forms of worship within the early Christian communities, even more

fig.66 **The Egyptian god of wisdom Thoth shown holding a staff formed of two solar cobras entwined in the Upper and Lower Egyptian heraldic plants, an early prototype of the snake-staff held by Hermes (see fig.65) whom the Greeks identified with Thoth. (Relief in the 19th Dynasty temple of Seti I at Abydos.)**

so after the people of Israel had rejected not only Jesus but also the proclamation of the gospel, necessitating the exodus from Jerusalem and Judaea to places further afield in the late first century. But there was no specific ritual tradition in Judaism on which to draw in order to experience the 'Word made flesh' and Christ's unique historical presence in the world as 'Son of God'. Nor was there in Judaism any sacramentalism through which Christ's redemptive love and rising from the tomb could be experienced. Yet this ancient Egyptian New Year ritual, centred on the king as the eternal son of Re, reigning at the vertical axis of the world, was perfectly in tune with early Christian soul life. Moreover, it offered to ritually inclined communities an age-old temple tradition in which heavenly divine life reached down to earthly beings, becoming accessible to them through the mediating power of love—Plutarch's 'third love' (see page 80). And in Christ's relationship with the woman who anointed him, with its hints of a love both human and eternal, Christians could experience anew this transforming mystery of 'love as strong as death'.

Yet this was not simply a straightforward translation, nor simply a matter of substituting one ritual form for another. For in the Christian tradition it is no longer a goddess who empowers the anointed king but an unknown woman or friend, even a sinner, through whom divine love is revealed in a world made flesh. Radically reinterpreted it may have been, but the *Gospel of Philip* shows how ancient Egypt's anointing ritual could be filled with a new indigenous content, and how its rites could become a new form of sacramental worship—as John's gospel had promised—for Christians honouring the 'Word made flesh'. Egypt's ancient wisdom had indeed

left the secrecy of the temples and become freely available to all. And whilst retaining its essential Egyptian core, it had become a powerful ritual experience drawing Christians into a living bond of union with Christ. Indeed, by transforming this secret knowledge, it had enabled it to be openly experienced by anyone with ears to hear, with eyes to see and with the knowledge of how to kindle the living flame of love in union with Christ.

In short, despite the fact that this ritual continuity has remained largely unacknowledged, there was a sacramental stream in early Christianity, detectable in both the Gospel of John and Philip's gospel, that drew on Egypt's profound New Year rites.[34] In itself, this transformation is no stranger than the way early Christians in Egypt built their churches in the precincts of the ancient temples. As David Frankfurter observed, 'Clearly something powerful, something axial, was being maintained in putting churches in temples, the Christians in a way grafting themselves to what was already long-sacred in the Egyptian world.'[35] Or, as St Augustine himself acknowledged, 'When Christ appeared in the flesh, the true religion already in existence received the name of Christian.'[36] The truth of his words is there to see in the *Gospel of Philip*. For ancient Egypt's sacred anointing tradition had indeed received a new 'name'.

Chapter 10

LOVE'S DYES:
HEALING ALCHEMY

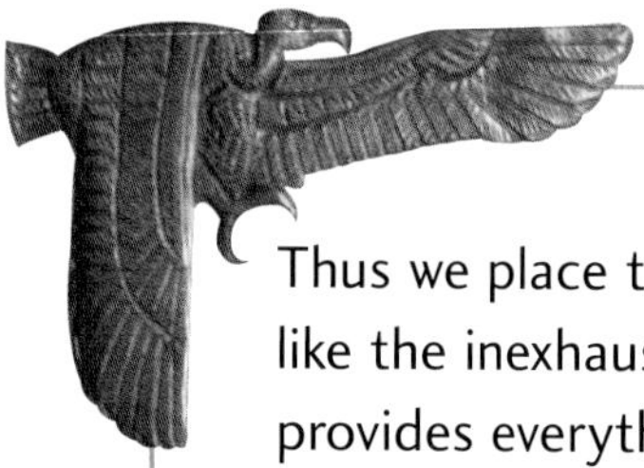

Thus we place the main thing at the centre of our work ...
like the inexhaustible source streaming in the midst of paradise
provides everything with a drinkable, fertilizing water and like the
midday sun at the zenith in one of the four quarters illuminates
the whole heavenly sphere without shade ... for without the liquid
of the philosophers it is impossible to complete the longed for things.[1]

(The Christian, an anonymous late antique alchemist)

Did not he who made the outside make the inside too?

(Gospel of Luke 11:40)

◀ *fig.67* **The alchemical Red King shown dressed in a red robe, wearing white sandals on his feet and holding a sceptre. The ancient Egyptian regenerated king was similarly attired at the close of the New Year ritual. Here the redness is the sign of completion in the alchemical work, symbolized also by the single red-gold poppy crowning the flask. (Illustration from the 15th-century** *Opusculum Alchemicum.* **Sloane 2560. British Library, London.)**

Why then has the *Gospel of Philip*'s 'Egyptianness' invariably been overlooked? For it has to be said that Nag Hammadi scholars searching for the gospel's sacramental origins have never seriously considered ancient Egyptian influence. And this despite the fact that the heresy-hunter Epiphanius gave an Egyptian clue when, in his *Panarion* or *Medicine Chest* against heresies, written in the fourth century, he stated he knew a *Gospel of Philip* in use among Egyptian gnostics.[2] To be sure, the extract quoted by Epiphanius is not included in the Coptic *Gospel of Philip* discovered at Nag Hammadi, but even so, his comment points towards a 'Philip connection' with Egypt, as does a strange encounter involving the evangelist Philip, recorded in the first century Acts of the Apostles (8:26–40). He has been in Samaria, preaching the Word, performing healing miracles in Christ's name, casting out demons, baptizing people and manifesting such healing power that he has even converted Simon Magus, whose

magic had previously captivated the region. Instructed by an angel to travel south from Samaria, he arrives at a crossroads where his path intersects with the Jerusalem–Gaza coast road to Egypt. With impeccable timing, he encounters an Ethiopian eunuch, a high official in charge of all the treasures of Candace, Queen of Ethiopia, who has been to worship in the Jerusalem temple and is now returning in his carriage and reading aloud the prophet Isaiah. (In antiquity, Ethiopia encompassed primarily the Egyptian-influenced lands of Nubia and Meroe, where Isis played a major role in the Meroitic divine pantheon, rather than the modern state of Ethiopia.)

Moved by the spirit to approach this Jewish pilgrim from the 'land of the burnt-faced people', Philip then interprets the puzzling meaning of Isaiah's words in the light of Christ's ignominious death and suffering. His wisdom so touches the pilgrim's heart that, reaching some water along the road, he asks Philip to baptize him. Both men plunge into the water. But

fig.68 **Four faces of Hathor on columns in her Graeco-Roman temple at Dendara.**

when they surface, Philip mysteriously vanishes and the pilgrim never sees him again. He goes on his way to Egypt, however, 'well content', returning perhaps through regions like Edfu and Elephantine in Upper Egypt, where there were strong Jewish communities, before reaching his southern queen's court in the land of the rising sun. Philip himself briefly reappears in Acts, living in Caesarea with his four mantic daughters, who evidently possessed the gift of prophecy received in dreams and visions (Acts 21:8–9), a mode of existence curiously evocative of Egypt's solar ruler

completely surrounded by 'four faces' of his beloved uraeus daughter, as in Hathor's 'house' at Dendara (fig.68).[3] Regardless of whether it was this evangelist who also wrote the *Gospel of Philip*, which commentators consider unlikely, this 'revelational' encounter involving ritual activity (baptism) connects a 'Philip tradition' directly with Egypt and southern lands.

Curiously, an enigmatic Philip figure appears in an apocryphal medieval Irish treatise entitled *In Tenga Bithnua*, 'The Ever-new Tongue', recounting a celestial revelation of the apostle Philip, which he

transmits to a multitude assembled on Mount Zion. So evocative of ancient wisdom is this medieval 'Philip' revelation, with its high-soaring praise of Christ's Easter resurrection attuned to the cosmic rebirth of the world in summer, and its graphic description of the sun's night journey between sunset and sunrise, it has been suggested its inspiration may have derived from late antique gnostic sources which preserved ancient Egyptian beliefs about the sun's night journey.[4]
If an underlying 'Egyptianness' can be detected in a medieval 'Philip revelation', why not then in a much earlier *Gospel of Philip*?

CRAFT SKILLS: HEALING RITES

But there are other important clues regarding the spiritual stream to which this gospel belongs. For it draws considerably on the principle of 'like to like', of 'sympathy' and 'antipathy', and knowing the correspondences running through the whole of nature, the secret charms by which one thing attracts another, which was so fundamental to ancient magical and healing practices. Significantly, too, it also draws on alchemy, a tradition with a deep reverence for Egyptian temple wisdom (see page 79).

Already in the *Gospel of Philip* we have seen the importance attached to marrying earth to heaven, of uniting the lower things with the gifts and properties of heavenly things (see page 101). Indeed, the gospel's author betrays considerable familiarity with Graeco-Egyptian alchemy and its wisdom of harmonizing different natures, of working with fire and infusing divine life into statues in order to 'make images live'.[5] But alchemists in antiquity were by no means concerned solely with 'chemical' transformation or allegorical interpretations of craft practices. Some also performed rituals, using a craft-based language to transmit their teachings of spiritual regeneration and unity with nature. For example, the influential partner of Zosimus of Panopolis, Theosebia, was herself a priestess, founding small initiatory groups in the early fourth century CE dedicated to the alchemical mysteries, though it is from the less well-known Syriac and Arabic alchemical treatises, rather than the Greek, that we can primarily detect this important 'ritual' stream, which looked both to Hermes and the Egyptian temples for its inspiration.[6]

This alchemical keynote is struck in the *Gospel of Philip*'s opening passage, which centres around generating 'like from like' and knowing how to 'sow and reap', themes that the gospel repeatedly returns to, as when it is stated 'a horse begets a horse, a human being begets a human being, a deity brings forth a deity.' Interestingly, striking parallels to this generation of 'like from like' occur in the alchemical letter of *Isis the prophetess to her son Horus*, in which Isis transmits the Hermetic secrets to her son.[7]

What concerns the gospel's author, moreover, is to move Christians from a perception simply of 'natural' generation to a universal kinship based on alchemical transmutation and divinization, a transformation of essence and change of identity in which a person passes from one state to another—in other words, a creation that has alchemically 'died' and been regenerated, changing from a base substance into a heavenly radiant new form, linked together with others through a chain of 'loving kinship', as Hermes calls it in the Hermetic treatise known as the

Asclepius.[8] This theme of alchemical transmutation runs as a leitmotiv throughout the gospel, written by someone seeking qualitative change and a blending of elements that have a living affinity to one another, sometimes despite 'natural' origins. For what is sought is the introduction of regenerative new qualities into the natural workings of sympathy and antipathy. 'You saw the spirit, you became spirit,' the gospel says. 'You saw Christ, you became Christ.'[9] In this 'marriage chamber' love is the great alchemy, able to change a Jew into a Christian and generate a completely new mode of existence through its visionary power.[10]

By the time this gospel was written, Jewish Christianity had entered the wider world of the Roman Empire, reaching out not only to Jews but also to people from a wide variety of cultural backgrounds—Greeks, Asians, Africans, Romans and Egyptians. Evidently, alchemy's 'kinship' language, with all its transformational wisdom of uniting different natures, could speak to Christian seekers in current terms, conveying to them the deeper meaning of their sacramental rebirth as well as the new relationship they shared with others in a spiritually united community.

So could alchemy's craft knowledge, especially the art of dyeing, which was vital to early alchemy, as seen in the numerous recipes for colouring metals and stones in Graeco-Egyptian alchemical texts. It must have been a highly visible activity in Egypt and the Levantine coastal regions where, for centuries, Phoenicia's 'purple people' had supplied the most luxurious 'purple' dye in history throughout the Mediterranean world. Obtained from sea creatures in the area around Byblos, it was used for dyeing expensive purple, violet or dark

red cloth, particularly for cult or royal use. It also symbolized the crown of the alchemical process, the 'royal' regenerated state, which the Isiac initiate in the mosaic from Antioch has also evidently attained (fig.65), for the precious robe draped over his shoulder would have been coloured with some kind of dye to evoke this prized royal 'red-purple'.

Here in the *Gospel of Philip* the 'Son of Man appears as a dyer', a bringer of colour changes who throws 72 different colours into the vat and takes them out 'all white'.[11] To alchemists dyeing is a 'nutritive' process, analogous to the body's absorption of food, giving nourishment to material substances whenever they successfully 'absorb' a new colour. It is also a healing process, since 'dyeing' imagery conveys healing power, suggested by the fact that the Greek word *pharmakon* not only means 'remedy' and healing 'charm' but also 'dyestuff'. To early Christians the eucharist was an immortalizing *pharmakon*, and Jesus himself became in patristic tradition the great doctor

▲ *fig.69* **Vats containing numerous coloured dyes for dyeing leather in present-day Morocco. Early Christians associated dyeing with baptismal transformation, since neophytes experienced a complete change in their nature, being dipped under the water like in the dyeing process. Ancient alchemists were highly skilled in the art of dyeing and two alchemical papyri from Thebes, dating to the third or early fourth century CE, list various dyeing recipes. In the Roman era the crafts still retained their religious character, and the various craft guilds formed in Egypt and elsewhere were instrumental in transmitting ancient ritual and craft secrets.**

who healed through his sublime medicine, restoring the body to health and good colour through his saving power.[12]

In Philip's sacramental gospel, however, this 'dyeing' imagery acquires baptismal significance, enhanced by the similarity in sound between the Greek words *baptein*, meaning 'to dip' or 'tinge', and *baptizein*, 'to baptize'. Thus an alchemist is both a 'baptist' and a 'dyer', as the gospel's original author well knew, drawing on this imagery to convey the transformational meaning of baptism. Intriguingly, the cryptic allusion to 72 colours thrown into the dyeing vat also recalls the creation of Adam as the divine likeness in the *Apocryphon of John*, which belonged in the same Nag Hammadi codex as the *Gospel of Philip*. Here 72 cosmic powers, under the guidance of seven angels, create the 72 parts of Adam's body from head to toe as a vehicle for his emotional soul, with its soul qualities pulsating in the eye, the blood, the skin and flesh.[13] But this archetypal first human being, Biblical

though he may seem at first sight, also has a distinctly ancient Egyptian ring about him, since, due to his familiarity with Egyptian star lore concerning the 36 decans and the rituals for deifying the bodily members, Joachim Quack could see the thinly disguised Egyptian influence underlying the *Apocryphon*'s creative process.[14]

Similarly, by specifying 72 colours in the 'dyeing' cauldron, the *Gospel of Philip*'s author graphically conveys a baptismal bath of bodily purification in which all previous colours are washed away in the symbolic waters of death. Conveyed, too, is very precise alchemical knowledge, since this transformation to 'all white' heralds the 'whitening' second phase in the alchemical journey from death to life, which is followed by the 'reddening' during the next stage of the work (fig.71). Thus, whenever early Christians plunged into the turbulent 'dyeing' waters, they alchemically cast off all blackness, rising forth to be clothed in the 'whiteness' of their baptismal garments before being irradiated with

▼ *fig.70* **Purification of Heruben, a temple priestess and granddaughter of the Theban high priest Menkherre. (Late 21st Dynasty papyrus, Egyptian Museum, Cairo.)**

light in the fiery anointing rites. In this alchemical gospel, 'dyeing' action and colour changes are completely joined to sacramental transformation and healing, for a person becomes 'immortal' through the divine 'remedies' (or 'colours') whenever 'God dips what he dips in water.'[15] Or, as the *Apocryphon of John* says, it is by being 'raised up' and 'sealed in the light of the water with five seals' that death is overcome.[16]

CLAY VESSELS: LIGHT BODIES

Furthermore, the *Gospel of Philip*'s author perceives the material body to be like a clay vessel, whilst the regenerated initiate is like a living vessel of glass. The breath of the glass-blower blowing a vase is life-giving *pneuma*, and whereas 'glass vessels are made again, if they break, since they were produced by breath *(pneuma)*, clay vessels perish if they break. For they were produced without breath.'[17] For centuries glass-makers had used fire to melt earth's substances, making beautiful fragile vessels alive with coloured light in the Syrian regions. But behind this unusual juxtaposition of clay and glass vessels is more than simply a 'craft' technique. What is emphasized is the power of life-bestowing breath to create living 'glass bodies' that can be renewed—the kind of Egyptian 'animating' craft knowledge, in other words, that Isis also teaches in the Hermetic treatise known as the *Koré Kosmou*, or 'Pupil of the Eye of the World'. Essentially, hers is an Egyptian alchemical wisdom, teaching how divine breath, fire and certain other 'unknown substances' are mingled together through 'secret incantations' to produce a subtle, pure and transparent material from which eventually souls are formed. The aim is to produce a shining living form of the kind created by craft workers, with

▲ *fig.71* **From Graeco-Roman times onwards the colour-changes of black, white and red, or black, white, red and gold, became fundamental to alchemy. Here the 'whitening', which follows the initial 'black' phase, is represented by nine ladies washing and laying out white sheets beside a river, perhaps in preparation for dyeing and tingeing in the final 'red' phase. The accompanying text speaks of the perfect whiteness, the 'spirit of the quintessence' called 'tincture', 'ferment', 'soul' or 'oil', which is achieved through purification and fire (or washing, cooking and roasting). Early Christians compared this 'whitening' process to being 'raised up' in the baptismal and anointing rites. A baptized initiate left behind the 'black' state and was clothed in a 'white' garment symbolizing new life. (Painted illustration from** *Splendor Solis* **by Salomon Trismosin.** *Harley MS 3469* **dating to 1582. British Library, London.)**

fig.73 **The potter god Khnum shapes the king's physical body and** *Ka* **on his wheel as Hathor holds out an** *Ankh*-**sign, enlivening them with her fiery solar beauty and vitality. (From the 18th Dynasty royal birth sequence in Luxor Temple.)**

fig.72 Polychrome glass vessel made by moulding the glass over a core which was later removed once the glass had cooled. Possibly the art of glassmaking was introduced into Egypt through increased contact with Syria in the New Kingdom, though the technique of glass-blowing was not developed until the Roman era when Egypt and Syria were renowned for their glassware. In the *Gospel of Philip* glass vessels are said to be endowed with 'life' because they are produced by a breath-spirit. (British Museum, London.)

vital breath and the heat of life from which eternal souls can draw nourishment. Alchemists themselves perceived this substance's raying whiteness to be translucent, comparing its milky qualities to dew, or honey or, better still, to glass, creating a living body, the 'water of glass' or 'water of fire', capable of truly sustaining all life.[18]

We find a similar wisdom, albeit expressed mythically, in the great *Hymn to Khnum* inscribed in the Graeco-Roman temple at Esna, in which the divine potter is praised as 'the god who forms bodies, the god who equips nostrils, the god who binds the Two Lands, so that they join their natures ... their *Ka* will not perish ... they are alive and abiding, like Re rising and setting'.[19]

Much earlier, the same craft wisdom is

at work in New Kingdom royal birth reliefs showing Khnum moulding the Egyptian king's physical body and *Ka* on his potter's wheel in the mysterious world of embryological growth. Seated across from Khnum as he forms these two bodies is the sun goddess Hathor, holding out to them an *Ankh*–sign in order to empower them with all her solar vitality and light-filled life (fig.73).

This is no lifeless clay 'image' that Khnum is shaping on his wheel, for the king's body is being formed together with his ever-renewing *Ka*, the vehicle of life for every living creature. It is the *Ka* which is the centre of a person's life energy and vitality. It is the *Ka*, too, that possesses the power of eternal renewal, being 'alive and abiding, like Re rising and setting' as the *Hymn to Khnum* says. Sustained by Hathor's heavenly radiance and fiery attraction, the king is blessed with a solar luminous body, with all the vital powers that link his *Ka* to the heavenly *Ba* and the whole of the living cosmos.[20] Receptive to the 'sweet breath of the north wind', to solar rays and regenerative life, he joyfully lives in this breathing light-filled solar world encompassed by a raying aura of light.

Indeed, to the Egyptians, such a solar luminous body 'shines' *(tjehen)*, gleaming with 'glass-like' qualities that arouse 'joy'. For the *tjehen*-root also occurs in the word *tjehenet*, a general term for 'glass' and also for the shiny glass-like blue or green glazed composition known as 'faience' *(tjehenet)*, a material much used by Egyptian craft workers, meaning quite literally 'that which gleams'.[21] Creating such a divinized living 'image', porous to life and light, lay at the heart of Egypt's temple cults—and the tradition of alchemy. And here in the *Gospel of Philip* this age-old ritual magic of creating 'living images' has been reworked within a Christian context.

So, too, this 'alchemical' gospel presents the relationship between Adam and Eve very differently from their punishment for disobedience in the Hebrew Bible's Garden of Eden. For it is Eve's 'separation' from Adam that is perceived to be the cause of the human mortal condition and death, and it is their reunion that restores life:

When Eve was in Adam, there
was no death.
When she was separated from him,
death arose.
Again, when they reunite and he
receives her to himself,
Death will be no more.[22]

Elsewhere the gospel says: 'If the female had not separated from the male, she and the male would not die. That being's separation became the source of death'.[23] Such a female, whilst perhaps recalling the Biblical creation of Eve from Adam's rib, taken from his body when he was in a deep sleep (Genesis 2:21–2), also brings to mind the archetypal 'separating female' who roves through alchemy. And indeed through Upper Egypt's Ptolemaic temples as the volatile Sun Eye who separates from Re (fig.50).[24] Again, it typifies the gospel's alchemical outlook, being a 'fall', not into sin, but into division, in which estrangement and separation bring death, but a love union brings life. And it is presented here by a Christian author displaying a distinct predilection for thinking in opposites: male and female, life and death, separation and union, seeking and finding—opposites that find unification and healing in the 'marriage chamber'. No lover can find union unless the beloved seeks it, unless the heart responds to the primordial call of love. And it is this 'seeking' and 'finding', this longing for healing and union in the soul, that draws a person to Christ in Philip's gospel.

With its emphasis on embodied spirituality, this regenerative gospel avoids the outright dualism and rampant negativity towards the female, Egypt and the 'flesh' so evident in certain gnostic and apocryphal Christian writings, with their distrust of sexuality and emphasis on the soul's need for purification from the body. For underlying its spirituality are those forces of 'sympathy' and 'antipathy' —the 'strife' that brings separation, the 'love' that brings union—that work together in the world in such a way that lovers are able to experience the mysteries of rejuvenating death whilst alive on earth. Indeed, if they 'do not first receive the resurrection whilst alive', the *Gospel of Philip*'s author says, speaking like an initiate who has experienced directly the mysteries of life and death, 'they will not receive anything when they die.'[25] This resurrection exists and manifests itself here and now; it is a resurrection in 'this life', a call to initiates to 'die before they die' through the deep mystery of transforming love. These early Christians were deeply imbued with the spirit of the cosmic Christ as the first-born of creation, the new Adam, whose words and deeds, death and triumphant resurrection recreated the world anew, and it is the regeneration through love, experienced in this life, that this alchemically inspired author skilfully weaves into the gospel's unification 'mystery'.

CLEOPATRA'S COLOURS: REBIRTH THROUGH IMAGES

In his detailed account of alchemy's origins in Graeco-Roman Egypt, Jack Lindsay drew attention to the striking similarities between alchemy, the mystery cults and the early Christian outlook.[26] We need but look at the 'marriage mystery' in an important alchemical treatise entitled the *Dialogue of the Philosophers and Cleopatra*, preserved in a Greek version, albeit showing signs of having been reworked by a later Christian Byzantine copyist, to appreciate the importance of this connection.[27]

Once again it is extremely difficult to pin down precisely when or where Cleopatra's dialogue was composed, though dates ranging from the second to the third century have been suggested. There is a hint too that it may well have originated in an Aramaic-speaking region, since Cleopatra first receives the teaching from the enthroned Komarios, whose name probably derives from the Aramaic 'Komar', meaning 'chief priest'.[28] It certainly belongs in an era when a deep Egyptian alchemical current was flowing into the Hellenistic and Roman world, bringing with it Egyptian divinization wisdom and craft knowledge of 'making statues live'.

The assembled philosophers have asked Cleopatra to teach them 'how the highest descends to the lowest, and how the lowest rises to the highest and is united with it', and how the 'beneficent waters descend from above to visit the oppressed dwellers in the darkness of Hades.' In lyrical evocative imagery, which Jack Lindsay observed had 'immemorial roots in Egypt', Cleopatra portrays the dead lying in caverns under the earth, waiting for the waters of resurrection to revive them, so that they may come forth clothed in 'various glorious colours'.[29] Rising up like springtime flowers from the seemingly dead earth, these Hades-dwellers' suffering is redeemed when the healing '*pharmakon* of life' enters, bringing the flowing waters. 'Rise up from the tomb, rouse yourself from darkness!' is the awakening call to them, beckoning them to come forth and reveal their hidden beauty, so bringing this threefold unification 'mystery' to completion:

And the soul rejoices in her home,
because, after
the body had been hidden in
darkness, she found it filled
with light. And she united with it,
for it had become divine
towards her and it is now her home ...
All have been united in love,
namely the body, the soul and the
spirit. They have become one,
and in this unity is the mystery
concealed. In their union is the
mystery completed, the sanctuary
has been sealed and a statue erected,
full of light and divinity.[30]

Here Cleopatra perceives divinity not as transcendence, but as embodied in a divinized light-filled statue, a regenerated body erected and sealed in its sanctuary 'full of light and divinity' at the completion of the work. Indeed, the whole atmosphere of this treatise retains a strong sense of Egyptian cult life and ritual animation of statues. Whoever this mystical female alchemist may have been, her beautiful dialogue, which Carl Jung said has 'all the characteristics of a regeneration mystery', teaches about an incandescent threefold love union, a manifestation of an imperishable reality, an indissoluble eternal essence shining at the heart of material creation.[31]

According to Cleopatra, fire is the active transforming agent at the heart of this divinization 'mystery'. For it is only when fire flames deep within 'plants, elements and stones', in the interiority of material creation, that their lustrous 'sought-for beauty' shines forth, transforming them into the 'divine state of fusion', alive with luminous colour and light. This fiery healing source of life is to be found deep in the earth, its flame forever revealing the hidden 'mystery':

And fire … brought them forth
from darkness into light,
from grief into joy, from sickness into
health and from death into life …
For in them has been hidden the
mystery which exists as something
divine and unchangeable.[32]

This dialogue, with its rebirth through flowing water and its marriage 'mystery', brings us very close to the spirit of Egypt's New Year ritual. And to the *Gospel of Philip*'s regeneration 'mystery', rooted in a sacramental wisdom of anointing with fire and 'rebirth through the image', of making the 'things below like the things above and the things outside like the things inside'. For it is when the waters flow again that the inert 'dead' rise forth from this primordial fount of life, flowering anew in glorious light-filled bodies, blessed with beauty, life and movement in a regenerated 'summer' world.

EPILOGUE

Much of what we find in Philip
...the author shares in common
with many of his Christian
contemporaries.[1]

(Elaine Pagels)

▶ *fig. 74* **Detail of
Tutankhamun from
the back of his
throne. (See fig. 15.)**

Cleopatra's dialogue displays a distinctive initiatory mode of transmission typical also of the Hermetic treatises from Roman-period Egypt, in which a pupil receives the secret teachings from Hermes Trismegistus, or sometimes Egyptian deities including Isis. Usually the pupils are male, related to the teacher as son. But here the priestly enthroned Komarios transmits this 'regeneration' mystery directly to Cleopatra, who then teaches the assembled philosophers, including the Persian alchemist Ostanes. Significantly, in the Graeco-Egyptian alchemical tradition, women like Cleopatra, Mary the Jewess and Theosebia, whom one modern commentator described as 'among the most influential exponents of alchemy in her day', were all prominent teachers of wisdom.[2]

Women were also particularly attracted to the redemptive mysteries of Isis. And we find a similar revelational mode of transmission in the Greek aretalogy of Isis from Cyme, in which the goddess says the wisdom she gives to the world was taught to her first by Hermes (see page 74). Likewise, in the *Gospel of Philip* it is Mary Magdalene who receives the living Word when Jesus kisses her (see page 96), indicative of her importance in the lineage and apostolic succession emanating from Christ.

In the nature of things it is very difficult to establish how the *Gospel of Philip*'s author(s) might have encountered alchemy. But by the time the gospel was composed, the Egyptian cults of Isis and Sarapis (which were closely linked to the healing cults of Asclepius/Imhotep and to alchemy) had spread to Syria, Phoenicia and Palestine. Certainly, Philo of Byblos, who lived in the early second century, not only emphasized the cultural ties between Egypt and Phoenicia but also displayed considerable familiarity with Hermes and Hermopolitan cosmogony as well as alchemy.[3] Also in the early Roman period, we find a young man called Thessalus travelling from the Levant to Alexandria and then to Thebes in search of healing wisdom, where he experienced a dream vision of Asclepius in a Theban temple chamber under the auspices of a native priest.[4]

According to Samuel Angus, it was the widespread cult of Asclepius, the physician who healed through love, that contributed a 'salvationist terminology and healing usages to the Christian Church'. Yet this same Asclepius was also closely linked with the Egyptian Imhotep, the deified sage and son of Ptah as well as the patron of alchemists under the name of Imouthes. He, too, was revered as a healer and saviour. Hence, followers of Asclepius, with their interest in botanical lore and healing remedies, would have been thoroughly at home in the world of alchemy and Egypt's therapeutic cults.[5]

In short, there must have been a variety of channels open to seekers of Egyptian wisdom, both in Egypt itself and in the wider Syrian region, including people belonging to the complex 'Philip traditions', with all their orientation towards ritual, healing and sacramental life.[6] Nevertheless, many of the teachings would have been perpetuated orally, coming through ritual and craft communications where the need for secrecy was paramount and where little was ever written down. But active in this transmission would surely have been Hellenized Greek-speaking Jews, since, according to the alchemist Zosimus of Panopolis, it was the Jews who first disclosed Egypt's gold-making secrets, taking this knowledge out of the temples into the wider alchemical world.[7]

It was, however, an elusive temple transmission that very carefully swept away traces of its footprints, leaving behind only hints and 'tiny scraps of evidence', some in later Arabic alchemical manuscripts. Interestingly, it is in the much-neglected writings of Islamic alchemists, who were often in touch with Syriac and Coptic sources, as well as the Hermetic tradition which still continued in Syria at places like Harran right through into Islamic times, that we can find graphic accounts of alchemical initiations in antiquity.

So, for example, an evocative Arabic treatise, the *Book of Krates*, describes a visit of Krates to a Sarapis temple, possibly in Alexandria or Memphis, in which he encounters the enthroned Hermes, clothed in white garments and holding a tablet in his hand. Then he is transported in a visionary state into an adjacent fiery Ptah temple where he beholds a statue of the mercurial love goddess in the sanctuary, evidently the vivifier of all Ptah's beautiful images, since she specifically begins to teach Krates about the vivification of bodies. Manifestly, what is being described here, amidst all the arcane alchemical language, is Krates' initiation into the mysteries of her loving-destructive power. For suddenly he falls into a fearful and wondrous trance, experiencing the full force of her arrow-shooting destructiveness, directed by her emissaries, who consider him to be unworthy of her temple secrets. Finally, though, her beneficence prevails, and the initiation culminates in the gift to Krates of a jewel-encrusted girdle, bestowed by a beautiful female attendant as a blessing from the all-encircling love goddess. Written in Arabic this may be, with the goddess herself named as Venus rather than Hathor-Aphrodite, yet preserved

121

▲ *fig.75* **Detail of Ankhesenamun's anointing gesture from the back of Tutankhamun's throne. (See fig.15.)**

centre of our work'. By the time this treatise was composed the *Gospel of Philip* would have long since been excluded from Christian canonical writings. Yet still preserved here by a Christian alchemist is that Heliopolitan vertical axis of the world, with all its echoes of the redemptive Egyptian New Year ritual and the age-old anointing mystery of 'finding the stone'.[9] A powerful current had flowed from the ancient temples into alchemy, bringing ancient Egyptian ritual traditions and craft mysteries. It had brought, too, knowledge of healing, regeneration and life-giving power. And it is this sacred New Year 'mystery' stream that we can glimpse in both Philip's gospel and the Gospel of John, powerfully shaping early Christian sacramental life.

RITUAL APPROACHES: EGYPT'S LEGACY

It would be a mistake because of its alchemical bias, to view this highly unusual *Gospel of Philip* as somehow peripheral to the mainstream of early Christian life. As Elaine Pagels emphasized, the author's spiritual outlook is no different from many of his Christian contemporaries.[10] She also notes how he betrays a belief in sacramental efficacy which 'engages human beings with spiritual forces hidden from ordinary perception—forces both diabolical and divine'.[11] In other words, this is a Christian author still very much immersed in the power of ancient ritual practice, seeking a healing form of worship that could bring human beings into true relationship with the divine. And Pagels had no hesitation in placing Philip's gospel in the mainstream of early Christianity—where it surely belongs.

Significantly, the *Gospel of Philip*'s overriding concern is not to emphasize

here in this Arabic treatise is not only an initiatory experience that has a totally authentic 'Memphite' ring about it, but also Islamic knowledge of Egyptian temple traditions as filtered through Hermetic 'cult' alchemy in the Hellenistic world.[8]

And should we need further confirmation that Egypt's New Year regeneration mystery indeed influenced Christian alchemists, we need but turn to a Greek alchemical gold-making treatise which is attributed to an anonymous author called simply 'the Christian', living perhaps in the sixth or seventh century CE. For, in the extract quoted at the beginning of chapter 10, it is the midday zenithal sun, shining in one of the four quarters and 'illuminating the whole heavenly sphere without shade', together with the eternal living water, the 'inexhaustible source streaming in the midst of paradise', that this alchemist singles out as 'the main thing at the conformity with orthodoxy but to interpret the beliefs underlying Christian sacramentalism. Its ritual healing form of worship, strongly rooted in knowledge of divine kinship, sees the life of Jesus as the sacramental paradigm.[12] Moreover, in this initiatory Christianity which encompasses more than baptism it is primarily the state of an individual's soul and relationship with heavenly life that determines how the sacraments are experienced.

But ritual practice, whilst instrumental in shaping shared values and a sense of community life, was also very diverse in early Christianity and evolved over time. It also provoked considerable controversy amongst Christians regarding which rites should be celebrated. And even though we can detect the influence of Philip's sacramentalism and the Gospel of John in the discreet house church at Dura-Europos on the banks of the Euphrates (see page 99), this form of worship is conspicuously absent from the work of Ignatius of Antioch, the influential leader and bishop of the Christians in Antioch who was martyred early in the second century. Antioch's early Christian community paid great attention to the development of liturgical worship and sacramental life. It was also an ecclesiastical hierarchy centred on the bishop, in which, according to Ignatius, the sacramental rites derived their validity through being performed by a bishop or an authorized official. Reflecting an increasing concern to bring Christians into conformity, this prevailing Antiochene orthodoxy sought to establish the Church as the sole mediator of the sacraments.

Significantly, whilst the form of worship advocated by Ignatius included baptism and the eucharist, anointing was not a separate sacrament. Nor was it prominent in an influential early work

called the *Didache* or *Teaching of the Twelve Apostles*, which was perhaps composed in Antioch during the second century. Showing detectable signs of Jewish-based ritual practices, the *Didache* displays little connection with the Johannine tradition. Again, whilst it affirms baptism and the eucharist, references to anointing are minimal, perhaps reflecting practices for initiation into the *Didache* community, and also the early Syriac-speaking Church, in which anointing with oil often preceded baptism, being considered as part of baptism rather than a separate rite.[13]

By contrast, Philip's gospel differentiates baptism and anointing, clearly regarding anointing as a separate fiery sacrament. Indeed, the fact that the gospel is so insistent on its importance is perhaps another pointer towards Egypt, since, as Carl Kraeling discussed, the separation of baptism and anointing in Christian ritual corresponds to the kind of liturgical ritual that seems to have originated in Egypt. Kraeling specifically contrasted what he called the 'Egyptian and Mediterranean' rite with the Syrian and Mesopotamian, as known from the *Didache* and Syrian writings.[14]

There seems to be little trace of Philip's sacramentalism, however, in the writings of the later church fathers, who by the fourth century were extremely keen to purge from Christianity everything contrary to orthodoxy or tinged with the slightest trace of ancient cults. Confident enough by this time to bring order into the ever-burgeoning groups and sects, they set themselves on a course irreconcilable with ancient ways. Probably the emphasis on inner guidance and personal moral responsibility, as well as Mary Magdalene's central role in Christ's life, would not have endeared Philip's gospel to church authorities, who by the fourth century honoured an all-male apostolic lineage. As Susan Haskins observed, along with the disappearance of writings like the *Gospel of Philip*, Mary Magdalene, the 'companion of the saviour', his 'spouse', 'consort' and 'partner' had vanished too, taking with her the powerful feminine element she, and other women in the gospels, had embodied in early Christianity.[15]

That it was a woman who specifically anointed Christ and enjoyed a loving relationship with him, with all its echoes of ancient cults, must have fuelled very ambivalent reactions in advancing Christianity. For not everyone was well disposed to the female in the Hellenistic and Roman world. Some gnostic sects regarded the female as the enslaving power, the source of all suffering in a 'fallen' time-world, keeping humanity in servitude. Fear of the female ran deep, not least of her sexual power to imprison the soul in the way of all flesh, weaving her earthly garments in which life languishes. Hence this ignorant female power had to be tricked and overcome, to the extent that some gnostics sought to transform the servile body into a purified heavenly garment, purged from feminine, as well as 'Egyptian', impurities.

That such views of the female were rife in the Hellenized world is evident in some Nag Hammadi treatises, as well as Philo of Alexandria's work, which exerted a strong influence in the early Christian Church. It was a view reflected also in Aristotle's influential notions of the female as inferior to the male, due in part to the 'coldness' of her nature. Unfortunately, Christianity early fell into similar views, veering towards an ascetic movement and repression of the feminine, apart from the maternal side embodied by Mary as Christ's mother.[16]

Rejection of the feminine was never the way of the ancient Egyptians. Nor was it the way of the alchemists, who saw the healing medicine of life, the well of living water, not as something to be sought as a means of escape from material existence but as the 'stone' which had to be drawn forth for the redemption of life here and now. It was the transformation of life here on a beautiful living earth, an earth honouring both male and female within creation, that concerned them, as it did some early Christians when they included this feminine rite of 'anointing'. For however these early Christians might have understood it, this deep-flowing Christian 'anointing' tradition affirmed the feminine dimension in Christ's life. It also affirmed that earthly elements like oil, bread, water and wine were reconcilable with a sacramental way of living uniting the human with the divine.

BURIED LIGHT: RETURNING TREASURES

Although it might seem on the surface that this anointing tradition disappeared, enough survives in Islamic and European 'marriage' alchemy to show that this 'wisdom of the queen' never really died out, but continued for centuries as an undercurrent to the religions that ruled on the surface. Indeed, when Islamic seekers of wisdom rediscovered Hermeticism and alchemy, often from Syrian sources, and eventually brought this ancient knowledge to medieval Europe, a fivefold sacramental wisdom very similar to the *Gospel of Philip*'s 'mystery' flourished in the work of medieval Christian alchemists.[17]

We see, too, in Christian medieval art a resurgent sensual Mary Magdalene appearing with her holy anointing vessel, her *alabastron*, filled with all her fragrant healing balm. Holding her ancient symbol of the eternal feminine, her sacred ointment jar containing the mysteries of life and death, she could have been for all the world a reborn Queen Ankhesenamun on Tutankhamun's Golden Shrine.

But that is not all. For there are echoes of this ancient 'mystery' still current to this day in an ancient homily about Christ's descent into the underworld as the wounded healer, which is read during the morning liturgy for Holy Saturday in the Roman Easter rites.[18] It opens with the words, 'What is happening? Today there is a great silence over the earth ... a great silence because the King sleeps.' And in this silent sleep Christ enters the darkness of the underworld bearing his cross. He comes as Adam's 'son' in order to seek out 'our first parent like a lost sheep' and to heal Adam and Eve, together with all their companions in the darkness, calling to them with the words:

Awake, O sleeper, and arise from the
dead … I am your God,
who for your sake became your son,
who for you and your
descendants now speaks …Come
forth, and those in the darkness.
Have light and those who sleep: Rise.

Entering as the healing medicine of life, the 'life of the dead', Christ seeks to cure Adam from the wound which arose when he 'brought forth Eve' from his side, healing him through his own wounded side and restoring all those dwelling with him to 'that first divine inbreathing at creation' and to cosmic unity. 'For you in me, and I in you, together we are one undivided person.' And this beautiful homily concludes with the promise of a heavenly throne and abundant food in the 'bridal chamber'.

This forms part of the Saturday morning liturgy that precedes the midnight lighting of a candle in the Easter vigil, the kindling of the new flame on the eve of the resurrection inaugurating Easter day, with all its triumphant celebration of resurrected new life. And perhaps here, in this liturgical celebration encompassing a 'redemptive descent', a celebration of the 'bridal chamber' and 'lighting of the flame', we can glimpse a little of the ritual meaning underlying the *Gospel of Philip*'s cosmic 'mystery'. And the paintings in the early house church at Dura-Europos, including representations of the three Marys lighting up the tomb with their candles, and Adam and Eve standing close to Christ as the good shepherd.

Strangely, this homily is often attributed to the fourth-century Epiphanius, who spent time in Egypt before becoming bishop in Salamis on the island of Cyprus and writing his *Medicine Chest* against all heresies (see page 110). Some have doubted that he could have written it.[19] But whatever the truth of its early origins, it is a homily haunted by remembrances of that much earlier 'medicine of life' in Cleopatra's alchemical dialogue (page 118), and of an ancient Egyptian king returning from the tomb, a king who also 'sleeps', being a 'son' whose redemptive healing quest in the New Year ritual not only restores his ancestral Osirian father to new life but also brings a revelation of cosmic undivided unity. So striking are the similarities that, surely, what has long remained largely unnoticed by us must have been known to initiates in this healing stream of early Christianity, namely that their sacramental life had

▶ *fig.76* **Detail of Ankhesenamun from the back of Tutankhamun's throne. (See fig.15.)**

arisen from the ancient Egyptian mysteries.

There is a certain irony, therefore, but also a sense of perfect timing and completion, in the fact that the unorthodox *Gospel of Philip*, which disappeared from sight once the canonical four gospels of the New Testament had been firmly established, surfaced again in modern times at Nag Hammadi in Upper Egypt, close to Dendara's temple of Hathor, only a few years after the discovery of Tutankhamun's Golden Shrine in the Valley of the Kings at Thebes and also around the time when the New Year ritual papyrus was formally registered in the Brooklyn Museum's Egyptian collection. This sacramental *Gospel of Philip*, preserved for posterity in an Upper Egyptian Coptic dialect, had indeed come full circle, being rediscovered in its original spiritual home close to the ancient dwelling of Egypt's love goddess.

It is hardly surprising that it should have caught the attention of an Egyptian long enough for it to have been translated into Coptic and then hidden away in a jar on the Nag Hammadi escarpment. For it holds precious clues to the continuity of ancient Egypt's New Year 'mysteries' in the early centuries of the Christian era, a tradition that had

been lovingly guarded by a goddess 'queen of the south' more than a 1,000 years before this gospel was ever written. Encircling Tutankhamun with all her beauty, wisdom and glory in her 'Great House' garden of delights, Queen Ankhesenamun could scarcely have known that her lovely golden flowers were to bloom anew in far distant lands, in a fragrant tomb of secrets freely revealed to every seeking human heart.

ABBREVIATIONS

CdE *Chronique d'Égypte: Bulletin périodique de la Fondation égyptologique Reine Élisabeth.* Brussels.

CT A. de Buck, *The Egyptian Coffin Texts.* 7 vols. Chicago 1935-1961.

GM *Göttinger Miszellen: Beiträge zur ägyptologischen Diskussion.* Göttingen.

HTR *Harvard Theological Review.* Cambridge (Mass.).

JAC *Jahrbuch für Antike und Christentum.* Münster.

JARCE *Journal of the American Research Center in Egypt.* Princeton.

JEA *The Journal of Egyptian Archaeology.* London.

JNES *Journal of Near Eastern Studies.* Chicago.

JWCI *Journal of the Warburg and Courtauld Institute.* London.

MDAIK *Mitteilungen des Deutschen Archäologischen Instituts, Abteilung Kairo.* Wiesbaden.

NHD See Schenke *et al.*, Nag Hammadi Deutsch.

NHL J.M. Robinson (ed.), *The Nag Hammadi Library in English.* Third revised edn. Leiden, New York, Copenhagen and Cologne, 1988.

OBC J. Barton and J. Muddiman (eds.), *The Oxford Bible Commentary.* Oxford, 2001.

OCB B.M. Metzger and M.D. Coogan (eds.), *The Oxford Companion to the Bible.* New York and Oxford, 1993.

PT K. Sethe, *Die altägyptischen Pyramidentexte.* 4 vols. Leipzig, 1908–22.

RdE *Revue d'Égyptologie publiée par la Société française d'Égyptologie.* Paris.

Urk. K. Sethe and W. Helck, *Urkunden der 18. Dynastie.* Leipzig and Berlin, 1906–58.

VigChr *Vigiliae Christianae.*

ZÄS *Zeitschrift für ägyptische Sprache und Altertumskunde.* Berlin and Leipzig.

ZDMG *Zeitschrift der Deutschen Morgenländischen Gesellschaft.* Leipzig and Wiesbaden.

127

NOTES

Chapter 1 *(pages 7–14)*

1 From an invocation to the Heliopolitan goddess Temet in the Edfu ritual for 'propitiating Sekhmet', see Goyon, *Rituel*, 70 (ll.8–9).

2 Carter Handlist no.108. The shrine measures approximately 50.5cm high, 26.5cm wide and 32cm deep. It was published by M. Eaton-Krauss and E. Graefe, *The Small Golden Shrine from the Tomb of Tutankhamun*. Oxford, 1985 (hereafter cited as Golden Shrine), with an analysis of the reliefs and relevant scholarly discussion. For two different proposals regarding the ancient craft techniques used to achieve the scenes on the gold sheets, see *ibid*. 2–3. It should be noted that my interpretation here, which develops the section on the Golden Shrine in my doctoral thesis (*Cult Objects of Hathor: An Iconographic Study* 1. [Unpublished thesis Oxford, 1984], 47–51), differs considerably from the analysis of Eaton-Krauss and Graefe, who downplay the shrine's royal and ritual meaning. Emphasizing its iconographic links with private tomb decoration, they maintain that Ankhesenamun's ideological role as Tutankhamun's queen is based on the wife's traditional role in ancient Egypt, albeit transposed into the royal sphere, see *ibid*. 29.

3 For solar religion in Akhenaten's reign, see Quirke, *Cult of Ra*, 143–70; Roberts, *Hathor Rising*, 132–68 (with further references).

4 For mythic allusions in Amarna art, see W. Helck's entry on Maat in *Lexikon der Ägyptologie* 3, col.1114; Roberts, *Hathor Rising*, 156–7, 160–3; Troy, *Patterns of Queenship*, 113.

5 For the importance of 'magic' *(heka)* in Ptah's creative activity, see Roberts, *My Heart My Mother*, 16–17 with n.13. See also below, chapter 2, n.26.

6 For Ramessid reactions to Akhenaten's reign, see Roberts, *ibid*. 2–27.

7 Note that Eaton-Krauss and Graefe consider it misleading to describe the shrine as the *Per-Wer*, *op.cit*. 2, n.10. However, the presence of Nekhbet's vultures on the roof points to the validity of this identification, as was recognized by I.E.S. Edwards in *Treasures of Tutankhamun*. British Museum, London, 1972, (no. 25). See also below, n.10.

8 On the New Kingdom goddesses inhabiting the coronation *Per-Wer* shrine, see Roberts, *Hathor Rising*, 41–2, 44–5.

9 Eaton-Krauss and Graefe (*Golden Shrine*, 30, n.146) refer to an unpublished work by A. Hermann, in which he suggested the shrine may have been a domestic chapel belonging to Ankhesenamun and housing her 'idol' of the king.

10 Kate Bosse-Griffiths first drew attention to the Golden Shrine's link with Weret-Hekau as the *Per-Wer* goddess, interpreting the scenes in a 'coronation' rather than 'domestic' context (*JEA* 59 [1973], 100–8; *JEA* 62 [1976], 181–2). Robert Hari also accepted this coronation context (*JEA* 62 [1976], 100–7), noting also that the queen appeared in some scenes like a priestess ministering to the king in the form of a cult statue. Their interpretations were criticized by Eaton-Krauss and Graefe (*op.cit*. 26–7). For Weret-Hekau's role as 'king-maker' at the coronation, see Roberts, *Hathor Rising*, 40–2, 46–7.

11 For Amun, Re and Ptah as members of the Ramessid era's important state triad, see Roberts, *My Heart My Mother*, 14.

12 On the pharaoh's identification with Re-Harakhti's 'attraction', symbolized by the gesture of offering a *menit*-necklace, see Roberts, *Hathor Rising*, 44–51. For the naos sistrum as a cult instrument of propitiation, see *ibid*. 54–64.

13 For the absence of traditional Hathor symbolism in the Amarna sun cult, see *ibid*. 157.

Chapter 2 *(pages 15–26)*

1 From the fourth treatise of the Fourth Ennead (Plotinus 4.4.40). Quotation from Kingsley, *Ancient Philosophy*, 300. For 'love' and 'strife' as the governing principles of magical operations in the ancient world, see *ibid*. 298–300, with n.32. The only limitation is Kingsley's omission of ancient Egypt from his discussion. Cf. Ritner, *Magical Practice*, 36, n.164, 66–7, 178, with n.828, for the circulation of 'love' and 'fear' in Egyptian magic.

2 This epithet occurs once on the left jamb on the front of the shrine and once on the back.

3 For the importance of seven in Hathor-Sekhmet's cult, see Roberts, *Hathor Rising*, 16, 173, n.25; Goyon, *Rituel*, 52–3 (6). See also chapter 8, n.14. For 'dread' and 'attraction' as qualities radiating from the solar king, see Roberts, *op.cit*. 45–50.

4 See below, n.28.

5 For Hathorian 'Eye' symbolism on throw-sticks in royal and private tomb-burial equipment, see Pinch, *Votive Offerings*, 295–98 (with further references).

128

6 A.M. Blackman, *The Rock Tombs of Meir 1: The Tomb-Chapel of Ukh-Ḥotp's Son Senbi*. London, 1914, pl.2. The fowling and fishing scenes are juxtaposed with a procession, which includes Hathorian female musicians and male Ihy-musicians, as well as offering-bearers bringing Hathor's sacred cult adornments to Senbi, notably a necklace, fragrant oil, a sistrum, a *menit*-necklace, a chest and bread.

7 Cf. O. Neugebauer and R.A. Parker, *Egyptian Astronomical Texts 1: The Early Decans*. London, 1960, 64 (text Ff), with pl.50. The text is to the right of Nut's head and states, 'The bird pools which are in the *Qebehu* of the sky.' Two ovals are also depicted, in one of which are three young birds. As the authors noted, these cosmic bird pools are clearly placed in the outermost limits of the heavenly waters. Illustrated also in Roberts, *My Heart My Mother*, 185, pl.143. For the return of the *Ba*-birds with Hathor, see *ibid*. 188.

8 This visual word-play between 'throw' and 'create, beget' was first observed by W. Westendorf, *ZÄS* 94 (1967), 142. Cf. also R.H. Wilkinson, *Symbol and Magic in Egyptian Art*. London, 1994, 182, who cites Westendorf's interpretation. For Tutankhamun's throw-stick as an allusion to Weret-Hekau, see *Golden Shrine*, 38. The authors compare it with a snake-headed boomerang depicted in Ay's royal tomb, which is similar to wands designated 'great of magic' in Middle Kingdom coffin friezes. For Weret-Hekau named in an inscription on a wooden throw-stick from Gurob, see Pinch, *op.cit.* 297.

9 See above, chapter 1, n.12.

10 For 'attraction' as the force uniting the Two Lands, see Roberts, *Hathor Rising*, 48–9.

11 Wolfhart Westendorf suggests Ankhesenamun is here the receptive partner, receiving the arrow from her husband and being impregnated by him (*op.cit.* 142). His interpretation is refuted by Eaton-Krauss and Graefe (*Golden Shrine*, 38, n.224).

12 For Ramesses II's identification with Sekhmet, see K.A. Kitchen, *Ramesside Inscriptions, Historical and Biographical* 2(1). Oxford, 1969, 318, 3–6. For the Thutmose III inscription, see W.K. Simpson (ed.), *The Literature of Ancient Egypt: An Anthology of Stories, Instructions, and Poetry*. New Haven and London, 1972, 280(7). For the king's relationship with Sekhmet, see also Germond, *Sekhmet*, 165–93; Roberts, *Hathor Rising*, 13.

13 The scene on the wooden chest is illustrated in [I.E.S. Edwards], *Treasures of Tutankhamun*. British Museum, London, 1972, (no. 21).

14 Wolfhart Westendorf first pointed out the visual puns and encoded symbolism in these 'water-pouring' and 'shooting' scenes (*op.cit.* 141–2), though the 'methodological shortcomings' of his interpretations were noted by Eaton-Krauss and Graefe (*op.cit.* 25, n.111). Cf. also H. Buchberger (*GM* 66 [1983]), 25–6), who criticized Westendorf for his ahistorical and selective approach which ignored the context of selected scenes within the shrine's overall decorative scheme. Whilst Buchberger's specific criticism is justified, it does not invalidate Westendorf's interpretation, which I have retained here in my discussion, though he connected the shrine with Tutankhamun's afterlife rather than his role as reigning king. See also below, n.22, for a similar juxtaposition of 'shooting' and 'generative' themes in Ramesses IX's tomb at Thebes.

15 For Ankhesenamun's gesture evoking the 'god's hand', see Troy, *Patterns of Queenship*, 62. This epithet is given to various goddesses, including Hathor, especially when she is identified with the Heliopolitan goddesses Iusaas or Nebet Hetepet as partners of Re-Atum. It also occurs in the titulary of 18th Dynasty queens and the priestess of Amun at Thebes known as the 'god's wife'. The ritual role of Hathorian royal women as the 'god's hand' is discussed by Troy, *ibid*. 91–102.

16 See Roberts, *Hathor Rising*, 137–8.

17 Both W. Westendorf (*op.cit.* 141) and L. Troy (*op.cit.* 62, 101) emphasized the generative meaning of this 'liquid-pouring' scene. Somewhat arbitrarily, Troy contrasted its 'domestic' context with the 'ritual' setting of other scenes on the shrine (*op.cit.* 101). Similarly, R. Wilkinson referred to the non-ritual nature of the king's gesture and its discreet reference to 'physical sexuality' (*op.cit.* 191), though he also associated it with the king's regeneration in the afterlife. My interpretation considers them all as 'ritual scenes' relating to Tutankhamun as the reigning king.

18 This allusion to nourishment was noted by Eaton-Krauss and Graefe (*op.cit.* 38), with reference to similar Old Kingdom private tomb scenes, which include the wife's words to her husband as she points to the thicket, namely her wish for a delicious bird. See, however, Lana Troy's discussion of the two nestlings as an allusion to the male-female duality arising from the generative act of creation, represented, for example, by Shu and Tefenet as Atum's offspring (*op.cit.* 62). Undoubtedly, the shrine's scenes can work on

129

different levels, both 'personal' and 'royal'. But inasmuch as Tutankhamun's role here is to integrate Sekhmetian energy within a life-giving 'nourishing' Heliopolitan cosmos (see chapters 3 and 4), Troy's interpretation highlights the scene's cosmic aspect. For Sekhmet manifesting as a 'nourishing' deity when invoked as Egypt's protectress, see Germond, *Sekhmet*, 282.

19 Here Troy's identification of Ankhesenamun's squatting figure with Maat in the 'shooting arrows' and 'water-pouring' scenes is perfectly apt (*op.cit.* 62). For Sekhmet's role in sustaining the way of Maat, see Germond, *op.cit.* 128–31, 275–7.

20 As noted by I.E.S. Edwards in *Treasures of Tutankhamun.* New York, 1976, 166, and quoted by Eaton-Krauss and Graefe, *op.cit.* 29, n.140.

21 For Aristotle's notions of the female as essentially passive and an 'infertile male', owing to the coldness of her nature, see Aristotle's *De Partibus Animalium I and De Generatione Animalium I (with passages from II,1–3).* Trans. D.M. Balme. Oxford, 1972, 46 (ch.19, 726b), 49 (ch.20, 728a). As Balme noted, the idea of females being colder than males was a commonplace which Aristotle accepted from tradition (*ibid.* 147). See also below, Epilogue, n.16.

22 For the destructive/creative aspects of Heliopolitan regeneration conveyed by 'shooting' symbolism in Ramesses IX's tomb, albeit in an Osirian context, see Roberts, *My Heart My Mother*, 132–4, with pl.107. In the middle register a solar scarab beetle sails in a boat, accompanied by a fiery sun Eye shooting forth arrows to vanquish enemies, whilst other

figures are evidently engaged in the procreation of new life. To the right is the huge outstretched figure of Osiris, with erect phallus and lying on the necropolis mound surrounded by a great serpent.

23 For iconographic similarities between the shrine's scenes and private tomb decoration, see *Golden Shrine*, 30–40. New Kingdom love poetry also extended beyond simply the 'private' sphere. Cf. Bernard Mathieu's comments about themes from hymns to deities incorporated into some poems and also the emphasis on the beloved's 'divinized' status (*Poésie amoureuse*, 232–40). For the love poetry's underlying magical aspects, see Mathieu, *ibid.* 226–232.

24 Quoted from a New Kingdom love charm invoking Re-Harakhti and the seven Hathors, see Borghouts, *Magical Texts*, 1 (no.1); Mathieu, *op.cit.* 227. For 'like to like' as an important principle underlying Egyptian magic and love poetry, see Mathieu, *op.cit.* 229. For 'attraction' as the dynamic magical power associated with the 'Great of Magic', see Mathieu, *op.cit.* 232, with n.774. See also above, n.1.

25 For a naos sistrum as a cult instrument of 'propitiation' and a loop sistrum as an instrument of 'praise', see Roberts, *Hathor Rising*, 56–7.

26 For this definition of *heka*, see Ritner, *Magical Practice*, 247. He pointed out the difficulties of defining Egyptian notions of *heka* according to Western notions of 'magic', since it had no connotations of a practice outside 'mainstream' religion, being rather intrinsic to the temple cults in all periods. The god Heka was the 'First of the creations of Re-Atum', appearing before the emanation of Hu (the creative word or Logos)

from the creator's mouth. It was this 'authoritative utterance', infused with magic vitality, that brought the gods and the cosmos into existence (*ibid.* 17). Ritner considered the 'Neoplatonist Theurgy', of the kind advocated by the Syrian philosopher Iamblichus, with its positive recognition of 'magic' as a technique within religion, to be closer to Egyptian notions of *heka* than Latin concepts of magic. He also noted that, as a sophisticated system of 'practical theology', a 'theurgy' in which the priest quite literally performed 'the works of god', Egyptian *heka*, within its own 'world view', was of far more 'exalted significance than its Coptic descendant or Western approximation' (*ibid.* 246–7).

27 For the importance of *heka* as the unifying 'thread' in creation, see C. Jacq, *Egyptian Magic.* Trans. Janet M. Davis. Warminster, 1985, 4, quoted also in Naydler, *Temple of the Cosmos*, 125. Frances Yates well encapsulates 'the erotic relation to nature' in Hermetic 'sympathetic magic': 'The Magus enters with loving sympathy into the sympathies which bind earth to heaven, and this emotional relationship is one of the chief sources of his power' (see F.A. Yates, *Giordano Bruno and the Hermetic Tradition.* London, 1964, 126–7).

28 A 'funerary' interpretation is advocated by Troy, *Patterns of Queenship*, 102; C. Desroches-Noblecourt, *Life and Death of a Pharaoh:Tutankhamen.* London, 1963, 269–70; W. Westendorf, *ZÄS* 94 (1967), 141; N. Reeves, *The Complete Tutankhamun.* London, 2007, 141. As Eaton-Krauss and Graefe observed (*Golden Shrine*, 25–6), the absence of any specific Osirian allusions in

the shrine's inscriptions makes a funerary context unlikely. Cf. also H. Buchberger, *GM* 66 (1983), 25, who links the Golden Shrine with 'temple' rather than 'tomb' scenes.

Chapter 3 *(pages 27–36)*

1 From a chant inscribed on an architrave in the Horus temple at Edfu, see Goyon, *Rituel*, 42 (Hymn C).

2 J.-C. Goyon, *Confirmation du pouvoir royal au nouvel an [Brooklyn Museum Papyrus 47.218.50]*. 2 vols. Cairo, 1972 (text), Brooklyn and Cairo, 1974 (plates) (hereafter cited as Goyon, *Confirmation*, with reference to vol.1). Why this particular collection of papyri was assembled is unknown. Stephen Quirke suggested the Wilbour Late Period Papyri survived because they were preserved in a tomb as burial equipment (*JEA* 83 [1997], 244). He also noted the same combination of literary, ritual, healing and technical texts in the Ramesseum cache of Middle Kingdom papyri, which were found in a tomb shaft, and in the New Kingdom Chester Beatty Papyri collection. Cf. also a similar cache from Thebes, dating to the third or early fourth century CE, comprising magical and alchemical papyri (Fowden, *Egyptian Hermes*, 168ff). Goyon surmised the Brooklyn ritual papyrus might have come from a temple 'House of Life' or even a magician's library (*op.cit.* 13–14, with n.4).

3 For the dating of the papyrus, see Goyon, *op.cit.* 7–8. He suggested it was copied from a New Kingdom liturgical manuscript, which also incorporated Middle Kingdom texts. For palaeographic reasons Goyon dated the Brooklyn papyrus to the end of the fifth or

beginning of the fourth century BCE (*op.cit.* 13).

4 See Goyon (*op.cit.* 5, n.7, 16, 44–6) for extracts from the ritual inscribed in Ptolemaic temples. He noted how certain chants that were only briefly mentioned in the Brooklyn papyrus were inscribed in more detail in the Horus temple at Edfu (*op.cit.* 17).

5 For this Theban 'rite of passage' confirming the king's power, see Roberts, *Hathor Rising*, 62–4.

6 For the Horus king's appearance on Geb's throne at Memphis, associated with the Moon Eye's restoration, see Roberts, *My Heart My Mother*, 39–41, 54, with further references.

7 Goyon, *Confirmation*, 55–6 (I.18–II.1). For the Egyptian fear that the dead might harm the living, see Roberts, *op.cit.* 152.

8 For this first chant, see Goyon, *op.cit.* 56 (II.2–3). The application of sacred unguents is well attested in Osirian cult rites. The *Pyramid Texts* mention an anointing ceremony involving seven unguents associated with the Eye of Horus (see A.M. Roth, *JEA* 78 [1992], 122–3; Naydler, *Shamanic Wisdom*, 195–7). Their ingredients were specified in later Ptolemaic inscriptions in the Horus temple at Edfu, by which time they comprised nine unguents (see L. Manniche, *Sacred Luxuries: Fragrance, Aromatherapy and Cosmetics in Ancient Egypt*. Ithaca, 1999, 108).

9 Protecting the king from Sekhmet's dangers is crucial in the annual rite of 'propitiating Sekhmet', which is preserved in Graeco-Roman temples, see Goyon, *Rituel, passim*; Germond, *Sekhmet*, 18–87, 194–274; Žabkar, *Hymns to Isis*, 121–7. Cf. also a New Kingdom sequence of seven love poems in which the theme of

Sekhmetian sickness and healing pervades the seventh stanza. The lovesick youth lies stricken with a malady which only his 'sister' can heal. She is both the source of his pain and the remedy. And his renewal comes in the first poem when his divinized lover appears before him on New Year's day, thus magically enclosing the poetic sequence in a sevenfold eternal cycle of annual renewal (see Roberts, *Hathor Rising*, 16).

10 Goyon, *Confirmation*, 63 (quoted from III.19–20). Goyon suggested sand from the Heliopolitan primordial mound may have been ritually strewn around the king to create a sacred zone under Heliopolitan protection (*ibid.* 21). For the magical use of sand to create the Egyptian cosmos, see Ritner, *Magical Practice*, 155–6.

11 For the reassertion of Ptah's craft wisdom in the aftermath of Akhenaten's reign, see Roberts, *My Heart My Mother*, 10–27.

12 Goyon noted the problematic interpretation of the hieroglyphic signs as a star, *Confirmation*, 109 (236). Nevertheless, some kind of celestial amulet would be appropriate here, symbolic of the Horus king's *Akh*-state. According to the *Pyramid Texts* (Utterance 77), when the king is anointed with seven oils, the sixth oil specifically transforms him into an *Akh*, a Horus ruler with power (*sekhem*) in his body, see Naydler, *Shamanic Wisdom*, 195–6. This sixth oil is also identified with the king's brow, where the uraeus resides.

13 Goyon, *op.cit.* 71 (extract from XVI.1–5). For a version of this chant in the Horus temple at Edfu, see Germond, *Sekhmet*, 83–7. For the Upper and Lower Egyptian Meret-goddesses identified with the solar Eye, see Troy, *Patterns of Queenship*, 87–8.

131

14 See Roberts, *Hathor Rising*, 54–64.

15 For this phase, see Goyon, *Confirmation*, 72 (XVI.6–7). There is a similar ritual sequence in the *Pyramid Texts* when the king asks Re to recognize him (Utterance 311), which is followed by a short food spell for bread (Utterance 312). See Naydler, *op.cit.* 279–83. For the importance of eating or swallowing a substance to acquire its benefits magically, see Ritner, *op.cit.* 102–10. For the creative use of saliva to transmit healing and blessing in Egyptian magical rites, *op.cit.* 78–80. Cf. also the ritual importance of bread in an ancient royal ritual performed for Senwosret I, preserved in the *Ramesseum Dramatic Papyrus*. Immediately after the king's ceremonial crowning, his very first ritual act was to share out half-loaves to the 'Great Ones of Upper and Lower Egypt', thus fulfilling his responsibility to provide nourishment for his people. The 'Eye of Horus', which immediately before the crowning ceremony had been offered up to the king in the produce of the land, was returned to the people as the bread of life. The king himself ate a sacred *Hetep*-meal (see Frankfort, *Kingship*, 130, 132).

Chapter 4 *(pages 37–46)*

1 Translation after Fox, *Song of Songs*, 93, 167–71 (commentary), who compared the wish to be the lover's seal with imagery in Egyptian love poems. Fox extensively studied the parallels between the *Song of Songs* and Egypt's love lyrics.

2 For the Horus-Seth conflict, see Roberts, *Hathor Rising*, 98–112, with further references.

3 Curiously, Eaton-Krauss and Graefe query whether Ankhesenamun's gesture symbolizes 'anointing', preferring to see it simply in terms of the queen's 'vivifying function' (*Golden Shrine*, 21, 38–39). They also dismiss Kate Bosse-Griffiths's interpretation because there is no conclusive evidence the king was ever anointed at his coronation (*ibid.* 39). Other scholars, however, refer to it as an anointing gesture, see *ibid.* 38, with n.226.

4 For the ancient Near Eastern custom of wearing a seal on the breast or upper arm as a protective amulet, see Keel, *Hohelied*, 247, also Fox, *op.cit.* 169. Fox noted that a seal-ring was like a signature and hence continually worn by an individual. When it was worn higher on the arm it became an amulet.

5 Goyon, *Confirmation*, 57 (extract from II.9–10).

6 *Ibid.* 58 (extract from II.11–13). For the uraeus-Eye and crown goddesses confirming the king's power, see Roberts, *op.cit.* 8–9, 46–7.

7 Goyon, *op.cit.* 60. The sycamore tree is sacred to Hathor, though Goyon here links the ritual's sycamore trees with the Bakhu and Manu horizon mountains (*op.cit.* 92 [84]). Cf. also chapter 109 of the *Book of the Dead*: 'I know those two trees of turquoise between which Re goes forth, which have grown up at the "supports of Shu", at that gate of the Lord of the East from which Re goes forth.' Interestingly, there is a diagram of the Heliopolitan temple of Hathor Nebet Hetepet, preserved on a fragmentary siltstone panel discovered at Heliopolis, which indicates a subsidiary shrine in the third court, possibly in the form of a platform approached by two short stairways, called 'house of Atum of the sycamore tree' (see Quirke, *Cult of Ra*, 104–5). Quirke noted the allusion to Hathor's Memphite epithet, 'Lady of the Southern Sycamore', and suggested that this part of Hathor's Heliopolitan temple may have been an open sun court with altars. The sequence of cult images shown on the panel includes Atum's cult image. The inventory also mentions a sistrum, Nefertem's emblem, Isis, Hathor, Lady of Heliopolis and two sceptre-like emblems named 'Power of Horus' and 'Power of Seth' (*ibid.* 103–4).

8 For this name of a scarab amulet, cf. the table of magical amulets in Ritner, *Magical Practice*, 52.

9 *Song of Songs* 1:2–4.

10 For Ankhesenamun's 'tying' gesture and 'assembling' the king's generative powers, see Troy, *Patterns of Queenship*, 101. She noted the term *tjes*, 'to tie/knot', had the same connotation as the verb *ip*, 'to assemble', specifically in the sense of gathering together powers for generation. For the protective aspect of 'tying' (*tjes*) and 'knots' (*tjeset*) in acts of creation and as protection from threatened dissolution, see Ritner, *op.cit.* 144, n.638 (with reference also to the root meaning of *tjes* as 'congeal/make firm/solidify').

11 Goyon, *Confirmation*, 61 (III.10). With regard to the temple rites for 'propitiating Sekhmet', Germond observed how it is only after the goddess has been propitiated, and her beneficent powers incorporated into service of the cosmic order, that the king then truly manifests as Atum, fulfilling his role to maintain the cosmos of the solar creator (see Germond, *Sekhmet*, 277).

12 *Ibid.* 61 (III.8). For Heliopolitan solar ascension and the king's identification with 'bull energy' when entering Re's presence in the Old Kingdom *Pyramid Texts* (Utterances 306–12), see Naydler, *Shamanic Wisdom*, 275–83. This Heliopolitan theme of 'restoring youth' reappears in much later Islamic and European alchemy. Cf. the 58th sermon of the *Turba philosophorum* concerning an old alchemist being restored to a state of eternal youth beneath the great fruit-bearing branches of a white tree, around which a house is built surrounded by dew: 'O how wonderful is nature which transforms the soul of that old man into the body of a youth, so that the father is become the son.' For the 'Egyptianness' of this passage, see Roberts, *My Heart My Mother*, 204, with nn.14,15. The theme of the *Turba's* next sermon is the volatile 'woman who flees'.

13 For the Heliopolitan symbolism of persea fruits associated with the returning inundation, see P. Derchain, *CdE* 50/99 (1975), 82–6. Derchain noted how the ripening of persea fruits required the dry midsummer conditions and hence they became a powerful 'natural' symbol of fecundity in a 'flood' context. If these are, in fact, persea fruits that Tutankhamun holds, it would further enhance the New Year connotations of his 'water-pouring' rite. The *Turba's* author may also have had in mind persea fruits when describing the union of the male with the 'woman who flees' in the context of the ripening of the perfect tree which needs the summer heat (see above n.12).

14 Goyon, *Confirmation*, 62 (III.16).

15 Jan Bergman noted how the king not only represented the land and his people at his coronation, but also embodied them, thus integrating them into the ceremony's divine cult actions (*Ich bin Isis*, 217). This embodiment is graphically conveyed by Tutankhamun holding a *rekhyt*-bird here on the Golden Shrine.

16 For Ptah's joyful embrace of Ramesses II, whom he creates as Re's living image on earth, see Roberts, *My Heart My Mother*, 25. To the Egyptians, praise-giving was itself a life-bestowing act, evoking the divine presence and releasing creative potential in the world.

17 For a different interpretation of the queen's *dwa*-gesture on the left door panel, see *Golden Shrine*, 30–1. The authors interpret the scene as a civil aspect of the queen's ideological function. They consider the queen's role here to be that of a 'mortal worshipping a deity' and indicative of the considerable gulf in status between herself and Tutankhamun. See above, n.16, however, for ritual 'praise-giving' as an essential complement to the 'birthing' of an image-king in the Memphite craft world.

18 M. Eliade, *The Myth of the Eternal Return*. Trans. Willard R. Trask. New York, 1954, 34.

Chapter 5 *(pages 47–58)*

1 Quotation from Plutarch's 'Dialogue on Love' (*Moralia 9*, section 762A). (See also below, chapter 7, n.18.)

2 See Goyon, *Confirmation*, 115 (282) for the royal predecessor as 'bull' identified here with Osiris-Wennefer. For Osiris as 'bull' in the New Kingdom *Book of Caverns*, see E. Hornung, *The Valley of the Kings: Horizon of Eternity*. Trans. David Warburton. New York, 1990, 117. Cf. also chapter 1 of the *Book of the Dead* for Osiris as 'Bull of the West'.

3 For the Lower Egyptian crown associated with Horus as Osiris's *Ba*, see Roberts, *My Heart My Mother*, 78–9.

4 As A. Gardiner noted, the 'divinely inspired writings' composed by scribes in the 'House of Life' had the power 'to vivify that which was dead' (*JEA* 24 [1938], 178).

5 This passage is cited by Thomas Taylor in a note to his translation of Iamblichus's *On the Mysteries of the Egyptians, Chaldeans, and Assyrians*. San Diego, 1984, 222. Cf. also the fire-spitting serpents guarding Osiris at night and repelling his enemies in the ritual of the House of Life in *Papyrus Salt 825* (see Ritner, *Magical Practice*, 224, n.1042). Ritner also noted an Egyptian magical spell against night terrors, which was uttered over four fire-spitting uraei made of pure clay and 'with lamps in their mouths', which were placed in the four corners of a room where a couple were sleeping. Four uraei also guarded the cardinal points in royal rituals at Edfu.

6 See K. Sethe, *Dramatische Texte zu altaegyptischen Mysterienspielen 2: Der dramatische Ramesseumpapyrus. Ein Spiel zur Thronbesteigung des Königs*. Leipzig, 1928, 139 (ll.34–5). For the tree's association with Osiris's procreative powers, see *ibid.* 145. For its Hathorian symbolism, see chapter 6, n.21. For particular stones and other materials enhancing the efficacy of amulets in Egyptian magic, see Ritner, *op.cit.* 38–40, 49–51.

7 Goyon commented on the strange description of the seals here, suggesting it was a later addition

133

by a private individual who adapted this royal rite for personal magical purposes, see *Confirmation*, 27–8, 115 (284). For a scene entitled 'Resting inside the tomb' in the Osirian phase of Osorkon II's Sed Festival 'secret rites', see E. Uphill, *JNES* 24 (1965), 378. The king is shown entering a chapel or shrine inhabited by the Heliopolitan deities. Other royal examples of the 'secret rites in the tomb' are discussed by Uphill, *ibid.* 377–80. See also Naydler, *Shamanic Wisdom*, 72–9.

8 For the Osirian ancestors and the inundation's return, see Roberts, *My Heart My Mother*, 67–8, 82–3, 150, 152–3, 194, 198. For Osiris as the rejuvenating water, cf a hymn to Isis at Philae: 'Her man is the pure water, rejuvenating himself at Biga at his time' (Žabkar, *Hymns to Isis*, 51). As Žabkar noted (*ibid.* 168, n.11), this is a recurrent theme at Philae and is encapsulated in a 'New Year' praise of the god: 'You (Osiris) are the inundation that returns at its time, who causes gods and men to live from his efflux, one who comes at his time, being born at his time, rejuvenating his limbs on the first of the year.' For the inundation as the resurrected Osiris's efflux, see Roberts, *op.cit.* 33.

9 Goyon suggested that this bed ceremony was either an incubation rite or a kind of 'funerary watch' during the night, with the king lying outstretched on the bed with the seals under his head (*Confirmation*, 115 [281]). For the importance of incubation in antiquity as a means of making contact with netherworld deities, see Kingsley, *Ancient Philosophy*, 284. He wrote: 'In antiquity the best way of actually making

contact with divinities of the underworld was through the practice of "incubation"—of awaiting a dream or vision while sleeping.' For possible New Kingdom evidence for incubation at Deir el-Bahri, see Pinch, *Votive Offerings*, 223 (with further references), though the examples are not from a royal context.

10 (Spell 228). From *CT* 3, 268–78.

11 Rundle Clark, *Myth and Symbol*, 160–1. He noted similarities with the Fisher King in the Grail legend.

12 Goyon, *Confirmation*, 73 (XVI.15).

13 Identification of the *Ibhet*-stone is problematic see below, chapter 6, n.3. For Thutmose IV 'finding a stone' as a confirmation of his royal power, see chapter 6, n.4.

14 (Spell 164). *CT* 3, 3c–d, quoted in DuQuesne, 'Raising the Serpent Power', 59.

15 For the magical practice of drawing enemy figures in ink on a new sheet of papyrus, see Ritner, *Magical Practice*, 185–6, 208, n.960.

16 (Spell 276). *CT* 4, 17. Cf. also inscriptions in the Middle Kingdom Theban tomb of Akhtoy, which praise Hathor as 'Gold', appearing in the solar day-boat as protectress of King Mentuhotpe. It is said that she 'loves Re', who comes forth in order to see her 'beauty', see A.H. Gardiner, *JEA* 4 (1917), 32. Hathor is often depicted in the solar boat's prow, but inscriptions also mention her holding the steering oar. See Derchain, *Hathor Quadrifrons*, 37–8.

17 H. Grapow, *Die bildlichen Ausdrücke des Aegyptischen: Vom Denken und Dichten einer altorientalischen Sprache*. Leipzig, 1924, 108. Grapow noted how the uraeus snake was called 'lock of hair' at Edfu. Cf. also chapter 99 of the *Book of the Dead* for the

provision of a ferry-boat to sail into the Field of Rushes. First, travellers must identify the mooring-post as the 'Lady of the Two Lands in the Shrine'. When they are subsequently asked the name of the bow rope, the reply is 'the lock of hair that Anubis makes fast' (see also below, n.22, for this spell). Cf. also the role of the female 'great mooring-post' (*menit*) in the *Pyramid Texts* (Utterances 437, 458, 461, 466, 483, 553, *passim*).

18 Goyon, *Confirmation*, 74 (XVI. 20–1). For the 'Tired Heart' as an epithet of Osiris, see Roberts, *My Heart My Mother*, 117–18, 236, n.3.

19 For Thoth's snake-staff, entwined with two crowned uraeus snakes, as a symbol of Osirian regeneration in the New Kingdom, see Roberts, *ibid.* 63–4. Jack Lindsay discussed the movement of life forces up and down the world pillar in the context of serpentine rebirth from the Osirian depths, comparing it with Indian religious practices of rousing serpent energy along the central spinal column: 'The Sun emerging at the end of the snake staff is both the dead man reborn and the newborn Sun (Khepri); the dead man emerges from the spinal column at the top of the skull, and is reborn' (see *Origins of Alchemy*, 190–1). For parallels between ancient Egyptian and Indian Tantric practices, see also Roberts, *Hathor Rising*, 63–4; DuQuesne, 'Raising the Serpent Power', 53–68.

20 Cf. a resurrection text invoking Khepri and Wadjet's 'papyrus plant' in the *Pyramid Texts*: 'O papyrus which came forth from Wadjet. You have gone forth from the king and the king has gone forth from you. The king is powerful through your strength' (*PT* §1875a–c).

21 For Seth's integration into a unified Egypt associated with the inundation, see te Velde, *Seth*, 70–1. For papyrus symbolizing the reconciliation of Horus and Seth, cf. a passage in the *Memphite Theology* describing how 'reed and papyrus were placed at the double door of the House of Ptah. That means Horus and Seth, pacified and united' (Lichtheim, *Literature* 1, 53 [15c]; Roberts, *My Heart My Mother*, 40). Immediately beforehand, the text affirms the 'sprouting of the two enchantresses' upon the royal brow. For a papyrus column amulet associated with 'greenness', 'flourishing life' and 'health', as well as Sekhmet's annual pacification, see Ritner, *Magical Practice*, 51, with n.240; Germond, *Sekhmet*, 267–70 (papyrus sceptre), 311–15. Germond also discusses Hathor-Sekhmet's relationship with the arrival of the inundation (*ibid.* 224–33).

22 For the importance of 'going forth' in a red garment, see M. Smith, *The Liturgy of Opening the Mouth for Breathing*. Oxford, 1993, 31(10), with commentary *ibid.* 46 (line 10,c). Here a person is told: 'You will accomplish the act of going forth by virtue of the dark red cloth. You will acquire the gift of sight by virtue of the bright red band.' Similarly, chapter 99 of the *Book of the Dead* invokes the 'Lord of bright red linen, who controls gladness of heart', see T.G. Allen, *The Book of the Dead or Going Forth by Day: Ideas of the Ancient Egyptians concerning the Hereafter as expressed in their own Terms*. Chicago, 1974, 80 (S2). In Utterance 254 of the *Pyramid Texts*, immediately after the king's meeting with the goddess called

the 'beautiful West', Re is released from his fetters by means of the 'amulet of the Great One which is in its red cloth' (*PT* §285d). For Hathor's association with red cloth, cf. a love charm invoking 'the seven Hathors who are clothed in wrappings of red cloth' (Borghouts, *Magical Texts*, 1 [no. 1]; Mathieu, *Poésie amoureuse*, 227). For Sekhmet as 'Lady of the red cloth' and protectress of the body in funerary rites (see Germond, *op.cit.* 352–3, with reference also to the cloth's symbolic associations with the sun, flame and blood). See also below, chapter 9, nn.28,29, for the importance of a red/purple cloth in rebirth rites in the Graeco-Roman era.

23 Goyon, *Confirmation*, 75 (XVI.24). The tradition of wearing white sandals was important in Egyptian ritual and carried though into Graeco-Egyptian magic (*ibid.* 120 [314]).

24 See Kingsley, *Ancient Philosophy*, 251–2, with n.6 (with further references to this unifying axis in Greek initiatory otherworld journeys and of descending into the depths in order to ascend). For the Heliopolitan vertical axis of the world and cosmic 'pillar', see B.H. Stricker, 'The Empire of Heliopolis' in *Proceedings of Colloquium, The Archaeology, Geography and History of the Egyptian Delta in Pharaonic Times, Wadham College, 29–31 August, 1988, Oxford*. Oxford, 1989, 295–300. For a well as the entrance to the netherworld, see Ritner, *Magical Practice*, 179, n.831. For this Egyptian midsummer heaven-deep earth axis in alchemy, see chapter 10, n.1.

25 For these swallow chants, see Goyon, *Confirmation*, 80–1 (XX.19–21). Cf. Spell 294 of the

Coffin Texts for transforming into a swallow with Hathor as the 'Flaming One … ascending in flame upon the ramparts of the sky.' Thus, a person is empowered to travel across the sky 'with the cat', whilst remaining grounded on earth 'by means of my sandals'. See Roberts, *My Heart My Mother*, 188, with nn.12–13, for this spell in the context of returning with Hathor from the Osirian realm.

26 For the necklace's association with Hathor-Maat, see Goyon, *Confirmation*, 128 (388). The text breaks off abruptly and this final rite is only very briefly mentioned. According to Goyon, the elliptic ending may be due to lack of space at the end of the papyrus, without the scribe having completely finished the ritual directions (*ibid.* 128 [389]).

Chapter 6 *(pages 59–72)*

1 Goyon, *Rituel*, 51 (Text 7).

2 F. Cumont, *Oriental Religions in Roman Paganism*. New York, 1956, 11.

3 Identifying the *Ibhet*-stone is problematic, see Goyon, *Confirmation*, 116–17 (289). Cf. also S. Aufrère, *L'univers minéral dans la pensée égyptienne* 1. Cairo, 1991, 247 (d), who noted the stone's magical aspect and association with Geb. He suggested it may have been some kind of diorite or green porphyry. But the 'smaragdite' has also been suggested. In Graeco-Roman temples it is connected with the ritual of *Filling the Eye*, see *ibid.* 246–7. See also below, chapter 7, n.16, for an 'emerald' specifically associated with Osiris's tomb in a Graeco-Egyptian magical text.

4 For Thutmose IV's inscription (*Urk.* 4, 1565, 3–6), see J. Baines and R.B. Parkinson, 'An Old

Kingdom Record of an Oracle? Sinai Inscription 13' in J. van Dijk (ed.), *Essays on Ancient Egypt in Honour of Herman Te Velde*. Groningen, 1997, 18. They suggest a stone was perhaps inserted into an opening in the naos, possibly to complete a sculpted figure of a falcon or standard. Cf. also the Roman-period funerary text known as the *Second Letter for Breathing*, in which an Osirian person is reborn from the mountains when 'the stone comes' and when 'the Great-of-Magic comes' (Roberts, *My Heart My Mother*, 194).

5 For this up-and-down flow of forces along the central axis, see chapter 5, n.19.

6 The *Myth of the Destruction of Humanity* graphically describes how Re 'grows old', his *Ba* withdrawing to the sky whilst his material body returns to its elemental form, becoming silver, gold and lapis-lazuli. Re's subjects on earth are also in rebellion, and to punish them, he sends out his Eye. But it results in Sekhmet's rampant power running amok until she is 'charmed' to return 'in peace' to the sun god. See Roberts, *Hathor Rising*, 10–11 (with further references).

7 For Sokar as the 'golden remedy in the temples', see Ritner, *Magical Practice*, 55, with n.257. For the religious connotations of the word *pekheret* meaning 'magical potion' or 'remedy' (*ibid.* 54–7). For the original meaning of the Greek word *pharmakon* as a 'charm', which could be either healing or poisonous, see Sonnedecker (ed.), *History of Pharmacy*, 16, 479. Later, under the influence of the Hippocratic theory of treatment, which was developed in Alexandria during the fourth and third centuries BCE, there was an

important shift in meaning. This theory emphasized the need to purify the body from illnesses producing excess of humours, bringing about a bodily catharsis or cleansing. Thus, rather than meaning primarily a healing 'charm', based on the healing magical 'sympathies' and 'antipathies' in nature, *pharmakon* increasingly came to mean a purifying remedy in a Hippocratic sense, used to dispel malign influences. For a possible ancient Egyptian derivation of the Greek word *pharmakon*, see R. Schmitz, *Geschichte der Pharmazie 1: Von den Anfängen bis zum Ausgang des Mittelalters*. Eschborn, 1998, 100; Sonnedecker, *op.cit.* 479.

8 For priests of Sekhmet, see Germond, *Sekhmet*, 304–9 (with further references).

9 For the sickness love causes when the beloved is absent in Egyptian love poetry, see Mathieu, *Poésie amoureuse*, 186–7; Fox, *Song of Songs*, 279–80. Fox noted that mixtures used to describe the feelings of love occurred also as medicines in Egyptian medical texts (*ibid.* 280).

10 For 'sympathy' and 'antipathy' in alchemy, see Lindsay, *Origins of Alchemy*, 105; Festugière, *Révélation*, 231–8; Kingsley, *Ancient Philosophy*, 298–9, 335–9. Kingsley refers mainly to the alchemical work of Bolus of Mendes, who applied the doctrine to the world of plants for purposes of magic, healing and ritual. He regarded the teachings of the Presocratic philosopher Empedocles to be the main influence on Bolus' doctrine (*ibid.* 299). Dating Bolus' lifetime is problematic, but he was probably a Hellenized Egyptian living in the second century BCE (see Fraser, *Ptolemaic Alexandria* 1, 440).

Curiously, whilst Fraser noted that 'there can be no doubt that Greek medicine adopted traditional Egyptian lore at an early date' (*ibid.* 344, with n.21), and how the Greeks turned to the Egyptian gods of healing (*ibid.* 374–5), he overlooked the possibility that Bolus' principles of 'sympathy' and 'antipathy' might also have derived from the same 'Egyptian lore', preferring to cite Theophrastus as the main influence (*ibid.* 442–3). For Bolus' importance in the transmission of Egyptian wisdom to Neoplatonic theurgists and Greek philosophers, see P. Eschweiler, *Bildzauber im alten Ägypten: Die Verwendung von Bildern und Gegenständen in magischen Handlungen nach den Texten des Mittleren und Neuen Reiches*. Freiburg and Göttingen, 1994, 273–4. A major difficulty in tracing Egyptian influence is the paucity of ancient botanical papyri. See, however, Stephen Quirke's discussion of plant descriptions preserved on fragments of a papyrus roll in the British Museum (EA 10547), written in hieratic script and dating from the fourth or third century BCE ('Colour vocabularies in Ancient Egyptian' in W.V. Davies (ed.), *Colour and Painting in Ancient Egypt*. London, 2001, 190–1). Not enough survives to determine whether this fragmentary roll was an Egyptian healer's manual. Nevertheless, referring to an analogous plant description in the New Kingdom *Ebers Papyrus*, Quirke cited these descriptions as important evidence for an indigenous tradition. For a Roman-period demotic papyrus, listing at least 86 plants including their medicinal uses, see F. Hoffmann, *Ägypten Kultur und Lebenswelt in griechisch-römischer*

Zeit: Eine Darstellung nach den demotischen Quellen. Berlin, 2000, 107–8. Hoffmann noted that the text preserved native Egyptian traditions, and seemed to refer specifically to healing plants. For Egyptian influence in early Greek medicine before the development of Hippocrates' theory of the humours, see *ibid*. 110–11.

11 Pliny, *Natural History* 5, 55. Trans. H. Rackham. London and Cambridge (Mass.), 1942, 261–3. See also above chapter 5, n.24 for this cosmic vertical axis.

12 *Aethiopica*, 9,10. See Heliodorus, *An Aethiopian Romance*. Trans. T. Underdowne, revised by F.A. Wright. London, 1928, 279.

13 See Fraser, *op.cit.* 1, 414–15 for Cleomedes's account of the discovery. Fraser refers to Pliny's information about the well and suggests Eratosthenes might have had access to similar information, (*ibid*. 2, 598–9 [308]). For his reliance on native Egyptian science, notably Egyptian information concerning the terrestrial distance between Alexandria and Aswan in making his mathematical calculations, see G. Priskin, *GM* 208 (2006), 79–81.

14 See Iversen, *Myth of Egypt*, 39–40, who noted how the Egyptians were quite capable of observing and registering natural phenomena. Rather than giving these 'theoretical' explanations, however, they expressed them in 'mythical' form. He wrote: 'The truth aimed at throughout the whole history of Egyptian thought remained always a concrete mythical truth' and was not 'a scientific or philosophical one, based on empirical observations and logic deductions' (*ibid*. 40). Iversen also noted the difficulties of post-Aristotelian Greeks in understanding Egyptian thought.

15 For the vast lost solar city of Re-Atum at Heliopolis, see Quirke, *Cult of Ra*, 73–114. As Quirke observed, despite 'all the utter destruction' at the site, 'one point does emerge with force—the sheer scale of the surviving precinct' (*ibid*. 91). For a reconstruction of the Heliopolitan temenos and location of the various shrines associated with the New Year ritual, see Goyon, *Confirmation*, 35.

16 For the ritual role of Egypt's royal women as priestess, see Troy, *Patterns of Queenship*, 73–102, who emphasized their identification with Hathor and the generative solar Eye.

17 The Sed Festival reliefs on Osorkon's gateway are discussed by E. Uphill, *JNES* 24 (1965), 365–83. The difficulties of reconstructing the order of the Sed Festival rites, based solely on reliefs shown on temple walls, is evident in Uphill's discussion. It is another reason why the Brooklyn Museum New Year ritual papyrus is so valuable, since it gives the precise order of the ceremonies, thus enabling a comparison with the Golden Shrine's iconography.

18 For Queen Teye's role in Amenhotep III's first Sed Festival, see Roberts, *Hathor Rising*, 32–6 (with further references).

19 See Roberts, *My Heart My Mother*, 72–88.

20 Goyon, *Confirmation*, 72 (XVI. 8–9). See also Ritner, *Magical Practice*, 38–40, for the importance of using the correct substances in Heka's realm.

21 For the *Ima*-tree symbolizing Hathor's unifying power, see Troy, *op.cit.* 83. Troy quotes a spell from the *Coffin Texts* for 'joining the river banks together', in which the *Ima*-tree effects a love union between the east and west banks (*CT* 6, 160c–h). See also Roberts,

Hathor Rising, 48–9 for Hathor's 'attraction' as the power 'coupling the Two Lands'. For the Eye's homecoming in the *Myth of the Destruction of Humanity*, see Lichtheim, *Literature* 2, 199, with n.13.

22 For Hathor's 'charm' and 'attraction' uniting together King Seti I and his heir, Ramesses II, at Abydos, see Roberts, *My Heart My Mother*, 51–6.

23 For Hathor's power to bring back the inundation waters, see Roberts, *Hathor Rising*, 12, 15–16.

24 For the importance of the 'seal of prophetship' in Islam associated with Muhammad's prophetic role as the beloved spiritual guide for his people, see Schimmel, *As Through a Veil*, 172. She wrote: 'He is the first thing created by God as well as the "seal" of all prophets, and brought with him the final and all-comprehensive revelation.' See also *ibid*. 175, for the consoling words of an Urdu poet: 'The person of the Seal of the Prophets is a guarantee for your salvation.' For further examples, see *ibid*. 196–7, 209, 211, 274, n.4.

25 The literature on Egyptian kingship is extensive, with different views regarding the extent of the pharaoh's divinity. See, for example, D.P. Silverman's contribution on 'Kingship and Divinity' in B.E. Shafer (ed.), *Religion in Ancient Egypt: Gods, Myths, and Personal Practice*. Ithaca, 1991, 58–87, with further references.

26 For this Hermetic treatise entitled 'A secret dialogue of Hermes Trismegistus on the mountain to his son Tat: On being born again, and on the promise to be silent', see Copenhaver, *Hermetica*, 49–54. For the rebirth experience initiated by the arrival of truth, see *ibid*. 51(9)ff.

27 Cf. also Treatise 10 of the *Corpus Hermeticum* describing the divinized power of a human to 'rise up to heaven', knowing 'what is in its heights and its depths', able 'to be on high without leaving earth behind, so enormous is his range' (*ibid.* 36 [25]).

Chapter 7 *(pages 73–84)*

1 For relevant bibliography on the Cyme aretalogy, see below, chapter 9, n.9.

2 For this half-hearted approach of the Egyptian priesthood, see *Lexikon der Ägyptologie* 2, col. 902.

3 For the Egyptian priesthood's role as upholders of Maat and continuing royal ideology during the Graeco-Roman period, see Bergman, *Ich bin Isis*, 299–300.

4 For extracts from the New Year ritual preserved in Graeco-Roman temple inscriptions, see chapter 3, n.4.

5 The hymn is translated by F. Daumas, *ZÄS* 95 (1968), 1. Cf. also Graeco-Roman temple reliefs depicting the birth of the divine child, which are based on New Kingdom scenes showing the pharaoh's birth in the palace and passage to crowning as son of Amun-Re and the Egyptian queen. In these later temples, however, a goddess replaces the queen as mother in the birth cycle (see Troy, *Patterns of Queenship*, 70). Troy also noted how earlier titles of queens were transferred to Isis, Hathor and other goddesses in Late Period temples. Similarly, the royal ritual of 'propitiating Sekhmet' becomes a divine ritual at Edfu, being transferred to Horus as the living falcon of the year (see Germond, *Sekhmet*, 11, 12, with n.3).

6 R.S. Bagnall, *Egypt in Late Antiquity*. Princeton, 1993, 268.

7 For the appropriation of traditional royal rites by private individuals, cf. a Late Period papyrus (BM 10081), in which a royal ritual for the destruction of enemies has been taken over by a private individual called Pawerem, with his name replacing the pharaoh's at the relevant places (see S. Schott, *MDAIK* 14 [1956], 181–2). See also above chapter 5, n.7. For the 'democratization' of the *Book of Night*'s netherworld journey (which first appears in New Kingdom royal tombs), and its adaptation in the Roman-period demotic *Second Letter for Breathing*, see Roberts, *My Heart My Mother*, 192–5, 243, n.10. On a more limited scale this process had already started by the end of the New Kingdom (see J. Baines, *JARCE* 27 [1990], 22–3). As Robert Ritner observed about Egyptian magic, however, the categories 'royal' and 'private' are essentially illusory, since the incantations were always priestly spells, being composed and preserved in a temple House of Life, and used for either royal or private benefit (*Magical Practice*, 204). Ritner noted similarities between a 'private' ritual in a *Coffin Text* spell and the same practice in a 'royal' context. Both derived from priestly authorship, the only difference being in the context and way they were applied (*ibid.* 205). For Late Period examples of temple papyri being appropriated by priests for 'private' use (*ibid.* 206, n.953).

8 For elements from royal enthronement and Jewish priesthood rites preserved in the Nag Hammadi writings, as well as the *Testament of Levi* and *Second Book of Enoch*, see Scopello, *Femme*, 79–113. Scopello noted their 'democratization' in the Hellenistic era, suggesting it was primarily through a process of 'interiorization' within the 'temple of the soul' rather than through actual enactments. For Mesopotamian royal rites as the underlying 'royal' influence in these Jewish and gnostic texts (see *ibid.* 83, 111). Nevertheless, the royal ritual pattern she discerned in the *Exegesis on the Soul* from Nag Hammadi (*ibid.* 90–6, 110), which incorporates the theme of the 'returning female womb' (*ibid.* 91), looks remarkably similar to the phases of 'purification', 'anointing', 'ascension' and 'return to cosmic origins' in the first part of the Egyptian New Year ritual. Though these have been interwoven with ideas about Aphrodite's trickery, as well as the 'fallen' feminine hypostasis of the divine, caught in matter and in need of redemption like the 'fallen' Sophia. This view of the female as 'fallen' is not Egyptian, being indicative of the distortions that could arise once Egypt's royal wisdom filtered through into groups from very different cultural backgrounds, some of whom were intensely hostile to Egyptian religion. For the distortion of Egypt's 'anointing tradition' in the gnostic *Hymn of the Pearl* (see chapter 9, with nn.30–1). For the theme of the 'wandering womb' in alchemy and the cult of Hathor-Sekhmet, see Roberts, *My Heart My Mother*, 204–5, 247, nn.16–17. For womb imagery and the 'unclean feminine' in *The Paraphrase of Shem* from the Nag Hammadi Library, and the text's underlying hostility to Egypt (*ibid.* 241, n.17).

9 See Griffiths, *Isis-Book*, 99ff. (Ch. 24). Whether this initiation was authentically 'Egyptian' has been much debated. See, however, Bergman, *Ich bin Isis*, 300, for Lucius appearing here as a solarized Horus, participating in formerly 'royal' mysteries. Cf. also a description of the wooden dais on which the triumphant solarized king appears in a Graeco-Roman inscription at Dendara, Goyon, *Rituel*, 56.

10 For Egyptian priests transmitting royal ideology and Maat wisdom into the Hellenized world of the Isis cults, see Bergman, *op.cit.* 299–300; Fowden, *Egyptian Hermes*, 16, 30, 53–4, 166–8, though Fowden's description of Egyptian priests as 'clerics of a learned bent', frequenting the schools of the Greeks in late antique Alexandria, seems wide of the mark (*ibid.* 167).

11 For Phoenicians at Memphis in Hellenistic times, see D.J. Thompson, *Memphis under the Ptolemies*. Princeton, 1988. 88–93. The integration of Phoenicians in the Egyptian cults is encapsulated in a beautiful Ptolemaic stela of Chaiapis from Saqqara (see fig. 53). The stela was formerly in Berlin, but unfortunately it was lost during the war of 1939–45. Chaiapis's connection with the Egyptian cults is discussed by G. Vittmann, 'Beobachtungen und Überlegungen zu fremden und hellenisierten Ägyptern im Dienste einheimischer Kulte' in W. Clarysse (*et al.,*), *Egyptian Religion The Last Thousand Years 2: Studies dedicated to the Memory of Jan Quaegebeur*. Leuven, 1998, 1244–6. Cf. however, the specific exclusion of foreigners from Hathor's temple crypt in an inscription at Dendara: 'No Phoenician should approach it, no Greek enter it, no Bedouin tread it, its magic *(heka)* should not be

seen within it' (quoted in Ritner, *Magical Practice*, 203, with n.940). Presumably, this inscription reflects the possibility that foreigners did have access to certain parts of Egyptian temples in the Graeco-Roman era.

12 Most of the information about Philo's account of Phoenician traditions comes from fragments preserved by Eusebius, the early fourth-century church historian and Christian bishop at Caesarea. For Philo's knowledge of Egyptian creation theology, especially Thoth's Hermopolitan cosmogony, see below chapter 9, n.27. For his knowledge of alchemy, see below Epilogue, n.3.

13 Berthelot, *Alchimistes grecs* 3, 129, quoted also in Jung, *Psychology and Alchemy*, 295.

14 Quoted in T. Burckhardt, *Alchemy: Science of the Cosmos, Science of the Soul*. Trans. W. Stoddart. Paperback edn. Shaftesbury, 1987, 101, with reference to Basilius Valentinus' interpretation of the alchemical keyword V.I.T.R.I.O.L: '*Visita interiora terrae; rectificando invenies occultum lapidem.*'

15 For the pattern of the Egyptian New Kingdom ancestor ritual exemplifying these lines from the *Emerald Tablet*, see Roberts, *My Heart My Mother*, 221–2, also *ibid.* 218–19, for the scholarly debate concerning alchemy's roots in ancient Egypt.

16 For these lines from the incantation, which is edited with extensive commentary by F. Maltomini, see M.W. Haslam (*et al.,*), *The Oxyrhynchus Papyri* 65. London, 1998, 105 (Recto, col.1, ll.30–4), 109 (English translation). Maltomini suggested the 'emerald' referred to the 'greening bed of Osiris', *ibid.* 117 (31–2). For the *Ibhet*-stone

associated with Osiris's tomb in the New Year ritual, see above chapter 5, n.13. For the importance of inscribing sacred texts on a 'green stone' in ancient Egypt and alchemy, see Roberts, *op.cit.* 219–20. See also above n.7 for the priestly origins of both royal rites and private magical spells.

17 This quest to reveal the hidden things pervaded the Egyptian temple mysteries. Thus, in Hathor's Graeco-Roman cult at Dendara, a sacred *menou*-drink was offered to the goddess, associated with her intoxicating power which 'opens the interior' *(wen-khen)* and makes manifest 'truth'. See F. Daumas, *RdE* 22 (1970), 76, who referred to Plutarch's statement that wine revealed the secret recesses of the soul. Cf. also the Theban Amun as the 'hidden' god whose concealed *Ba*-power manifests in the threefold cosmos in Ramessid Amun theology (see J. Assmann, 'Primat und Transzendenz: Struktur und Genese der ägyptischen Vorstellung eines "Höchsten Wesens", in W. Westendorf [ed.], *Aspekte der spätägyptischen Religion*. Wiesbaden, 1979, 7–42). Assmann considered this Amun-theology to have been an influential current flowing through into later alchemy, Hermeticism and Neoplatonism (*ibid.* 38).

18 From Plutarch's 'Dialogue on Love' (*Moralia* 9, section 762A). See also above chapter 5, n.1.

19 *Ibid.* (section 765A). For the statement about the sun as Eros associated with Aphrodite (section 764B).

20 For this Osirian oracle, see Berthelot, *Alchimistes grecs* 3, 103. Discussed also by M.-L. von Franz, *Alchemy: An Introduction to the Symbolism and the Psychology*. Toronto, 1980, 82–6.

Olympiodorus's 'soldering gold' treatise forms a section in a longer work entitled *On the Sacred Art*. Scholars differ as to when he lived. Some identify him with a sixth-century follower of Plato by the same name, who taught in Alexandria, others with a fifth-century historian, diplomat and native of Thebes called Olympiodorus.

21 Berthelot, *op.cit.* 103–4. I am indebted to the late Dr Ulla Jeyes for verifying Berthelot's translation of the Greek text and her comments, especially as it is translated differently by von Franz, *op.cit.* 82, and Vereno, *Studien*, 80–1.

22 For scholarly dismissal of Olympiodorus as a charlatan, see Kingsley, *Ancient Philosophy*, 61 (with further references). Kingsley rightly rejected this view, noting the 'self-conscious principle of composition' in Olympiodorus's discussion of the Presocratics preserved in his 'soldering gold' treatise, *ibid.* 64.

23 The ancient Egyptian use of 'chrysocolla' (or ground copper carbonate), mixed with glue or gum, for joining together gold granules or larger sheets of gold in the method known as colloidal hard soldering is well described by C. Aldred, *Jewels of the Pharaohs: Egyptian Jewelry of the Dynastic Period*. London, 1978, 28. The term 'chrysocolla' (which in Greek means literally 'gold glue') was applied by ancient writers to various materials used in soldering gold. For its association with *wadj* in ancient Egypt, often identified with 'malachite', see *Lexikon der Ägyptologie* 1, col. 971. The term can also refer to various copper-based substances. For Hathor's links with copper-mining regions, see Pinch, *Votive Offerings*, 49, 59–70.

24 Plutarch, *op.cit.* (section 765B–C).

25 For Aphrodite residing at the place where the immortal is blended with the mortal, see section 764D.

26 For Aphrodite's identification with the moon and her ineffectiveness without Eros, see section 764D. For Greek notions of the female as 'cold' and 'passive', see above chapter 2, n.21.

27 The tangled complex of Egyptian Eye goddess symbolism in the Hellenistic world and Isis as a lunar goddess is well discussed by Howard Jackson, with reference to the role of Isis in the *Koré Kosmou*, see *CdE* 61/121 (1986), 116–35, esp.123ff. As Jackson noted, it is the association of Isis with the sun that is repeatedly stressed in late Egyptian sources (*ibid.* 130). See also below chapter 10, n.18. Cf. Joan Engelsman's comment that Hathor 'could not be a great goddess of the Hellenistic period because she is so strongly identified as a cow' (see J.C. Engelsman, *The Feminine Dimension of the Divine*. Wilmette, Illinois, 1987, 70, with n.67). She particularly noted Plutarch's antipathy to Egypt's animal deities (*ibid.* 166, n.67).

Chapter 8 (pages 85–94)

1 For discussion of these episodes, see M. Barker, *Temenos Academy Review* 9 (2006), 104–5, who links them with power shifts in the Second Temple period when the prerogatives of the 'sons of Aaron' and 'Mosaic law' prevailed, with Miriam separated off from the priesthood. Referring to the curious Miriam episode, Barker wrote: 'Moses represents the Law, Aaron the high priesthood and so the temple, and Miriam represents someone—perhaps an office or institution—that disappears from

the picture.' She suggests Miriam may have represented Wisdom in the First Temple rites (*ibid.* 105, with n.16).

2 See Haskins, *Mary Magdalen*, 23–6, for the different 'anointing' accounts in the canonical gospels and the conflation of the different women performing the rite in Christian tradition.

3 According to first-century Jewish rabbis, the verses were collected together by court officials in Hezekiah's reign, who attributed them to Solomon (see Keel, *Hohelied*, 9). Most commentators date the song's composition, or at least the compilation of the final text, no earlier than the Second Temple era, see *OBC*, 429 (with bibliography, *ibid.* 433, 1335). But there was probably an oral tradition long before the songs were gathered into their canonical form.

4 See Haskins, *op.cit.* 63–7, for Hippolytus's Christian interpretation. Jewish and Christian commentators in Alexandria favoured an allegorical approach, influenced also by the revered first-century Rabbi Aqiba. Amidst the controversy in Judaism as to whether the *Song of Songs* was a sacred text at all, he declared, 'All the writings are holy but the *Song of Songs* is the Holy of Holies.' Cf., however, Theodore of Mopsuestia's view that it was a secular love poem written on the occasion of Solomon's marriage to Pharaoh's daughter see D. Z. Zaharopoulos, *Theodore of Mopsuestia on the Bible: A Study of His Old Testament Exegesis*. Mahwah, 1989, 49–52. Like other Syrian church fathers Theodore refused to interpret the *Song of Songs* as an allegory, though his radical views were condemned by the Second Council of

Constantinople. Evidently, though, this highly influential Syrian commentator recognized its connection with Egypt. A similar 'secular' approach is widely favoured by modern-day commentators, see A. Brenner (*OBC*, 429): 'The songs/poems are secular love poems about heterosexual, erotic, passionate relationships.'

5 See below, n.10. For the importance of Pharaoh's daughter in the conception of Solomon's temple, see C.V. Camp, *Wise, Strange and Holy: The Strange Woman and the Making of the Bible*. Sheffield, 2000, 182, though she also interpreted this Egyptian presence negatively, stating it meant that 'The temple is at best a tarnished crown to Solomon's wisdom.' She also noted how this foreign influence 'sets the seeds of its destruction' (*ibid.* 171). Camp also observed how it was 'no accident' that Sheba's story followed closely after mention of 'Pharaoh's daughter' (*ibid.* 176), linking both women with the 'seductive strangeness' of foreign women and the female embodiment of Wisdom in the 'strange woman'. She saw the Queen of Sheba as uniting both 'wisdom' and 'strangeness' in her person. The situation seems to be more complex, however, since Solomon's temple was built with the help of Phoenician craftsmen, coming from a region with close cultural and trade ties to Egypt (see below chapter 9, n.27).

6 J.S. Kloppenborg, *HTR* 75 (1982), 78. Kloppenborg's discussion (*ibid.* 57–84) developed Burton Mack's study of the Sophia (Wisdom) tradition in Hellenistic Judaism, in which he saw the influence of Egyptian goddesses, especially Maat and Isis (see Mack, *Logos*

und Sophia, 34–42, 185–8). Similarly, W. Horbury (*OBC*, 659) noted Egyptian influence in the *Wisdom of Solomon*. For the influence of the therapeutic Isis cults and the emergence of Wisdom (Sophia) in Hellenistic Alexandria and Philo's work, see also Witt, *Isis*, 194–5.

7 For the use of the Egyptian sun disk and scarab in royal Judaean tradition, particularly associated with the solar falcon god Horus of Edfu, as divine royal protector, see J.G. Taylor, *Yahweh and the Sun: Biblical and Archaeological Evidence for Sun Worship in Ancient Israel*. Sheffield, 1993, 42–56, 261. Taylor noted the difficulties of interpreting the meaning of this Egyptian solar symbolism within the Judaean context.

8 For similarities between Amarna hymns and Psalm 104, see *ibid.* 225–30. Taylor observed 'the remarkable availability of the Egyptian tradition' within the context of the worship of Yahweh centuries after the time of Akhenaten (*ibid.* 229, with n.2). For the serpent healing staff of Moses (Exodus 4:2–4 and 7:8–12) and its links with Egyptian practices, see Ritner, '"And each staff transformed into a snake"', 205–25. He also noted how Moses set up a bronze serpent on a pole to heal snakebite (Numbers 21:8–9) and how the revered serpent staff placed in the Jerusalem temple became an object of worship before being removed (2 Kings:18:4). Referring to these episodes, Ritner wrote: 'In this direct adoption of iconography, healing methodology and temple setting, Israelite tradition enshrines the staff of Egyptian divinity' (*ibid.* 217).

9 See O. Keel, *Die Weisheit spielt vor Gott*. Freiburg, 1974, 63–8. For the Eye of Re as the instrument of Re's activity in the world, see Roberts, *Hathor Rising*, 8–9 *passim*. For the playful role of daughter goddesses in the royal solar cult, see *ibid.* 54–64. For the Egyptian conceptions of Maat underlying Wisdom's role here in Proverbs, see also C. Kayatz, *Studien zu Proverbien 1–9: Eine Form- und Motivgeschichtliche Untersuchung unter Einbeziehung ägyptischen Vergleichsmaterials*. Neukirchen-Vluyn, 1966, 93–119, and Burton Mack (*op.cit.* 34–8). For the problematic translation of the Hebrew word 'master craftsman' in Proverbs 8, see K.T. Aitken, *OBC*, 411 (though without mention of possible Egyptian influence in this section of Proverbs). See, however, John Collins' brief statement that Wisdom in Proverbs 8 'may be influenced by Egyptian prototypes' (*OBC*, 682). Biblical commentators are extremely cautious about acknowledging Egyptian influence in the Hebrew Bible and New Testament.

10 For Solomon's marriage to Pharaoh's daughter, see 1 Kings 3:1; 7:8; 9:16, 24; 11:1; 2 Chronicles 8:11. Walter Dietrich (*OBC*, 236) interpreted the marriage as 'diplomatic', noting that an Ammonite became the mother of Solomon's heir, not an Egyptian. For her connection with Solomon's temple, see above, n.5. For Theodore of Mopsuestia's view that the *Song of Songs* was composed as a love poem celebrating Solomon's marriage to Pharaoh's daughter, see above, n.4.

11 Cf. Stephen Smalley's entry in *OCB*, 375, where he notes the importance of two second-century papyri from Egypt for establishing

141

the gospel's likely date of composition, i.e. at the beginning of the second century, and probably earlier. Cf. also the four further papyri discovered at Oxyryhnchus edited by W.E.H. Cockle, dating to the third century and preserving fragments of John's gospel (see M.W. Haslam [*et al.*,], *The Oxyrhynchus Papyri* 65. London, 1998, 10–20 [with further references to the other 23 published papyri preserving versions of the gospel]).

12 The importance of this exact 'sixth-hour' parallelism was emphasized by R.H. Lightfoot, *St. John's Gospel: A Commentary.* Oxford, 1956, 122, though not in connection with Egypt.

13 See C.H. Dodd, *The Interpretation of the Fourth Gospel.* Cambridge, 1954, 313. He noted how the Jewish prophets stigmatized the 'adulterous' syncretistic cults of Samaria in which worship of the God of Israel was combined with pagan elements. For Egyptian cults in Samaria, see Bricault, *RICIS* 2, 510–11; Witt, *Isis*, 195, 258, 322, n.18. It is beyond the scope of this book to consider how far the episode of the Samaritan woman beside the well relates also to the teachings of Simon Magus in Samaria, as preserved by Hippolytus. These included awakening the 'seventh power' within the human being and also knowledge of the eternal 'Standing One', who 'stands above in the unbegotten power' and 'stands below in the stream of the waters'. These themes are also strongly interwoven with ideas about the 'fallen' feminine hypostasis of the divine, paralleling the 'fallen' Sophia in gnostic sources who is in need of redemption. For a summary of Simon's teachings, see Welburn, *Gnosis*, 156–7, 177(17).

14 For 'seven' symbolizing 'rebirth' in mystery religions, see Reitzenstein, *Hellenistic Mystery-Religions*, 312–13. Cf. also the passage about rebirth in Treatise 13 of the *Corpus Hermeticum* in which the arrival of truth as 'the seventh' power signifies that 'the good has been fulfilled' and presages the initiate's rebirth see Copenhaver, *Hermetica*, 51 (9–10), 190. For the parallels between John's gospel and Hermetic writings, see Dodd, *op.cit.* 10–53 *passim.*

15 This Egyptian tradition of seven 'utterances' is discussed by Ritner, *Magical Practice*, 46–7. For the seven phases of Memphite regeneration rites in Seti I's temple at Abydos, see Roberts, *My Heart My Mother*, 58–88. For seven as the Egyptian magical number of rebirth, see F.R. Herbin, *Le livre de parcourir l'éternité.* Leuven, 1994, 335. See also above, chapter 2, n.3. For seven as an organizing principle underlying Egyptian royal temple inscriptions, see Mathieu, *Poésie amoureuse*, 215, with n.695.

16 For the *Memphite Theology*, see Roberts, *op.cit.* 14–20, with further references.

17 J.P. Allen, *Genesis in Egypt: The Philosophy of Ancient Egyptian Creation Accounts.* New Haven, 1988, 46.

18 See Frankfort, *Kingship*, 29. For Ptah's mode of creation associated with the Logos doctrine, see also E. Iversen, *Egyptian and Hermetic Doctrine.* Copenhagen, 1984, 12.

19 For the absence of references to Egypt, cf. *OBC*, 833–4, 961–3. The prologue's themes of the descent of the cosmic Logos and the 'seeking' of a dwelling on earth' are also characteristic of Jewish Wisdom theology. As Burton Mack pointed out, however, underlying this Jewish

Wisdom theology is also 'Isis-Wisdom' and the Egyptian *Ba*-theology of heavenly deities descending to unite with their temple images in 'bird' form, so that the temples become their 'resting places' (*Logos und Sophia*, 41–2). For Egyptian influence in early Christianity, see below, n.20.

20 See J.M. Hull, *Hellenistic Magic and the Synoptic Tradition.* London, 1974, 110–11. He drew extensively on F. Preisigke's earlier important research into Egyptian kingship and its influence on early Christianity (*Die Gotteskraft der frühchristlichen Zeit.* Berlin and Leipzig, 1922). Preisigke considered Egypt to be the main source for the early Christian outlook, noting how early Christians were firmly rooted in the religious practices of the pagan world (*ibid.* 5). Cf. also Andrew Welburn's discussion of Hull's views (*Beginnings of Christianity*, 270–5). Whilst he accepted that ancient Near Eastern general notions of cosmic kingship helped to shape John's gospel, he also minimized the specific Egyptian contribution (*ibid.* 274–5). For parallels between Egyptian healing practices and Jesus's healing miracles, see Ritner, *Magical Practice*, 90–1. For the Osirian mythic roots of Christianity, see R.G. Bonnel and V.A. Tobin, 'Christ and Osiris: A Comparative Study' in Sarah Israelit-Groll (ed.), *Pharaonic Egypt, the Bible and Christianity.* Jerusalem, 1985, 1–29.

21 For the difficulties of recognizing 'transformed Egyptian material' when expressed in a Greek idiom, see Iversen, *Myth of Egypt*, 39–41. Iversen also noted the loss of the 'magical' dimension when Egypt's 'mythical' truth began to be interpreted allegorically, which he described as an 'utterly

un-Egyptian' mode of interpretation created by Greek philosophy and poetry (*ibid.* 40). He maintained that there was far greater direct Egyptian inspiration and influence in Greek philosophy and thought than is generally acknowledged. Cf. also Garth Fowden's remarks about the 'paring down' of Egyptian mythological symbolism in Graeco-Egyptian magic (*Egyptian Hermes*, 66–7). He wrote: 'What we are seeing here is not a cultural break, but precisely that "rendering plausible" of Egyptian material for the benefit of a Greek audience' who might have had difficulties relating to the 'plethora of arcane divinities one encounters in the Pharaonic texts'. His words hold true for Egyptian influence in early Christianity.

Chapter 9 *(pages 95–108)*

1 St. Augustine, *The Retractations* (Ch.12). Translation from Sr. M.I. Bogan, *Saint Augustine: The Retractations*. (The Fathers of the Church series, vol. 60). Washington, 1968, 52. I am grateful to Jack Herbert for this reference.

2 For an English translation of the treatises, see J.M. Robinson (ed.), *The Nag Hammadi Library in English*. Leiden, New York, Copenhagen and Cologne, 1988 (hereafter cited as *NHL*). For the events surrounding the discovery at Nag Hammadi, see *ibid.* 22–6.

3 The *Gospel of Philip* (Codex II,3) is translated by Wesley W. Isenberg in *NHL*, 141–60. It is now in the Coptic Museum, Cairo. See also Bentley Layton's translation, which includes useful thematic headings, *Gnostic Scriptures*, 329–53. For this relationship of Jesus and Mary Magdalene, *NHL*, 148 (63–4). The literature about the gospel is

extensive, see H.-M. Schenke (*et al.*,), *Nag Hammadi Deutsch 1: NHC I,1–V,1*. Berlin–New York, 2001, 183–4, for a bibliography (hereafter cited as *NHD* 1). It is beyond the scope of this book to enter into a detailed analysis of the gospel. My aim here is to present a meaningful Egyptian ritual context for its sacramental 'mystery'.

4 For Syria, more specifically Antioch, as the gospel's possible place of origin, see Gaffron, *Studien*, 69. For a less specific Syrian origin, see also Isenberg, *NHL*, 141; Schenke, *NHD* 1,187 (east Syria, possibly Edessa). Dating when the original text was written is extremely difficult. A third-century dating is based on the assumption that the gospel is a gnostic Valentinian work and postdates Valentinus's lifetime in the second century. Bentley Layton, for example, suggests some sayings may derive from Valentinus himself (*op.cit.* 325). For a second-century dating, see Gaffron, *op.cit.* 70; Schenke, *NHD* 1, 187. Likewise, Einar Thomassen pointed out that the gospel's author 'appears to draw on older materials and traditions', though still saw the gospel as conforming to Oriental Valentinian teaching (see Thomassen, 'How Valentinian is the Gospel of Philip?', 279). Here it is worth noting Layton's comment about the myth of the soul underlying the Thomas literature, namely that it was 'to some extent compatible with more complex systems like the gnostic or Valentinian myth', but it does not 'necessarily presuppose such a system' (*op.cit.* 360). His words apply equally to Philip's gospel, for which there is also no need to presuppose a developed Valentinian system. As Andrew

Welburn tellingly observed, there are no allusions to the complex Valentinian aeonology in Philip's gospel (*Gnosis*, 268–9). He plausibly suggested it was a 'tradition of Christianity that was rooted in the Mysteries', that was subsequently taken up by Valentinian groups, though he saw Mandaean and Iranian, rather than Egyptian, influence in the gospel. The fact, though, that the Egyptian god Ptah appears as the Mandaean demiurge Ptahil (see Jonas, *Gnostic Religion*, 98), suggests that the Mandaeans themselves were not immune to Egyptian traditions, even if they evaluated these negatively in terms of the material world.

5 *NHL*, 155 (77). See also *ibid.* 142 (52). The 'world' here is not 'world' in a gnostic or ascetic anti-material sense, but rather represents everything that is opposed both to God and to those who belong to God. See *OBC*, 1276, for a similar conception of 'the world' in the First Epistle of John.

6 For fire and the creation of beauty, see *NHL*, 150 (67). For freedom through love, see *ibid.* 155 (77).

7 *Ibid.* 147 (62). Cf. also 153 (74) for the anointing of Christ in the bridal chamber.

8 *Ibid.* 145 (59).

9 This aretalogy, in which Greek and Egyptian elements are combined, is inscribed on a white marble stela found in the Iseum at Cyme and is now in the Izmir Museum, see Bricault, *RICIS 2*, 422–4 (302/0204) for the Greek text and a French translation, with relevant bibliography. Bricault suggested the text was probably composed in the third or second century BCE. For these lines about the Isiac genealogy, *ibid.* 422–3 (ll.5–8). A Memphite prototype for the aretalogy, anchored in

143

royal and Maat ideology, was proposed by Bergman, *Ich bin Isis*, 218–19, *passim*. He suggested it reflected the concern of Memphite priestly circles to interpret this theology for the wider Hellenistic world. This Memphite origin is accepted by Bricault, *op.cit.* 424; Fowden, *Egyptian Hermes*, 46–7. The scholarly debate concerning its Egyptian or Greek origins is well summarized by Žabkar, *Hymns to Isis*, 135–7. He considered Ptolemaic hymns to Isis at Philae may have been the main influence, pointing to thematic similarities between the Philae Isis hymns and the Greek aretalogies (*ibid.* 158–9). For an English translation of the Cyme aretalogy, see *ibid.* 140–1.

10 For this mythic prototype in Egypt, consisting of two sisters associated with a contrasting female figure, or as a mother and two daughters, see Troy, *Patterns of Queenship*, 48–9. She emphasized the importance of the family structure to express regeneration, noting how the aspects of mother, wife, sister and daughter provided the 'cyclical continuum that ensures the renewal of the life force in the family, and the resurrection of the individual' (*ibid.* 50). For these aspects embodied by Hathorian queens (see *ibid.* 53–72). For their transformational significance in the diurnal solar cycle, see Roberts, *Hathor Rising*, 66–8. Einar Thomassen interpreted the *Gospel of Philip*'s generational theme metaphysically: 'Thus we are to understand the spiritual life which has been realized with the advent of the Savior as one in which the redeemed are simultaneously children, partners in a spiritual marriage, and fathers of spiritual offspring, in a mode of being where there is no distinction between these roles' (*op.cit.* 272).

11 For a detailed discussion of the room's decoration, see Kraeling, *Excavations*, 40–88, with pls.17–45; Hopkins, *Dura-Europos*, 109–17. Contrary to Kraeling, who noted there was space on the wall for other figures, Hopkins considered only three Marys were depicted beside the sarcophagus (*ibid.* 114).

12 Whilst accepting Kraeling's association of the south wall with holy oil and anointing (Kraeling, *op.cit.* 151, 190), Hopkins suggested that the scroll of the New Testament would have been placed in the niche, with the oil kept together with the eucharistic sacraments on the ledge below the niche (*op.cit.* 115–16). Interestingly, Hopkins saw this niche and its paintings as the focal point of the entire room (*op.cit.* 115–16). Nevertheless, neither author linked the architectural and iconographic details on the west wall (baptism) and south wall (anointing) with Philip-centred traditions in which baptism (water) and anointing (fire) are differentiated rites. Kraeling's interpretation of the room, which was influenced by the Syrian baptismal liturgy (*op.cit.* 195), saw anointing with oil as a preparatory action before baptism and he maintained that the niche scenes on the south wall were only concerned with the baptism rite (*op.cit.* 195), hence his description of the room as a 'baptistery'. He did, however, link the niche scenes with the resurrection scene directly opposite on the north wall. As such, it is a decorative scheme more in tune with Philip's gospel, which specifically associates 'anointing' with 'naming' and the resurrection (see also below, Epilogue, n.14). For oil protecting against hostile powers, see below, Epilogue, n.11.

13 For this inscription, see Hopkins, *op.cit.* 91, 96, 115–16.

14 *NHL*, 153 (74). Cf. also 'From the olive tree comes the anointing, and from the anointing comes resurrection' (*NHL*, 153 [73]). On the basis of a fragment of parchment discovered in debris a short distance away from the house church, which preserved Greek extracts from the *Diatessaron* (composed by Tatian in Syria in the latter part of the second century as a synthesis of the four gospels into a single narrative), Hopkins suggested Dura's Christianity to be based on Tatian's work (see Hopkins, *op.cit.* 93, 108–9). Yet the paintings and lay-out of the so-called 'baptistery' are more consistent with a Philip-centred sacramental tradition, especially the location of the three Marys on the north wall, specifically across from the south wall niche that probably contained the oil.

15 *Ibid.* 150 (67).

16 *Ibid.*

17 See E. Segelberg's study of the sacraments as a fivefold structure, *Numen* 7 (1960), 189–200, esp.191, 198. W. Isenberg interprets the sacraments as 'five stages of a complete initiation' (*NHL*, 140). Similarly, Schenke, *NHD* 1, 191. See, however, D.H. Tripp, 'The "Sacramental System" of the Gospel of Philip' in E.A. Livingstone (ed.), *Studia Patristica* 17 (1). Oxford, 1982, 251–60. He considered the 'mystery' to be threefold, namely 'baptism', 'anointing' and 'eucharist', with baptism and anointing representing the 'redemption rite' and the eucharist representing the 'bride-chamber', see *ibid.* 256. Egyptian influence in the gospel has never been pursued ever since H.-G. Gaffron's analysis of the

gospel's sacraments, in which he discounted Schenke's observations about the Egyptian 'colour' in the gospel (see Gaffron, *op.cit.* 27). Whilst Gaffron recognized there was a close connection between Egypt and Syria in the second century (*op.cit.* 70), he rejected Near Eastern or ancient Egyptian influence (*op.cit.* 199). Curiously, whilst noting that the author's predilection to think in opposites was neither specifically gnostic nor Valentinian (*op.cit.* 15), he still interpreted the gospel primarily as a branch from the Valentinian stem (*op.cit.* 171). However, he was unable to offer any explanation for the fivefold sacramental sequence.

18 Cf. also the five books or 'Scrolls', including the *Song of Songs*, which are gathered together in one collection near the end of the Hebrew Bible. The important non-canonical *1 Enoch* is also arranged as a pentateuch. Thus, the *Gospel of Philip*'s five sacraments follow a recognizable Jewish 'literary' form, but their ritual content, unlike anything in Mosaic law, conveys a new ritual paradigm for Judaism.

19 For the *Apocryphon of John*'s five seals, see *NHL*, 122: 'And I raised him up and sealed him in the light of the water with five seals, in order that death might not have power over him from this time on.' See also R. Charron, *VigChr.* 59 (2005), 453–4 (and below chapter 10, n.29). For ancient Egyptian influence in the *Apocryphon*, see below chapter 10, n.14.

20 For the introduction of the Isis cults in Antioch, see G. Downey, *A History of Antioch in Syria from Seleucus to the Arab Conquest.* Princeton, 1961, 91–2. An overly cautious view of early Isis cults in Antioch before the Roman period

is adopted by Dunand, *Culte d'Isis*, 123–4, though, as Dunand noted, the evidence concerning the Isis cults in Syria is very scattered (*ibid.* 125) and it is difficult to know how they actually functioned. For the Memphite background of the Isis aretalogy, see above n.9. For the Red Sea trading links in the Ptolemaic era, see Fraser, *Ptolemaic Alexandria* 1, 176–80. For early Ptolemaic connections with Antioch, see also A.K. Bowman, *Egypt after the Pharaohs.* London, 1986, 155–6.

21 The finds relating to the Isis and Sarapis cults in Syria, Phoenicia and Palestine are listed (with relevant bibliography) in Bricault, *RICIS* 2, 501–10; *Atlas de la diffusion des cultes Isiaques (IVe S. av. J.-C.–IVe S. apr. J.-C.).* Paris, 2001, 70–6. For the second-century BCE priest in charge of incubatory dreams at Athens, see Dunand, *op.cit.* 140, 155.

22 The mosaic is now in the Hatay Archaeological Museum, Antakya (Inv. 849). It was first published by Levi, *Antioch Mosaic Pavements* 2, pl.8b. For the Isiac context of the scene, see *ibid.* 1, 49–50. It is difficult to date the mosaic precisely since no other material was found in its vicinity.

23 The evidence is discussed by F.W. Norris, *HTR* 75 (1982), 189–207. He also noted the discovery of a statue of Sarapis at Seleucia, the port city on the coast near Antioch. The statue is now in the Antakya Museum, *ibid.* 194. See also above n.21.

24 The mosaic is now in the Princeton University Art Museum (Acc. no. 1965–217), see Levi, *op.cit.* 2, pl.33a. The mosaic's diagonal patch is a repair to the extensive damage caused when a pipeline was installed through the house. For the mosaic's association

with the Isis mysteries, see Levi, *op.cit.* 1, 163–4; *Berytus* 7(1) (1942), 19–36, 54–5, with pl.1(1); F.C. Albertson, *JAC* 38 (1995), 129–30. Levi's interpretation is retained in Princeton's Antioch exhibition catalogue, see S.A. Takács, 'Pagan Cults at Antioch' in C. Kondoleon (ed.), *Antioch: The Lost Ancient City.* Princeton, 2000, 199, with reference also to the initiation of Lucius in the *Golden Ass.* Similarly, F. Le Corsu, *Isis: Mythe et Mystères.* Paris, 1977, 238, who suggests it depicts the Isiac initiate's coming forth from the death chamber accompanied by the high priestess of Isis. How far the Graeco-Roman Isis mysteries retained genuine links with ancient Egyptian traditions has been much debated among scholars, see Quaegebeur, 'Diodore I, 20 et les mystères d'Osiris', 160, with n.21 (including extensive bibliography).

25 See Norris, *op.cit.* 189–207, esp. 201ff. Similarly, Griffiths, *Isis-Book*, 300. S. Campbell, *The Mosaics of Antioch.* Toronto, 1988, 75–6, with pl.212, simply refers to the possibility the figure may be either Demeter or Isis. In contrast to Levi's dating of the mosaic to *c.*193–235 CE, Campbell proposed a mid-third century date for the House of the Mysteries (*ibid.* 74). That the Greeks identified Isis with Demeter is well-known (see Griffiths, *op.cit.* 151). But it is Isis who is closely linked with Hermes rather than Demeter (see below, n.26). For representations from Egypt of the snake-bodied Isis-Thermouthis or Isis-Renenutet shown with Demeter's torch, see D.M. Bailey, *JEA* 93 (2007), 267, with n.21, 269, with n.31. For Egyptian rituals of 'lighting a flame' for the solar Eye goddess, symbolizing rebirth and return from the Osirian realm, see Roberts, *My Heart My Mother*, 83–5, 188.

26 Diodorus's statement is the starting-point for an insightful discussion by Jan Quaegebeur, *op.cit.* 157–81. Noting how the statement had received little scholarly attention, he traced the connection of Isis and Hermes (Thoth) through into ancient Egyptian sources, especially in two late-period funerary texts known as the *First and Second Letters for Breathing* attributed to Isis and Thoth respectively. See also Fowden, *Egyptian Hermes*, 32–3, 35, for Isis and Hermes in the Hermetic-alchemical tradition. For a second-century BCE dedication to Isis, Sarapis and Hermes at Alexandria, depicting an ibis bird (sacred to Thoth) holding the god's healing snake-staff (caduceus), see Ritner, '"And each staff transformed into a snake"', 216. For Thoth and Hermes in the context of healing, see *ibid.* 216. For a much earlier representation of Thoth holding a snake-staff in Seti I's temple at Abydos, see fig.66; Roberts, *op.cit.* 63. For citations of Isis and Hermes in Greek hymns to Isis, see D. Levi, *Berytus* 7(1) (1942), 20–1.

27 For Thoth-Hermes in Philo's work, see Baumgarten, *Philo of Byblos*, 68–72; Fowden, *op.cit.* 216–7. For Philo's knowledge of the Hermopolitan cosmogony, see Baumgarten, *op.cit.* 110, 115–17, 120–1, 130. The extent to which Phoenicians incorporated the 'content' of Egyptian religion is often played down by scholars. Cf., however, a scarab discovered in Sardinia which combines a Phoenician inscription with Hermopolitan elements in its decoration (see Vittmann, *Ägypten und die Fremden*, 79–80, with

fig. 41), which Vittmann discussed in connection with Philo's cosmogony. However, he regarded Egyptian influence in Phoenicia to be more within the sphere of 'personal piety' and 'folk beliefs' than in the official state religion, (*ibid.* 81–2). For the adaptation of Egyptian forms in Syrian-Phoenician art, see also H. Frankfort, *The Art and Architecture of the Ancient Orient*. Harmondsworth, 1969, 194–5. Frankfort observed how the Phoenicians, 'a people without pictorial traditions', drew on ancient Egypt's 'mature school of art' in order to express their own religious conceptions. Certainly, there were close ties between Phoenicia, Cyprus and Egypt in the first millennium, fostered also by the copper trade (see Vittmann, *op.cit.* 44–83). This would have helped to make the region receptive to the diffusion of Egyptian cult knowledge and Hermeticism in the Hellenistic era. (See also below, Epilogue, n.3).

28 For a detailed description of the mosaic's colours, including the red cloth over the initiate's shoulder, see Levi, *Berytus* 7(1) (1942), 28–9. In a personal communication to me, Michael Padgett, curator of ancient art at Princeton's Art Museum, kindly confirmed there are traces of red still visible on the cloth.

29 See above, chapter 5, n.22, for the ancient Egyptian 'going forth' in a red robe from the Osirian tomb. For the importance of a red/purple robe as the symbol of a world or spiritual ruler in the Hellenistic era, see Vereno, *Studien*, 252, with n.304. He also cited examples of a purple robe being worn in the cult of Isis. Cf. a statue from Cyrene showing a snake-crowned Isiac female figure wearing a purple

robe over a green chiton. The tunic has bands criss-crossing it like mummy bands, see Levi, *op.cit.* 24, with pl.2(1). In the ancient world purple could encompass a range of different shades, including a deep, almost crimson, colour. It was also sometimes associated with the colour of blood. This ambiguity is evident in Egyptian descriptions of the 'red cloth' associated with Sekhmet, which is sometimes described as 'violet', see Goyon, *Rituel*, 54 (18).

30 For this comment on the hymn's 'charm', see *OBC*, 1327. For a translation of the Syriac version, which includes details omitted in the Greek version, see P.-H. Poirier, *L'Hymne de la perle des Actes de Thomas: Introduction Texte –Traduction Commentaire*. Louvain-la-Neuve, 1981, 343–8. Poirier includes an extensive survey of earlier scholarship and commentary. For translations based on the Greek version, see J.K. Elliott, *The Apocryphal New Testament: A Collection of Apocryphal Christian Literature in an English Translation*. Oxford, 1993, 488–91 (with bibliography, *ibid.* 445–6); Layton, *Gnostic Scriptures*, 371–5. My summary is based on the Syriac version.

31 The hymn's negativity towards Egypt was noted by Poirier, who contrasted it with the positive approach to Egypt found in the *Corpus Hermeticum* and other writings (*op.cit.* 416–17). He was perplexed about the Syriac version's description of the youth, whom the prince encountered in Egypt, as an 'anointed one' (see *op.cit.* 421–22). But it suggests the author's concern with ancient anointing rites, albeit within the context of hostility to Egyptian royal traditions. Cf. the remarks

146

of Hans Jonas about the tendency in gnostic allegory to subvert ancient knowledge: 'Instead of taking over the value-system of the traditional myth … it tries, not to demonstrate agreement, but to shock by blatantly subverting the meaning of the most firmly established, and preferably also the most revered, elements of tradition', (see *Gnostic Religion*, 92). Some scholars see the hymn as a completely gnostic work. For its Iranian and Manichaean links, and subsequent inclusion in the *Acts of Thomas*, see Poirier, *op.cit.* 312–20.

32 For the gospel's themes arranged around its sacramental 'mystery', see Welburn, *Gnosis*, 262. His approach differs from that of scholars who downplay the gospel's sacramental aspects. See, for example, M.L. Turner, *The Gospel according to Philip: The Sources and Coherence of an Early Christian Collection*. Leiden, New York and Cologne, 1996, 259, who refers to the gospel as a 'tinker's collection of odds and ends' gathered together as 'materials' useful for developing further insights and approaches. Turner minimized the sacramental aspect (*ibid*. 178). Cf.also R.McL. Wilson's entry on the Nag Hammadi Library in *OCB*, 544, in which he describes the gospel as 'a rather rambling discourse whose continuity seems largely due to catchwords or the association of ideas'. Wesley Isenberg expressed a similar view in *NHL*, 139–40, describing the gospel as 'eccentrically arranged'. See, however, Layton (*Gnostic Scriptures*, 326), who wrote: 'Especially striking are the many references to sacraments ("mysteries")'.

33 Doresse, *Secret Books*, 225. Cf. also the comments by J.S. Kloppenborg about the underlying Isis-Horus mythic cycle in the *Wisdom of Solomon* which influenced the figure of Sophia (Wisdom) without her being recognizably Egyptianized, thus making it attractive to Hellenized Jews. He wrote: 'The biblical account is thereby allowed to participate in the *mythic power* of the symbol of a savior deity, but without acquiring the explicit aspects of the Egyptian myth' (see *HTR* 75 [1982], 72).

34 For Egyptian influence in the development of early Christian art, including depictions of the 'Raising of Lazarus' which appear from the third century onwards, see F.C. Albertson, *JAC* 38 (1995), 123–32, with particular reference to the Antioch mosaic of the *mors voluntaria* (fig. 65) as the prototype for the Lazarus scenes.

35 Quoted from D. Frankfurter, *Religion in Roman Egypt: Assimilation and Resistance*. Princeton, 1998, 266. A similar point is made by Robert Ritner regarding the reappearance of Egyptian healing and magical practices in Coptic literature. He wrote: 'With the Christianization of Egypt, ancient concepts were adapted to the new faith' (see *Magical Practice*, 90). Cf. also Witt, *Isis*, 184, who noted that 'The ritual of the Christian Church owes a considerable and unacknowledged debt to the Egyptian religion that preceded it in the Graeco-Roman world.' Witt particularly referred to the importance of the New Year Festival of Isis on 5 March, with its water rites of renewal, which he noted were echoed in the Orthodox liturgy.

36 See above, n.1.

Chapter 10 *(pages 109–119)*

1 Berthelot, *Alchimistes grecs* 3, 383 (2).

2 Epiphanius (*Panarion* 1.26.13, 2). See F. Williams (ed.), *The Panarion of Epiphanius of Salamis Book 1 (Sects 1–46)*. Leiden, New York, Copenhagen, Cologne, 1987, 94. The ascetically-inclined Epiphanius is hostile to the group using this Philip gospel, whom he had encountered in Egypt and identified as licentious gnostics. The influence of Philip-centred traditions is omitted from the discussion of early Christianity in Egypt by B.A. Pearson (*Gnosticism and Christianity in Roman and Coptic Egypt*. New York and London, 2004, 1–81), who briefly describes the *Gospel of Philip* as a third-century work from Syria incorporating Valentinian writings (see *ibid*. 68). It should be noted that the 'confusions' between the apostle Philip and the evangelist Philip who appears in Acts, as well as the various traditions associated with Philip in uncanonical writings, are extremely difficult to disentangle, and there is no scholarly consensus about their relationship.

3 For a detailed discussion of Hathor as the goddess with 'four faces' in Graeco-Roman temples, see Philippe Derchain's fine monograph, *Hathor Quadrifrons*, *passim*.

4 This Egyptian link is argued persuasively by John Carey, who compares the treatise's description of the sun's night voyage with Re's netherworld journey in the *Amduat*, see *JWCI* 57 (1994), 14–34, esp. 26ff. For a possible transmission via gnostic groups in Roman Africa and then into Spain, regions which were in close touch with Ireland in the seventh century, see *ibid*. 32–3. Dr Carey's

147

new edition of *In Tenga Bithnua* will be published by Brepols as part of their Series Apocryphorum. I am grateful to him for sending me copies of his articles.

5 Andrew Welburn noted alchemy's importance in the *Gospel of Philip* (*Beginnings of Christianity*, 170, 321, n.7; *Gnosis*, 282 [43], 284 [51], 306 [115]). He also cited alchemical imagery in the writings of the Syrian church fathers, (*ibid.* 282 [43]), though he regarded Mithraic and Mandaean influence to be decisive in Philip's gospel. See also R. Charron and L. Painchaud, 'God is a Dyer', 47–50 (without reference, however, to Welburn's earlier comments). For the importance of alchemical imagery more generally in the Nag Hammadi texts, particularly the *Apocryphon of John*, see R. Charron, *VigChr* 59 (2005), 438–56. Charron concluded, albeit without reference to ancient Egypt, that 'the question of the relationship between the Graeco-Egyptian alchemical writings and Gnosticism deserves to be revisited' (*ibid.* 455). She also noted the use by Valentinians of many technical alchemical terms (*ibid.* 455, with n.72).

6 For this Syriac information about Theosebia as a 'priestess', see M. Berthelot, *La chimie au moyen âge 2: L'alchimie syriaque*. Paris, 1893, 308; Fowden, *Egyptian Hermes*, 167. See also Fowden, *ibid.* 125–6, for the founding of initiatory secret groups by Theosebia. The cult dimension of her alchemy is evident in the Arabic *Missive of Secrets*, in which Hermes teaches her an ancient wisdom of alchemical transformation. See Vereno, *Studien*, 136–59, who includes many references to ancient Egyptian cult wisdom and the Isis

mysteries in his commentary on the Arabic text.

7 *NHL*, 154 (75). Cf. the lines in the letter of *Isis the prophetess to her son Horus*: 'Go to the farmer Achaab and learn from him what is the sowing and what is the reaping, and you will discover that the one who sows wheat reaps wheat, that the one who sows barley reaps barley ... consider all creation and generation and know that it is the condition of a human being to generate a human being, a lion to engender a lion, a dog to engender a dog.' See Berthelot, *Alchimistes grecs* 3, 33 (6–7); Festugière, *Révélation* 1, 259. This letter is important evidence for the connection of Isis with Graeco-Egyptian alchemy. Cf. also Isis heating a furnace in a Coptic magical papyrus (*Papyrus Berlin 8313*), which Tonio Richter interprets in the context of late antique alchemical practices (see T.S. Richter, *JEA* 93 [2007], 259–63.) For the principle of 'like to like' in magic and Egyptian love poetry, see above chapter 2, nn.1, 24, 27. It was, of course, a widespread magical principle in the ancient world.

8 Copenhaver, *Hermetica*, 90 (38).

9 *NHL*, 147 (61).

10 See Schenke, *NHD* 1, 207 (102b). The theme of love's transforming power appears in the alchemically inspired work of Rumi, the 13th-century Islamic mystic, who tells how love can transform an 'Armenian into a Turk' and 'turn copper into gold', see Schimmel, *As Through a Veil*, 124.

11 *NHL*, 148 (63).

12 For *pharmakon* as 'dyestuff', cf. Sonnedecker (ed.), *History of Pharmacy*, 479. For the eucharist as an immortalizing *pharmakon*, see Lindsay, *Origins of Alchemy*, 359.

13 See *NHL*, 113–14 (15–17).

14 See Quack's detailed discussion (with reference to other scholarly interpretations) in *JAC* 38 (1995), 97–122, esp. 97–8, 101. The number 72 is also highly symbolic in Biblical sources. Cf. the mission of the 72 whom Jesus sent into the world (Gospel of Luke 10:1). According to Jewish tradition there were also 72 translators who translated the Hebrew Bible into Greek on the orders of Ptolemy II and 72 different languages of the world. These allusions would have resonated with the *Gospel of Philip*'s 72 colours, enhancing their significance. Given the gospel's emphasis on sacramental life, however, a bodily transformation through baptism is more likely to have been the primary meaning, paralleling the 72 parts of the body in the *Apocryphon of John*, which belongs in the same codex as the *Gospel of Philip*. For references to the importance of 72 in other Nag Hammadi texts, see Quack, *ibid.* 101–2.

15 *NHL*, 146 (61). Régine Charron and Louis Painchaud highlighted the subtle 'dyeing' vocabulary in their translation of this passage: 'Since his dyes are immortal, they become immortal by means of the drugs prepared by him. God baptizes those he baptizes in water and power' (see 'God is a Dyer', 44, 48). As Charron noted, the Coptic word for 'dyes' is the equivalent of the Greek word *baphé*, complementing the subsequent 'drugs prepared', which is based on the Greek word *pharmakon*. It is a shift conveying the healing transformation of the baptized 'dyed' one. (For *pharmakon*, see also above, n.12, and chapter 6, n.7). See also Lindsay (*op.cit.* 380) for

alchemical allusions to *baptein*, 'dip', and *baptizein*, 'baptize'.

16 See above, chapter 9, n.19, for these five seals.

17 *NHL*, 147 (63).

18 For this alchemical imagery in the *Koré Kosmou*, associated with creating a pure transparent substance which possesses animating power, see Festugière, *Hermétisme*, 230–4. The treatise is preserved in the *Anthology* of John Stobaeus from Macedonia. For discussion of its title, see H. Jackson (*CdE* 61/121 [1986], 116–35), who connects it primarily with Isis as the ancient Egyptian 'pupil of the solar eye'. For Hathor's various manifestations as the 'pupil of the eye' of the cosmic creator, Re-Atum, in Graeco-Roman temple inscriptions at Dendara and Edfu, see Goyon, *Rituel*, 121–3. She is both his 'mother' and 'daughter', protectress and 'female sun', eternally renewing him and being renewed by him, who conceals him in the 'interior of her pupil'. Goyon also noted, with reference to Jackson's study, the preservation of this Egyptian tradition concerning Isis-Hathor in the *Koré Kosmou* (see *ibid*. 123, with n.222). For regenerative 'breath' in the Osirian resurrection mysteries, cf. the vivifying power of Isis's breath in the New Kingdom 'Great Hymn to Osiris'. Here the goddess 'made shade with her plumage, created breath with her wings, rejoiced and joined her brother, raised the weary one's inertness, received the seed, bore the heir' (see Lichtheim, *Literature* 2, 83). The idea of life being breathed into forms is, of course, attested more generally in the ancient world. Cf. the Hebrew Bible's book of Genesis where it is said that the first (male) human is

made from the earth, probably clay, into which a living soul is breathed, the 'breath of life' (Genesis 2:7). The destruction of the heathen is also compared to a shattered potter's vessel in Psalm 2 of the Hebrew Psalter. But here in the *Gospel of Philip*, it is a very specific juxtaposition of 'clay' and 'glass', typical of an alchemical outlook. For the juxtaposition of glass and clay in an Arabic alchemical letter attributed to Hermes of Dendara, see Vereno, *Studien*, 160 (5), 300, 304(d), where the imagery refers to pliable glass which can bend like clay because of its plasticity.

19 Lichtheim, *Literature* 3, 115.

20 For the *Ka*'s regenerative power, see Roberts, *Hathor Rising*, 93–4. For Hatshepsut's rulership of Egypt expressed in terms of this light-filled *Ka*-theology in her temple at Deir el-Bahri, see *ibid*. 122–6.

21 For the association of *tjehenet*, 'faience', with shining qualities and joy, see G. Fecht, *ZDMG* 106/31 (1956), 40–7.

22 *NHL*, 150 (68). Here I have followed the translation of R.M. Grant, *VigChr.* 15 (1961), 134. Cf. also *NHL*, 151 (70) where it is explicitly said that 'Christ came to repair the separation which was from the beginning and again unite the two, and to give life to those who died as a result of the separation and unite them.'

23 *NHL*, 151 (70). See also Layton, *Gnostic Scriptures*, 343 (70).

24 For the Egyptian 'fleeing' Sun Eye, see Roberts, *Hathor Rising*, 10–13. The relationship of Sekhmet with both life and death is evident in an invocation to her at Edfu. As the returning goddess, she is the 'Lady of life of the Two Lands who causes death' (see Germond, *Sekhmet*, 281). For the alchemical 'fleeing female',

who separates from the male and whose return brings life and creation, see Roberts, *My Heart My Mother*, 204–5. There is also a resonance with the fleeing Lilith in Hebrew legend.

25 *NHL*, 153 (73). This mystery of a rejuvenating death, 'to die before you die', is also a powerful theme in Islamic mysticism, including Rumi's poetry, which is strewn with alchemical imagery, see Schimmel, *As Through a Veil*, 70, 132.

26 See Lindsay, *Origins of Alchemy*, 358–9. For parallels between the alchemical *Dialogue of the Philosophers with Cleopatra* (n.27 below) and St Paul's writings, see Reitzenstein, *Hellenistic Mystery-Religions*, 399–400, although he emphasized Mandaean and Iranian influence in the *Dialogue*.

27 See Berthelot, *Alchimistes grecs* 3, 278–87, text re-edited by R. Reitzenstein, *Zur Geschichte der Alchemie und des Mystizismus*, Göttingen, 1919, 14ff. Translated also by Festugière, *Hermétisme*, 241–6; Lindsay, *op.cit.* 254–60. When Cleopatra's dialogue was composed is unclear. Festugière dated it to the end of the third century CE (*op.cit.* 209–10).

28 See Reitzenstein, *Hellenistic Mystery-Religions*, 398, for the suggestion that the dialogue may have been translated from Aramaic into Greek by an Egyptian-Greek editor. For 'Komar' in Aramaic meaning 'chief priest' (*ibid*. 165, n.68), see also Lindsay, *op.cit.* 253.

29 For the dialogue's 'essentially Egyptian' character and links with the Osirian mysteries, see Lindsay, *op.cit.* 255; Roberts, *My Heart My Mother*, 68, 202. That it belongs to an 'Egyptian' alchemical stream is suggested by Cleopatra's name, which she shares with Egyptian Ptolemaic

149

queens. Moreover, among the philosophers she teaches, only Ostanes, a well-known Persian adept in the Hellenistic alchemical tradition, is specifically mentioned by name, thus drawing attention to his (and Persian) dependence on Cleopatra's wisdom. See below (Epilogue, n.3) for Ostanes learning his wisdom from Taautos (Thoth). For the similarities between the *Dialogue* and the *Koré Kosmou*, see Festugière, *Hermétisme*, 246. See also Régine Charron's discussion of the *Dialogue* (*VigChr.* 59 [2005], 443–54), in which she compares Cleopatra's regeneration 'mystery' with the pattern of redemption in the 'Pronoia Hymn' in the *Apocryphon of John*, noting how the two texts share 'numerous liturgical terms and motifs' (*ibid.* 450). Though, importantly, she also noted the absence of specific 'Gnostic' elements in the *Dialogue*, notably the soul's release from the prison of the body (*ibid.* 451). Like the ancient Egyptians, Cleopatra teaches an embodied spirituality, culminating in the resurrection of a divinized living 'statue' or 'image'.

30 Berthelot, *Alchimistes grecs* 3, 284. For an Egyptian New Kingdom parallel to the call of 'awakening', cf. the introductory tableau to the *Book of Night*, which shows Horus bringing life and 'awakening' to the recumbent Osirian king lying on a bed. Above the king is a hieroglyphic sign meaning 'awake' (see Roberts, *My Heart My Mother*, 112, with pl.86).

31 Jung, *Psychology and Alchemy*, 359.

32 Berthelot, *op.cit.* 284–5.

Epilogue *(pages 120–126)*

1 Quotation from Pagels, 'Ritual in the *Gospel of Philip*', 281.

2 For this description of Theosebia, see Fowden, *Egyptian Hermes*, 125.

3 For Philo's knowledge of Thoth-Hermes and Hermopolitan cosmogony, see above chapter 9, n.27. For hints of his alchemical knowledge, cf. the reference to Agathodaimon and to Ostanes, whom Philo says took his knowledge from the Phoenician Taautos (Thoth), see Baumgarten, *Philo of Byblos*, 258–9. For Ostanes specifically named among the philosophers in Cleopatra's *Dialogue*, see chapter 10, n.29. Philo also enigmatically refers to 'Mot', which probably means 'mud' or the putrefaction of a watery mixture from which all fertile life emerges and which is reformed into the cosmic egg (see Baumgarten, *ibid.* 111–13, 123, 133–4, including the importance of 'mud' in Egypt [*ibid.* 113] and in Greek sources [*ibid.* 123]). See also H.W. Attridge and R.A. Oden, Jr., *Philo of Byblos, The Phoenician History: Introduction, Critical Text, Translation, Notes.* Washington, 1981, 76–7, n.29, for various suggestions concerning the meaning of 'Mot', including a possible reference to the Canaanite god Mot as 'Lord of the Underworld'. They also note how Isis is called 'Mouth' by Plutarch (see *De Iside et Osiride* [Ch.56]). Interestingly, they also cite the ancient Egyptian word *m3wt* as a term for land newly emerging from the Nile flood. In alchemy, the 'black earth' is a powerful symbol of the *prima materia*, being sometimes identified with Isis and also with female alchemists. For the mud-coated object in the Osirian phase of the Egyptian New Year ritual, see

p.51. Cf. also the reference to 'rebirth from the egg' in the swallow's speech in the New Year ritual's final phase (p.58), offering a parallel to Philo's 'mud' reforming into the cosmic egg (see Baumgarten, *op.cit.* 133).

4 For this visit, see Roberts, *op.cit.* 245, n.36, with further references.

5 See Angus, *Mystery-Religions*, 307–9. He also noted how votive inscriptions for Asclepius were adapted for use by early Christians. For the healing love of Asclepius, see *ibid.* 229–30, with reference also to the healing kindness of Isis and Sarapis. For the links between Asclepius and Imhotep in Graeco-Roman Egypt, see Roberts, *op.cit.* 196.

6 For the emphasis on healing in the 'Philip' traditions, cf. the apocryphal fourth-century *Acts of Philip*, in which the apostle Philip acclaims Jesus as 'my medicine, the healer of illnesses'. He also displays his own miraculous healing power during a sea journey from Ethiopia to Palestine when he calms a raging storm, much to the amazement of the sailors travelling with him. On arrival in Palestine, he immediately heals the eye complaint of a nobleman's daughter. These two episodes (*Acts of Philip* 3:15 and 4:4) are discussed by Scopello, *Femme*, 317–46. For Philip's praise of Jesus as 'my medicine', see *ibid.* 343.

7 Zosimus's statement about the Jews transmitting Egyptian secrets is preserved in his treatise *The Final Count*, see Berthelot, *Alchimistes grecs* 3, 98, 231; Festugière, *Révélation* 1, 277(2); Lindsay, *op.cit.* 335. Zosimus explains to his 'sister' Theosebia that the Egyptian priests were forbidden to disclose their secrets as they would have contravened royal orders and they were anyway careful of their secrets.

8 Though the love goddess is here named as Venus, her presence in a Ptah temple, combined with the kind of power she manifests, points unmistakably to an identification with Hathor-Sekhmet or Hathor-Aphrodite. See Roberts, *My Heart My Mother*, 22–7, for Hathor's power to vivify the bodily forms created by Ptah. For this episode in the *Book of Krates*, see M. Berthelot, *La chimie au moyen âge 3: L'alchimie arabe*. Paris, 1893, 61–4, also D. Kahn, *Hermès Trismégiste: La Table d'Émeraude et sa tradition alchimique*. Paris, 1994, 118–22. It is noteworthy that Arabic alchemical treatises associated with Hermes preserve a far stronger sense of Egypt's mythic cult temples than in the Greek alchemical corpus, perhaps reflecting Islamic alchemy's indebtedness to Syriac sources, which were closer to ancient ritual and cult practices.

9 See chapter 10, n.1. Ingolf Vereno specifically associated this liquid with the Nile flood, noting how the Christian author placed the completion of the alchemical work in conjunction with the return of the Nile inundation and the heliacal rising of Sothis/Sirius (see *Studien*, 274–5). See also Lindsay, *op.cit.* 371–2. In Arabic alchemy the king's coming forth, the waters and the purple/red garment are frequently associated (see Vereno, *op.cit.* 210–11, 275–9). Vereno associates this imagery with Egyptian cult practices. Cf. also the 'coming forth' of the regenerated Red King in European alchemy, see Jung, *op.cit.* 358–9, for a relevant passage from the *Tractatus aureus*.

10 See above, n.1. Andrew Welburn also emphasized the gospel's place within the 'mainstream liturgical development of the Church's sacraments, at an early stage when they are close to the forms of the pagan Mysteries' (see *Gnosis*, 19). He also noted there was no evidence that it was addressed to a minority group: 'If there is Gnosticism in the *Gospel of Philip*, it had not yet been isolated and pushed out of the Church. It is still present as a part of the way the experiences of the ritual-sacramental life of the Christian could be understood' (*ibid.* 19).

11 Pagels, *op.cit.* 283. This ritual contact with hostile powers is vividly conveyed by a painting of David fighting Goliath in the house church at Dura-Europos. It is placed directly beneath the niche which probably contained the holy oil for anointing, see chapter 9, p.99. For oil protecting against hostile powers in Syriac sources, see Kraeling, *Excavations*, 189–90.

12 This aspect is emphasized by Elaine Pagels: 'What matters to Philip is less to delineate the action of each sacrament than to show that the initiate first re-enacts Jesus' divine birth, then his resurrection, and, finally, his reunion with his *syzygos*' (see Pagels, *op.cit.* 286). As such, it highlights yet again the author's roots in a magical and 'mythic' world-view.

13 For the *Didache*, see the summary by J.K. Elliott in *OBC*, 1308–11 (with further references). Elliott noted that links with the Johannine tradition were not a prominent feature of the *Didache*. Also, the brief prayer over oil is omitted from the *Didache*'s Greek version and occurs only in the Coptic (*ibid.* 1310). Elliott also

referred to the New Testament connection of oil with the anointing of Jesus as a Messiah-making event and also its use in the mysterious 'sealing' rite referred to in the second-century apocryphal Acts, though he omits its importance in Philip's gospel. Unlike the lengthy section devoted to the *Gospel of Thomas* in *OBC*, 1316–19, the *Gospel of Philip* does not even feature in the *OBC*'s index, even though it belongs in the same codex as the *Gospel of Thomas*.

14 See Kraeling, *op.cit.* 151–3. He wrote, 'The baptismal ritual used in Syria and Mesopotamia differs in certain salient particulars from that used elsewhere' (*op.cit.* 152). He linked the house church at Dura-Europos with this Syrian-Mesopotamian tradition and the early Syriac-speaking Church, as well as the *Didache* and other writings. Yet, as Kraeling himself observed, the decoration at Dura was strongly influenced by John's gospel (*op.cit.* 185), which suggests a tradition other than the *Didache*. (For the absence of any specific links between the Johannine tradition and the *Didache*, see above, n.13). The Dura house church's decoration is, however, in tune with Philip-centred traditions, cf. its scenes of Christ stilling the storm and performing a healing miracle, which are placed above the tomb scene (Kraeling, *Excavations*, pls.34–7). These parallel episodes in the *Acts of Philip* (see above, n.6). The *Gospel of Philip*'s categorical emphasis on anointing is evident: 'The anointing is superior to baptism, for it is from the word "anointing" that we have been called "Christians", certainly not because of the word "baptism". And it is because of

the anointing that the "anointed one" (Christ) has his name' (see *NHL* 153 [74]).

15 Haskins, *Mary Magdalen*, 53–7. As Haskins noted, the dominant view of Mary Magdalene in later Christianity changed from being Christ's beloved companion to that of 'a repentant whore' (*ibid.* 57). It was not until the medieval period, in 1215, that the seven sacraments of the Catholic Church were officially named by the Fourth Lateran Council. Before then church fathers could differ considerably as to what constituted Christian 'sacraments'. For example, St Ambrose saw both baptism and foot-washing as sacraments, whilst St Augustine regarded the creed, the Lord's Prayer, baptism and the eucharist as sacraments.

16 See above, chapter 2, n.21. For Aristotle's influence on medieval Christian theologians and their views of the female, see Haskins, *op.cit.* 148–50, 178. The *Gospel*

of Philip's approach is more nuanced than in 'negative' gnosis, since the author is very careful to avoid outright dualism seeking rather the 'middle' way. But perhaps a similar view towards the female is evident in the statement: 'Whereas in this world the union is one of husband and wife—a case of strength complemented by weakness [?]—in the aeon the form of the union is different, although we refer to them by the same names' (*NHL* 154 [76]). However, the translation is uncertain. It is noteworthy that the gospel strives throughout to maintain a balanced approach to the 'flesh', as, for example: 'Fear not the flesh nor love it. If you fear it, it will gain mastery over you. If you love it, it will swallow and paralyze you' (see *ibid.* 149 [66]). Moreover, there is a strong emphasis on the spirit as feminine and Mary Magdalene's role.

17 The transmission of Egypt's transformational wisdom through

Islamic alchemy into medieval Europe will form part of my forthcoming book *Nefertari's Love Wisdom: An Egyptian Alchemy of Life.*

18 See *The Divine Office, The Liturgy of the Hours according to the Roman Rite 2.* London, 1974, 320–22, where it is cited as an anonymous homily (see below n.19)

19 For the homily's origins, see J. Kroll, *Gott und Hölle: Der Mythos vom Descensuskampfe.* Berlin, 1932, 100, who doubted its attribution to Epiphanius and referred to its author as 'Pseudo-Epiphanius'. Kroll cited numerous early Christian writings concerning Christ's journey into Hades. He also observed significant differences between the homily's version and the account, for example in the *Gospel of Nicodemus* (see *ibid.* 104). See also above chapter 10, n.30 for an ancient Egyptian call to 'awakening'.

SOURCES OF THE ILLUSTRATIONS

All illustrations not listed here were supplied by the author

1, 6, 10, 12, 28, 37, 38—Robert Partridge: The Ancient Egypt Picture Library; **2, 15, 27, 31, 59, 68**—courtesy of Kurt Lambelet; **4** F.J.Gladstone; **5** Uni-Dia slide (no.32584); **7** © the Trustees of the British Museum, London; **9** drawing after É Chassinat, *Le temple de Dendara* 3. Cairo, 1935, pls.219, 223; **14** drawing James Lawrence; **16** Brooklyn Museum papyrus 47.218.50—bequest of Theodora Wilbour from the collection of her father, Charles Edwin Wilbour; **18** Uni-Dia slide (no.22217); **19** Uni-Dia slide (no.30810); **30** drawing James Lawrence; **32** drawing after A.H.Gardiner, *JEA* 24 (1938), 169; **33** Alexandre Piankoff, *Egyptian Religious Texts and Representations* 3 © 1957 Princeton University Press, 1985 renewed PUP. Reprinted by permission of Princeton University Press; **34** Uni-Dia slide (no.30845); **44** Gerald Eedle; **53** courtesy of the Staatliche Museen zu Berlin SPK, Ägyptisches Museum und Papyrussammlung; **54** RMN © Hervé Lewandowski; **55** courtesy of the Petrie Museum of Egyptian Archaeology, UCL; **56** © 1990 Photo SCALA, Florence; **57, 62** Women at the tomb. Reconstruction at Yale University Art Gallery, Acc.nos.ds-4, z-107. Dura-Europos Collection, Yale University Art Gallery; **58** drawing after Kraeling, *Excavations*, pl.40(2); **60** © 1990 Photo SCALA, Florence; **61** map James Lawrence; **63** drawing after Kraeling, *Excavations*, pl.45(2); **64** Antioch Expedition Archives. Department of Art and Archaeology, Princeton University; **65** Gift of the Committee for the Excavation of Antioch to Princeton University; **66** Uni-Dia slide (no.30282); **67** © British Library Board. *Sloane 2560, f.15*; **69** courtesy of Lyn Haward; **70** Uni-Dia slide (no.32803); **71** © British Library Board. *Harley Manuscript 3469*; **73** drawing after L. Lamy, *Egyptian Mysteries: New Light on Ancient Knowledge*. London, 1981, 25; **74–6** details of **15**

SELECT BIBLIOGRAPHY

Note: Sources appearing here are cited more than twice in the notes; all others receive full entries in the notes.

Angus, S. *The Mystery-Religions and Christianity: A Study in the Religious Background of Early Christianity.* New York, 1925.

Baumgarten, A.I. *The Phoenician History of Philo of Byblos: A Commentary.* Leiden, 1981.

Bergman, J. *Ich bin Isis: Studien zum memphitischen Hintergrund der griechischen Isisaretalogien.* Uppsala, 1968.

Berthelot, M. and Ruelle, C.-É. *Collection des anciens alchemistes grecs.* 3 vols. Paris, 1888.

Borghouts, J.F. *Ancient Egyptian Magical Texts.* Leiden, 1978.

Bosse-Griffiths, K. 'The Great Enchantress in the Little Golden Shrine of Tut'ankhamūn'. *JEA* 59 (1973), 100–108.

Bricault, L. *Recueil des inscriptions concernant les cultes Isiaques (Ricis).* 3 vols. Paris, 2005.

Charron, R. 'The *Apocryphon of John* (NHC II, I) and the Graeco-Egyptian Alchemical Literature'. *VigChr.* 59 (2005), 438–56.

Charron, R. and Painchaud, L. '"God is a Dyer." The Background and Significance of a Puzzling Motif in the Coptic *Gospel according to Philip* (CG II,3)' in *Le Muséon* 114 (2001), 41–50.

Clark, R.T. Rundle. *Myth and Symbol in Ancient Egypt.* Reprinted paperback edn. London, 1978.

Copenhaver, B.P. *Hermetica: The Greek Corpus Hermeticum and the Latin Asclepius in a new English Translation, with Notes and Introduction.* Paperback edn. Cambridge, 1998.

Derchain, P. *Hathor Quadrifrons: Recherches sur la syntaxe d'un mythe égyptien.* Istanbul, 1972.

Doresse, J. *The Secret Books of the Egyptian Gnostics: An Introduction to the Gnostic Coptic manuscripts discovered at Chenoboskion. With an English Translation and critical evaluation of The Gospel According to Thomas.* London, 1960.

DuQuesne, T. 'Raising the Serpent Power: Some Parallels between Egyptian Religion and Indian Tantra' in T. DuQuesne (ed.), *Hermes Aegyptiacus: Egyptological Studies for B H Stricker on his 85th Birthday.* Oxford, 1995, 53–68.

Dunand, F. *Le culte d'Isis dans le bassin oriental de la Méditerranée 3: Le culte d'Isis en Asie mineure, clergé et rituel des sanctuaires Isiaques.* Leiden, 1973.

Eaton-Krauss, M. and Graefe, E. *The Small Golden Shrine from the Tomb of Tutankhamun.* Oxford, 1985.

Festugière, A.-J. *La Révélation d'Hermès Trismégiste 1: L'astrologie et les sciences occultes.* Reprinted second edn. Paris, 1989.

— *Hermétisme et mystique païenne.* Paris, 1967.

Fowden, G. The *Egyptian Hermes: A Historical Approach to the Late Pagan Mind.* Paperback edn. Princeton, 1993.

Fox, M.V. *The Song of Songs and the Ancient Egyptian Love Songs.* Madison (Wis.), 1985.

Frankfort, H. *Kingship and the Gods: A Study of Ancient Near Eastern Religion as the Integration of Society & Nature.* Paperback edn. Chicago and London, 1978.

Fraser, P.M. *Ptolemaic Alexandria.* 3 vols. Oxford, 1972.

Gaffron, H.-G. *Studien zum koptischen Philippusevangelium unter besonderer Berücksichtigung der Sakramente.* Bonn, 1969.

Germond, P. *Sekhmet et la protection du monde.* Basle and Geneva, 1981.

Goyon, J.-C. *Confirmation du pouvoir royal au nouvel an [Brooklyn Museum Papyrus 47.218.50].* 2 vols. Cairo, 1972 (text), and Brooklyn and Cairo, 1974 (plates).

— *Le rituel du sḥtp Sḥmt au changement de cycle annuel: D'après les architraves du temple d'Edfou et textes parallèles, du Nouvel Empire à l'époque ptolémaique et romaine.* Cairo, 2006.

Griffiths, J. Gwyn. *Apuleius of Madauros: The Isis-Book (Metamorphoses, Book XI).* Leiden, 1975.

Haskins, S. *Mary Magdalen: Myth and Metaphor.* Paperback edn. London, 1994.

Hopkins, C. *The Discovery of Dura-Europos.* New Haven and London, 1979.

Iversen, E. *The Myth of Egypt and its Hieroglyphs in European Tradition.* Paperback edn. Princeton, 1993.

Jonas, H. *The Gnostic Religion: The Message of the Alien God and the Beginnings of Christianity.* Paperback edn. Boston 1963.

Jung, C.G. *Psychology and Alchemy.* Paperback edn. London, 1980.

Keel, O. *Das Hohelied.* Zurich, 1986.

Kingsley, P. *Ancient Philosophy, Mystery, and Magic: Empedocles and Pythagorean Tradition.* Oxford, 1995.

Kraeling, C.H. *The Excavations at Dura-Europos conducted by Yale University and the French Academy of Inscriptions and Letters: Final

Report VIII, Part II: The Christian Building, (edited by C. Bradford Welles). New Haven, 1967.

Layton, B. *The Gnostic Scriptures: A New Translation with Annotations and Introductions.* London, 1987.

Levi, D. *Antioch Mosaic Pavements.* 2 vols. Princeton, London, The Hague, 1947.

Lexikon der Ägyptologie. 7 vols. Wiesbaden, 1975–1992.

Lichtheim, M. *Ancient Egyptian Literature: A Book of Readings.* 3 vols. Paperback edn. Berkeley, Los Angeles and London, 1975–80.

Lindsay, J. *The Origins of Alchemy in Graeco-Roman Egypt.* London, 1970.

Mack, Burton L. *Logos und Sophia: Untersuchungen zur Weisheitstheologie im hellenistischen Judentum.* Göttingen, 1973.

Mathieu, B. *La poésie amoureuse de l'Égypte ancienne: Recherches sur un genre littéraire au Nouvel Empire.* Cairo, 1996.

Naydler, J. *Temple of the Cosmos: The Ancient Egyptian Experience of the Sacred.* Rochester, 1996.

— *Shamanic Wisdom in the Pyramid Texts: The Mystical Tradition of Ancient Egypt.* Rochester, 2005.

Pagels, E. 'Ritual in the *Gospel of Philip*' in J.D. Turner and A. McGuire (eds.), *The Nag Hammadi Library after Fifty Years: Proceedings of the 1995 Society of Biblical Literature Commemoration.* Leiden, New York and Cologne, 1997, 280–91.

Pinch, G. *Votive Offerings to Hathor.* Paperback edn. Oxford, 1993.

Plutarch, 'The Dialogue on Love' in *Moralia 9.* Trans. E.L. Minar, F.H. Sandbach and W.C. Helmbold. London and Cambridge (Mass.), 1961.

Preisigke, F. *Die Gotteskraft der frühchristlichen Zeit.* Berlin and Leipzig, 1922.

Quack, J.F. 'Dekane und Gliedervergottung. Altägyptische Traditionen im Apokryphon Johannis'. *JAC* 38 (1995), 97–122.

Quaegebeur, J. 'Diodore I, 20 et les mystères d'Osiris' in T. DuQuesne (ed.), *Hermes Aegyptiacus: Egyptological Studies for B H Stricker on his 85th Birthday.* Oxford, 1995, 157–81.

Quirke, S. *The Cult of Ra: Sun-worship in Ancient Egypt.* London, 2001.

Reitzenstein, R. *Hellenistic Mystery-Religions: Their Basic Ideas and Significance.* Trans. John E. Steely. Third edition. Pittsburgh, 1978.

RICIS, see Bricault, *Recueil des inscriptions*

Ritner, R.K. *The Mechanics of Ancient Egyptian Magical Practice.* Chicago, 1993.

— '"And each Staff transformed into a Snake": The Serpent Wand in ancient Egypt' in K. Szpakowska (ed.), *Through a Glass Darkly: Magic, Dreams and Prophecy in Ancient Egypt.* Swansea, 2006, 205–25.

Roberts, A.M. *Cult Objects of Hathor: An Iconographic Study.* 2 Vols. Unpublished thesis. Oxford University, 1984.

— *Hathor Rising: The Serpent Power of Ancient Egypt.* Reprinted edn. Rottingdean, 2001.

— *My Heart My Mother: Death and Rebirth in Ancient Egypt.* Rottingdean, 2000.

Schenke, H.-M. (*et al.,*), *Nag Hammadi Deutsch 1: NHC I,1–V,1.* Berlin and New York, 2001.

Schimmel, A. *As through a Veil: Mystical Poetry in Islam.* Paperback edn. Oxford, 2001.

Scopello, M. *Femme, Gnose et Manichéisme: De l'espace mythique au territoire du réel.* Leiden, 2005.

Sonnedecker, G. (ed.), *Kremers and Urdang's History of Pharmacy,* Fourth edn. Philadelphia and Toronto, 1976.

te Velde, H. *Seth, God of Confusion: A Study of his Role in Egyptian Mythology and Religion.* Leiden, 1977.

Thomassen, E. 'How Valentinian is The Gospel of Philip?' in J.D. Turner and A. McGuire, *The Nag Hammadi Library after Fifty Years: Proceedings of the 1995 Society of Biblical Literature Commemoration.* Leiden, New York and Cologne, 1997, 251–79.

Troy, L. *Patterns of Queenship in Ancient Egyptian Myth and History.* Uppsala, 1986.

Vereno, I. *Studien zum ältesten alchemistischen Schrifttum: Auf der Grundlage zweier erstmals edierter arabischer Hermetica.* Berlin, 1992.

Vittmann, G. *Ägypten und die Fremden im ersten vorchristlichen Jahrtausend.* Mainz am Rhein, 2003.

Welburn, A. *Gnosis, the Mysteries and Christianity: An Anthology of Essene, Gnostic and Christian Writings.* Edinburgh, 1994.

— *The Beginnings of Christianity: Essene Mystery, Gnostic Revelation and the Christian Vision.* Paperback edn. Edinburgh, 1995.

Westendorf, W. 'Bemerkungen zur "Kammer der Wiedergeburt" im Tutanchamungrab'. *ZÄS* 94 (1967), 139–50.

Witt, R.E. *Isis in the Graeco-Roman World.* London, 1971.

Žabkar, L.V. *Hymns to Isis in her Temple at Philae.* Hanover and London, 1988.

INDEX